ORDINARY ECSTASY

It has been said that John Rowan's *Ordinary Ecstasy* is a unique resource in the field. It is especially so some twenty-five years later, for we are in a time when "positive psychology" and other developments have seemed to diminish humanistic psychology's once unique stance.

For a brief period of time in the 1970s, there were a handful of texts about humanistic psychology, Rowan's being one of them. There are not many more now, and this one is still unique in its range and depth. It is also very up-to-date with the current controversies in the field.

Here are some of the features of his text that have made it useful for me as a teaching tool. First, it has the advantage that a single text has over assembling a group of readings: a coherent voice surveys the entire field. Second, the book is full of references, which offers the student an entry into their own scholarship and further exploration into the field. Third, Rowan frequently 'editorializes' with his own strong opinions on the subject matter. Such opinions stimulate the student to think about viewpoints, to realize that he is not merely reading a set of facts, but there are opinions, different ways to look at the facts, different ways to study the material. Reading Rowan's text helps the student to realize that there is something at stake, something to care about, and it makes it easier for me to engage the students in a dialogue about what difference it all makes. Not many texts can do that.

Henry Reed, Ph. D.
Professor of Transpersonal Studies,
Atlantic University, Virginia Beach, Virginia

John Rowan is the author of a number of books, including *The Reality Game: A Guide to Humanistic Counselling and Psychotherapy*, *Discover Your Subpersonalities: Our Inner World and the People in It*, *The Transpersonal: Psychotherapy and Counselling*, and *Healing the Male Psyche: Therapy as Initiation*. He has co-edited *The Plural Self: Multiplicity in Everyday Life* with Mick Cooper. He is a Fellow of the British Psychological Society and a Fellow of the British Association for Counselling.

ORDINARY ECSTASY

The dialectics of humanistic psychology

Third edition

John Rowan

BRUNNER-ROUTLEDGE
ALERE · FLAMMAM
Taylor & Francis Group

First published in 1976
Second edition published 1988
Third edition published 2001
by Brunner-Routledge
27 Church Road, Hove, East Sussex, BN3 2FA

Simultaneously published in the USA and Canada
by Taylor & Francis Inc.,
325 Chestnut Street, Philadelphia, PA 19106

Brunner-Routledge is an imprint of the Taylor & Francis Group

Typeset in Times by Mayhew Typesetting, Rhayader, Powys
Printed and bound in Great Britain by TJ International Ltd, Padstow, Cornwall
Cover design by Sandra Heath
Cover illustration by Nick Orsborn

British Library Cataloguing in Publication Data
A catalogue record for this book is available from the British Library

Library of Congress Cataloging in Publication Data

Rowan, John
Ordinary ecstasy : the dialectics of humanistic psychology / John Rowan. — 3rd ed.
p. cm.
Includes bibliographical references and index.
ISBN 0-415-23632-0 (hardbound) — 0-415-23633-9 (pbk.)
1. Humanistic psychology. I. Title.

BF204 .R68 2001
150.19'8—dc21
00–064039

ISBN 0–415–23632–0 (hbk)
ISBN 0–415–23633–9 (pbk)

Contents

CONTENTS

CONTENTS

Figures and tables

Introduction

At the heart of humanistic psychology lies the spirit of paradox. Its thinking is fundamentally dialectical thinking. This is the kind of thinking which Ken Wilber has called vision-logic. 'Vision-logic is not yet transrational but, we might say, lies on the border between the rational and the transrational, and thus partakes of some of the best of both' (Wilber 1998, p. 132). He is saying, and I am saying too, that humanistic psychology is just at the cusp of the transpersonal: it is the last stage of the personal, and at the same time the first stage of the transpersonal. In the terms of Beck and Cowan (1996), it is the last level of the first tier (which essentially comes out of conventional thinking), and the first of the second tier, which is more to do with postconventional thinking. This makes it hard to grasp, and hard to live out, and hard to understand. This why most people, including eminent folk like Ernesto Spinelli (1994), do not understand it, and reduce it to nothing but Maslow and Rogers.

Abraham Maslow and Carl Rogers are great thinkers and were eminent men, but they do not define humanistic psychology. Nor do Jacob Moreno, Fritz Perls or Alexander Lowen. Let us go back a step, and think about dialectics.

Dialectics is a form of thought which goes back a long way. In the West, Heraclitus in Ancient Greece was aware of it, and in the East, there are a number of thinkers who practised it. The *Tao Te Ching* is a good example of dialectical writing.

Dialogue is not the same as dialectics, and the Ancient Greeks, for example, were not dialectical thinkers in the modern sense, even though they were very interested in dialogue.

In more recent times the greatest exponent of it is of course Hegel: 'vision-logic evolutionarily became conscious of itself in Hegel' (Wilber 1998, p. 132). Numbers of Hegelians followed his example. The most famous of these was of course Marx, though Engels and Lenin actually made more use of it, and Mao Tse-tung made contributions too. The British Hegelians were more right-wing politically, so there is nothing essentially left-wing about it. Adorno (1973) and others emphasized negative dialectics.

1

DIALECTICAL THINKING

The first characteristic of dialectical thinking is that it places all the emphasis on change. Instead of talking about static structures, it talks about process and movement. Hence it is in line with all those philosophies which say 'Let's not be deceived by what it is now as we perceive it – let's not pretend we can fix it and label it and turn it into something stiff and immutable – let's look instead at how it changes'. Hence it denies much of the usefulness of formal logic, which starts from the proposition that 'A is A', and is nothing but A. For dialectics the corresponding proposition is 'A is not simply A'. This is even true for things, but much more obviously true for people. A person is surely a person, but is also a number of potentials beneath the surface which want to be experienced. Alvin Mahrer, the great theorist of humanistic psychology, has spelt this out very fully (Mahrer 1989).

But the second characteristic, which sets it apart from any philosophy which emphasizes smooth continuous change or progress, is that it states that the way change takes place is through conflict and opposition. Dialectics is always looking for the contradictions within people or situations as the main guide to what is going on and what is likely to happen. There are in fact three main propositions which are put forward about opposites and contradictions.

The interdependence of opposites This is the easiest thing to see: opposites depend on one another. It wouldn't make sense to talk about darkness if there were no such thing as light. I really start to understand my love at the moment when I permit myself to understand my hate. In practice, each member of a polar opposition seems to need the other to make it what it is.

The interpenetration of opposites Here we see that opposites can be found within each other. Just because light is relative to darkness, there is some light in every darkness, and some darkness in every light. There is some hate in every love, and some love in every hate. If we look into one thing hard enough, we can always find its opposite right there. To see this frees us from the 'either-or' which can be so oppressive and so stuck. Mary Parker Follett (see Graham 1995), a great and recently rediscovered writer on management who was a closet Hegelian, used to say 'Never let yourself be bullied by an either-or'.

The unity of opposites So far we have been talking about relative opposites. But dialectics goes on to say that if we take an opposite to its very ultimate extreme, and make it absolute, it actually turns into its opposite. Thus if we make darkness absolute, we are blind – we can't see anything. And if we make light absolute, we are equally blind and unable to see. In psychology, the equivalent of this is to idealize something. So if we take love to its extreme, and idealize it, we get morbid dependence, where our whole existence depends completely on the other person. And if we take hate to its extreme, and idealize it, we get morbid counterdependence, where our whole existence again depends completely on the other person. This appreciation of paradox is one of the strengths of the dialectical approach, which makes it superior to linear logic, formal logic, many-valued logic and even fuzzy logic.

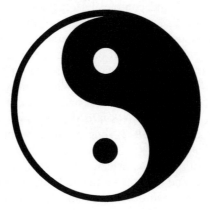

Yin-yang symbol

A good symbol for these three processes is the yin-yang symbol of Taoism (see above). The interdependence of opposites is shown in each half being defined by the contours of the other. The interpenetration of opposites is expressed by having a black spot in the innermost centre of the white area, and a white spot in the innermost centre of the black area. The unity of opposites is shown by the circle surrounding the symbol, which expresses total unity and unbroken serenity in and through all the seeming opposition. It is, after all, one symbol.

PRACTICAL PHILOSOPHY

The lessons of the dialectic are hard ones. It tells us that any value we have, if held to in a one-sided way, will become an illusion. We shall try to take it as excluding its opposite, but really it will include it. And if we take it to its extreme, and idealize it, it will turn into its opposite. So peace and love, cosmic harmony, the pursuit of happiness, positive psychology and all the rest are doomed, if held to in this exclusive way. (This is of course what constructivism and postmodernism also say, but from a different angle.)

The only values which will be truly stable and coherent are those which include opposition rather than excluding it. And all such values appear to be nonsense, because they must contain paradoxes. As a psychotherapist I practice humanistic psychology, which comes from existentialist and phenomenological roots, but also incorporates dialectical thinking. It takes from Hegel (see Rowan 1992) and Goldstein and Maslow the concept of self-actualization, and this is one of those paradoxical concepts that are so characteristic of dialectical thinking. The concept of the self is self-contradictory, paradoxical and absurd. (More on this in Chapter 13.) The self is intensely personal and completely impersonal at one and the same time. It is the lowest of the low and the highest of the high at the same time. It is single and particular and a mass of subpersonalities at the same time. It is completely individual and just part of a field at the same time. And this is why, when we contact the self in a peak experience, our description of what happened is invariably a paradoxical one. When put into words, it breaks out of the realm of common sense. The whole idea of a peak experience, where we get taken out of ourselves into the realm of ecstasy, was written about at length by Maslow (1973), one of the few thinkers able to do it justice.

There is a logic of paradox, which enables the intellect to handle it without getting fazed, and its name is the dialectic. It is complex because it involves holding the spring doors of the mind open – hence it often tries to say everything at once. But it shows how we do not have to give up in the face of paradox and abandon the intellect as a hopeless case.

How does one actually use dialectical thinking in everyday life? Some say that dialectics is not for everyday life at all – it has to do with 'ideas of the horizon' where we are dealing with concepts that are at the very limits of human thought. For everyday life, they say, formal logic is good enough. But I think humanistic psychology has shown us that you can use dialectical thinking even for walking, or driving, or eating, or playing tennis, or any other everyday activity. Take these four points for example:

TAKE NOTHING FOR GRANTED This is one of the most important principles of humanistic psychology. All the time one is questioning the fixed categories, the rigid 'shoulds', the congealed knowledge – what the exponent of humanistic psychology Jacob Moreno used to call the cultural conserve – that stops one seeing the world. Our beliefs are the greatest obstacle to clear perception, and the more we can unfocus from them, the more we can let in. Fritz Perls, one of the classic humanistic writers, was particularly clear about this.

SPONTANEITY Again a crucial concept, which dialectical thinking makes easy to understand and easy to do. Spontaneity is obviously a paradoxical quality, which you can only aim at by letting go. The great writer about this was Jacob Moreno. In recent times there have been many writers on games and sports who have made use of such insights. We do not make the mistake, of course, of confusing spontaneity with impulsivity.

TRANSFORMATION OF QUANTITY INTO QUALITY This important idea states that by simply emphasizing and holding fast to things, we can eventually arrive at something quite different. In therapy, going intensively into one side of a conflict often brings us more vividly into the other; and if we push the whole conflict hard enough and far enough, a whole new vision may appear. In other words, we do not have to import something different from elsewhere: the answer is right there in the phenomenon itself. Gestalt therapy is particularly good on this, and the work of Beisser (1972) is often quoted here, with the concept of paradoxical change, which he got from Fritz Perls. But psychoanalysts like Aaron Esterson (1972) have also used such ideas.

BREAKING PATTERNS So the main practical application of the dialectic is in breaking fixed patterns of thought and behaviour. Every time you adopt a regular and unaware pattern of washing, dressing, eating and so on, you are avoiding reality. But if awareness of these activities increases, the amount of play involved in them is also likely to increase. Taking responsibility for our actions is choosing our life, and this usually feels good. You can be responsible and playful at the same time, and this is one of the paradoxes in which dialectics delights. Carl Rogers used to write about this particularly well; James Bugental and Alvin Mahrer and John Enright are other writers in the humanistic-existential tradition who have made much of it. In management theory Mary Parker Follett (Graham 1995) made it central in her thinking.

In this volume we shall be applying these ideas chapter by chapter as we go through. Nothing will be left untouched in the end.

Part 1

WHAT IS HUMANISTIC PSYCHOLOGY?

1

HUMANISTIC PSYCHOLOGY IS AND IS NOT PSYCHOLOGY

Humanistic psychology is and is not psychology. This paradox lies at the heart of humanistic psychology, and helps to make it what it is.

If we ask where humanistic psychology comes from, it comes from the Old Saybrook conference in 1964. There was a long build-up to this, starting in the 1930s or even before, and people like Abraham Maslow, Carl Rogers, Rollo May, Gordon Allport and James Bugental were key figures in making this happen (DeCarvalho 1991). But it was at this conference that the American Association for Humanistic Psychology took shape. And it did not consist entirely of psychologists.

It was Maslow who actually took the main initiatives in starting up the movement now known as humanistic psychology. In the spring of 1949 he and Anthony Sutich met for the first time. Out of their discussions emerged an agreement to work together on developing a psychology which would get away from the then current emphasis on less-than-fully-human behaviour. Maslow had already published his first paper on self-actualization, and Sutich had written one on growth experiences, which was published soon after.

In 1954 Maslow organized a mailing list for the purpose of circulating duplicated copies of articles that could not be published in the official journals because of the commitment of these journals to the behaviourist orthodoxy, or, on the other wing, to the psychoanalytic orthodoxy. The papers dealt with the wider possibilities of the human person, in areas like creativity and autonomy, and with topics like love and growth.

In the summer of 1957 Maslow and Sutich agreed that the time had come to launch a journal. What should its title be? Suggestions included: *Journal of Growth Psychology*, *Journal of Ortho-Psychology* (one meaning of 'ortho' is 'to grow or cause to grow') and *Journal of Self Psychology*. Carl Rogers suggested *Journal of the Human Person*; Herbert Marcuse proposed the name *Journal of Human Studies*.

It took until 1961 before the first issue of the *Journal of Humanistic Psychology* appeared. It was sponsored by Brandeis University, which helped with the costs. Within three months, more than 150 letters had come in, suggesting that an Association be formed. An organization committee was set up, and took a year to drum up possible members, write a constitution and arrange a founding meeting, which took place in 1963. The Association, whose first President was James Bugental, began as a subsidiary of the journal and was directly responsible to the editors. This enabled Brandeis University to help again with the expenses.

THE OLD SAYBROOK CONFERENCE

It was at the Old Saybrook conference, organized by Bugental, that things really came together. The list of attenders was remarkable:

Allport, Gordon, Harvard University
Barzun, Jacques, Columbia University
*Bennis, Warren, MIT
Bugental, J. F. T., Psychological Services Associates, Los Angeles
Buhler, Charlotte B., University of Southern California Medical School
Butterfield, Victor, Wesleyan University
DuBos, Rene, Rockefeller Institute
Kelly, George, Ohio State University
Knapp, R. H., Wesleyan University
Lasko, A. A., Psychological Service Associates, Los Angeles
*MacLeod, Robert, Cornell University
Maslow, A. H., Brandeis University
Matson, Floyd, University of California, Berkeley
May, Rollo, New York City
*McClelland, D. C., Harvard University
Moustakas, Clark E. Birmingham, Michigan
Murphy, Gardner, Menninger Foundation
Murray, H. A., Harvard University
Rogers, Carl, Western Behavioral Sciences Institute
*Sarbin, T. R., University of California, Berkeley
Shoben, E. J., Columbia University
Tratch, Roman, State University College, Oswego, NY
White, R. W., Harvard University
*Note: Bennis, MacLeod, McClelland and Sarbin, according to Allport's notes, were not there. However, we also know that attending the conference were Anthony Sutich, Miles Vich and Norma Rosenquist (Lyman), among others (Taylor 1998).

This was a rich mixture. And it ensured that humanistic psychology had roots in literature, philosophy, education and letters generally, not only in psychology. In fact, people in the field have often referred to novels and poetry, philosophy and Eastern wisdom, and not only to psychology.

In 1965 the Association severed its link with Brandeis and became a charity, and in 1969 the control of the journal was transferred to the Association for Humanistic Psychology (AHP), which in the same year dropped the word American from its title, and became an international organization, some more of whose story is given in Chapter 12.

EASTERN THOUGHT

We have seen how important the Old Saybrook conference was in this history. But there is one important strand in the life of humanistic psychology which is not very obviously represented there, though in my opinion it was implicit: Eastern thought. The reason why this was so was perhaps because in Eastern thought psychology, philosophy and spirituality are not so separate as they are in most Western thought. In the 1950s and 1960s there was a great wave of interest in such things in the literary world. Humanistic psychology also wants to hold these things together, rather than keep them apart.

The so-called Beat Generation included poets like Ginsberg, Ferlinghetti and Corso, and novelists like Kerouac and Burroughs. They were all deeply taken by Eastern philosophy and religion, and in particular by one aspect of it – the emphasis on spontaneity and mistrust of the intellect as a controller. But the crucial thing was that these people did not just read Suzuki and the *Tao Te Ching*: they acted on what they found there.

This was quite new. For many years cultured people had appreciated Eastern art and metaphysics, and had occasionally joined some official Buddhist cult – but to go right to the heart of Zen and Taoism and act out what one found there – that was different. Of course the established intelligentsia reacted with scorn: these young people didn't really understand what they were doing, they were immature and shallow, and besides it was dangerous.

It is clear in Rogers' approach to therapy that the therapist or counsellor may or may not have a great deal of knowledge or experience, but the important thing is to leave it all behind in the actual therapy session with a client. (This is not really very different from the practice of the best psychoanalysts, such as Bion, as Bergantino (1981) makes clear.) The important things is to be all here now, totally present to the client. And this means letting go of knowledge, of theory, even of experience of similar cases. Rogers actually gives this quote from a film-maker, Frances Flaherty:

> What you have to do is to let go, let go every thought of your own, wipe your mind clean, fresh, innocent, newborn, sensitive as

11

unexposed film to take up the impressions around you, and let what will come in. This is the pregnant void, the fertile state of no-mind. This is non-preconception, the beginning of discovery.

(Quoted in Rogers 1990, p. 270)

In terms of our social stereotypes, this approach is much more feminine than masculine. This is an important theme which we shall return to again and again. To the extent that we can actually live and work in this way, we begin to exemplify a quality which the Chinese call tzu-jan (spontaneity, nature). Another example would be the artist painting a picture who accidentally splashes paint on to the canvas, and instead of rubbing it out or covering it up, makes it into an integral part of the finished painting. This is taking responsibility for our actions. It is my mistake, which I made; I do not blame an external clumsiness, or an external brush, or an external self who wanted something else. I take it into my whole situation as a part of that situation, neither minimizing it nor exaggerating it. It is there, and has its own meaning, which I must now take into account.

This is opposed to a theory of painting which holds that the artist has a picture in the imagination which is then put on to canvas as accurately as possible, and still more to a theory of painting which holds that the artist is there to represent as accurately as possible what is out there in the world. But these theories of painting are not held by many artists today, though they are held by many non-artists who want artists to conform to them. In fact, many artists are very much influenced by the Taoist approach which is also found in Zen and some of Tantra. As the six precepts of Tilopa put it:

No thought, no reflection, no analysis,
No cultivation, no intention;
Let it settle itself.
(Quoted in Watts 1957, p. 99)

Zen is all about letting go. One of the key terms is *wu-wei* (non-action, non-making, non-doing, non-striving, non-straining, non-busyness) which is in some ways not all that far from the Western idea of 'not pulling up the roots to see how the plant is getting on'.

One of our characteristic and very masculine beliefs in the West is that if we have a problem, the correct thing to do is to face it, grapple with it and deal with it. In this way we do two new things: we turn the problem into a thing (usually giving it a name, which helps considerably in this) and a dangerous thing at that; and we raise up an opponent of some kind, which becomes equally real and hard and definite. Medicine is an excellent example of this, as Inglis (1964) has spelt out in some detail. This almost invariably has the same result – the problem and its opponent become institutionalized and permanent.

12

In psychology this happens all the time. A problem arises, like the reliability of a battery of questions. It is found that reliability can be increased by adding items to the battery. Now we have so many items that the battery can only be used on very special occasions; also the meaning of the words keeps changing with time, and so on.

The Zen approach is to let go of your problems, rather than tackling them. Does the word 'reliability' make sense? Does the whole idea of giving the 'same' test to two different people make sense? It would be convenient if human beings were like machines, because we know how to handle machines, and 'we' want to handle human beings in the same way. But do we? Who is the 'we' who want to predict and control human beings? Do you want to be predicted and controlled?

If we can ask enough of these simple Zen questions we can perhaps start to let go of some of our psychological assumptions.

In recent years the word Zen has become rather too popular for its own good, and we have even had books like *Zen and the Art of Motor Cycle Maintenance* which are not about Zen at all, and are even quite opposed to Zen. One of the classics remains the book of stories edited by Reps (1961), which is beautiful and unpretentious. I also liked Watts (1957), because of its explanation of the Chinese characters. Kapleau (1967) is very helpful and explicit. And it seems to me, in spite of all the controversy, that *Roots and Wings* (Rajneesh 1979) goes to the heart of the matter. It is full of the spirit of paradox, which is so fundamental to humanistic psychology.

Another of the Eastern influences has been Taoism. One of the assumptions often made in psychology is that we have to concentrate the powers of our intellect upon the things we want to study. We have to see them clearly and distinctly, and talk about them unambiguously. Only in this way can we prove them true or false.

There is a whole other approach which we find in the Tao (Rawson and Legeza 1973). This is that we can only start getting close to something when we unfocus our eyes. As long as we stay focused and single-minded, we are limited by the categories which our intellect (or someone else's, in really bad cases) has already set up. We are at the mercy of old knowledge, which has become fixed and inflexible. When we unfocus, we let in the object, and we let out our other faculties – feeling, intuition, remote associations, creativity.

The *I Ching* (Walker 1986) is the classic Taoist way of demonstrating this. If we want to make a difficult decision, we prepare ourselves to throw the coins or stalks, ask the question while casting the objects, and then interpret the pattern set up, referring to the traditional wisdom on the subject. If we can do this in an intuitive and centred way, an answer either comes or it does not. If it comes, it is probably the best decision we could have made, because our whole self is involved, and not just one cut-off part of ourself. If it does not come, we are not ready to make that decision yet; and that is important too.

Many of us have had a similar experience when doing crosswords, particularly the more difficult ones. If we laboriously puzzle over each clue, trying to make logical sense of it, nothing much happens. But if we unfocus, and let the words play around in our minds in an intuitive way, this is often much more productive, particularly if we are familiar with that specific series of puzzles.

I mentioned the word 'centred' earlier, and this is a crucial word in Taoism. Mary Caroline Richards writes movingly about how centring in the person is like centring in pottery:

> As I grow quiet, the clay centres. For example, I used to grieve because I could not make reliably a close-fitting lid for a canister, a teapot, a casserole. Sometimes the lid fitted, sometimes it didn't. But I wanted it to fit. And I was full of aggravation. Then a GI friend of mine who was stationed in Korea sent me an ancient Korean pot, about a thousand years old. I loved it at once, and then he wrote that he thought I might like it because it looked like something I might have made. Its lid didn't fit at all! Yet it was a museum piece, so to speak. Why, I mused, do I require of myself what I do not require of this pot? Its lid does not fit, but it inspires my spirit when I look at it and handle it. So I stopped worrying. Now I have very little trouble making lids that fit.
>
> (Richards 1969, pp. 22–23)

In Taoism centring has a very precise meaning. In the body there are three 'crucibles' where energy is processed, and they run down the centre of the body. The function of Taoist meditation is to connect up these three crucibles (*tan-t'ien*) so that the energy may flow freely and produce a state of ecstasy.

In Maslow's book on science, he says that if we want to know more about how to do genuinely human science (the experiential kind) we can go to Taoism and learn about receptivity.

> To be able to listen – really, wholly, passively, self-effacingly listen – without presupposing, classifying, improving, controverting, evaluating, approving or disapproving, without dueling with what is being said, without rehearsing the rebuttal in advance, without free-associating to portions of what is being said so that succeeding portions are not heard at all – such listening is rare.
>
> (Maslow 1969, p. 96)

But if we can do it, says Maslow, these are the moments when we are closest to reality. Contemplation is something which is hard to learn, but it can be learned, and it is an essential moment in the scientific process as

14

Maslow sees it. And again recent thinkers such as Anderson and Braud (1998) agree with him.

The discipline of T'ai Chi is a moving meditation which is deeply wound into Taoist philosophy and practice. It is carried out every morning by many thousands of people in China today. It is often taught as a fixed series of exercises which have to be learned and practised exactly until the pupil matches the master. But as Ma-Tsu said many years ago:

> The Tao has nothing to do with discipline. If you say that it is attained by discipline, finishing the discipline turns out to be losing the Tao . . . If you say there is no discipline, this is to be the same as ordinary people.
>
> (Quoted in Watts 1957, p. 117)

Note carefully what this is saying. It is not saying that the Tao is attained by discipline, and it is not saying that the Tao can be attained without discipline. The collateral Indian phrase is *neti neti* (not this, not that) and this expresses an important truth about the Tao – it escapes all opposites. Maslow talks in various places about 'dichotomy-transcendence' and this is another way of putting it. In philosophical terms, we are talking about a dialectical approach to the world, which can do equal justice to the masculine and to the feminine, and which is not taken in by apparent opposition and contrast. This is symbolized in the well-known yin-yang symbol, as we saw in the Introduction. The two shapes are contrasted and unified at the same time. Nothing could be more different, nothing could be more similar. As the philosopher Hegel says:

> Thus essentially relative to another, somewhat is virtually an other against it: and since what is passed into is quite the same as what passes over, since both have one and the same attribute, viz. to be an other, it follows that something in its passage into other only joins with itself. To be thus self-related in the passage, and in the other, is the genuine Infinity.
>
> (Hegel 1892, p. 176)

This may sound difficult, but what he is saying is that the old idea of infinity, where something just goes on for ever, is a bad infinity – it can never really be infinite, because it excludes the finite, and the finite therefore limits it forever. But when one thing – or one person – finds itself in another, that is the good infinity. And this is really a statement about love rather than about mathematics. If I meet another person, and instead of finding alienation find myself, that is the true infinity; or true love. If I meet another person, and find that the more of myself I give away, the more I get back, that is the true infinity – which may also be ecstatic. (And this is

15

actually the philosophical background to the idea of synergy, which we shall meet further on.)

So the yin-yang symbol can be very powerful in what it suggests, once we are able to look at it with the kind of insight which dialectics gives us. It is also extremely simple, as Huang (1973) makes clear. In recent years Tao has again become very popular, and we have had such titles as the Tao of Physics and even the Tao of Pooh. Ken Wilber has an excellent critique of such attempts to use the Tao for illegitimate purposes. His interviewer sums up at one point: 'Reduce all things to material particles, then discover the particles are holoarchic, then claim that the holoarchy is the Tao' (Wilber 1982, p. 260). Wilber agrees that this sort of thing is nothing much to do with the Tao at all, and goes on to criticize many of the New Age thinkers who are actually very one-sided, whereas the whole essence of the Tao is not to be one-sided.

But there was also another current from the East which went into humanistic psychology. This was the Tantric tradition, running through various Hindu centres, strong in Tibet, and found in other forms among the Hopi Indians, the Sufis, the Theosophists and Rosicrucians. The best-known form is the Kundalini system.

There are seven chakras, or centres, in the body, and the energy passes through them. It is important to understand that these chakras are not just nodes or points – they are locations of the person (Bruyere 1989). It is as if the person had seven brains, instead of one; or as if there were seven subpersonalities which had to be contended with; or seven ego-states which could be entered into.

And it seems that we cannot enter into the higher ego-states until we have dealt properly with the lower ones. Here is the order in which they stand. There are many versions of this, but this is the one which makes most sense in my experience:

Chakra	Meaning	Location
7	Cosmic consciousness, bliss	Top of head
6	Intuition	Level of pineal body, 3rd eye
5	Communication and expression	Level of throat
4	Affection, love	Level of heart
3	Assertiveness, anger, aggression	Level of navel, solar plexus or spleen
2	Sexual energy	Level of genitals
1	Primitive energy, grand potential	Base of spine

Here is an example to show how this schema can actually be used in group work. Will Schutz says:

A man in an encounter group is having difficulty establishing a love relationship (fourth chakra) with a woman in the group. She reports that she feels some phoniness in his approach and feeling. What frequently results is that he has a sexual desire (second chakra) for her and is not acknowledging that this issue must be dealt with first. Or sometimes he has great hostility toward women (third chakra) that he is also not dealing with.

(Schutz 1971, p. 65)

Schutz feels that the general principle that one cannot skip over chakras at will has been extraordinarily illuminating for him. Certainly it gives much food for thought to anyone who is seriously concerned with communication: we are continually trying to communicate (fifth chakra) without entering into any real relationship with the other person – as I am doing now, for example.

In the work of healing, the chakras can be very important, but that area lies rather outside the scope of this book. We have looked at Zen, at the Tao and at Tantra.

SCIENCE AND RESEARCH

It seems easy enough to see how these Eastern approaches could be used in group work. It is also easy to see how they could apply to art – and it is interesting to see here how jazz and rock music fulfils all the demands more than most other art forms – but less easy to see how it could be used in science.

Maslow (1969) wrote a very important book on science, which is still of great interest today (Reason and Bradbury, in press). He divided his book into ten sections, each one dealing with a dilemma which faces everyone trying to work on research with human beings. In most cases he resolves this dilemma by grasping both sides of it in a typically Eastern manner.

(1) *Humanism vs. mechanism.* Science is often seen as mechanistic and dehumanized. Maslow sees his work as about the rehumanization of science. But he conceives this to be not a divisive effort to oppose one 'wrong' view with another 'right' view, nor to cast out anything. He tells us that his conception of science in general and of psychology in general, is *inclusive* of mechanistic science. He believes that mechanistic science (which in psychology takes the form of behaviorism, of cognitive science and of the empirical approach generally) to be not incorrect but rather too narrow and limited to serve as a general or comprehensive philosophy (Maslow 1969, p. 5).

(2) *Holism vs. reductionism.* If we want to do psychology, in the sense of learning about people, we have often in practice to approach one person at

a time. What is the state of mind in which this is best done? This is one of my favourite quotes from Maslow:

> Any clinician knows that in getting to know another person it is best to keep your brain out of the way, to look and listen totally, to be completely absorbed, receptive, passive, patient and waiting rather than eager, quick and impatient. It does not help to start measuring, questioning, calculating or testing out theories, categorizing or classifying. If your brain is too busy, you won't hear or see well. Freud's term 'free-floating attention' describes well this non-interfering, global, receptive, waiting kind of cognizing another person.
>
> (Maslow 1969, pp. 10–11)

If we adopt this approach, Maslow says, we have a chance of being able to describe the person holistically rather than reductively. In other words, we can see the *whole* person, rather than some selected and split-off aspect of the person. But this depends crucially on the *relationship* between the knower and the known. We have to approach the person as a person:

> This is different from the model way in which we approach physical objects, i.e. manipulating them, poking at them, to see what happens, taking them apart, etc. If you do this to human beings, you *won't* get to know them. They won't *want* you to know them. They won't *let* you know them.
>
> (Maslow 1969, p. 13)

My own view is that this is a basic point which has to be taken on board by anyone studying people.

(3) *I–Thou vs. I–It*. Maslow was way ahead of his time in recognizing the importance of Martin Buber's distinction between two ways of approaching another person. It is only today that this idea is being taken up by many other people as important for research.

He takes the I–Thou and compares it with the more conventional starting-point of spectator knowledge. He makes it clear that he sees immense value in the I–Thou approach. Not only for studying human beings:

> But I wish to raise the more radical question: can *all* the sciences, *all* knowledge be conceptualized as a resultant of a loving or caring interrelationship between knower and known? What would be the advantages to us of setting this epistemology alongside the one that now reigns in 'objective science'? Can we simultaneously use both? My own feeling is that we can and should use both epistemologies

as the situation demands. I do not see them as contradictory but as enriching each other . . . Reality seems to be a kind of alloy of the perceiver and the perceived, a sort of mutual product, a transaction.

(Maslow 1969, pp. 108–111)

This is bold thinking, and many of us are still catching up on it. Maslow never mentions Merleau-Ponty, but the thinking is clearly related to phenomenological ideas (Valle 1998).

(4) *Courage vs. fear*. Most research and most knowledge, he says, comes from deficiency motivation. That is, it is based on fear, and is carried out to allay anxiety; it is basically defensive. Maslow enumerates 21 cognitive pathologies which emanate from this basic stance (Maslow 1969, pp. 26–29).

(5) *Science and sacralization*. Science is notorious for the way in which it seems to oppose religion and also such emotions as reverence, mystery, wonder and awe. Maslow suggests that deficiency-oriented science has a need to desacralize as a defence.

The question Maslow wants to ask is: is it in the intrinsic nature of science or knowledge that it must desacralize, must strip away values in a way that he calls 'countervaluing'? On the contrary, says Maslow. And in this he is close to the recent thinking of Ken Wilber (1998), who in his book *The Marriage of Sense and Soul* is making some very similar points (see also Braud and Anderson 1998). Recently Bentz and Shapiro (1998) have adopted a specifically Buddhist approach to scientific research.

(6) *Experiential knowledge vs. spectator knowledge*. The world of experience can be described with two languages; a subjective (first-person) one and an objective (third-person) one. 'In his presence I feel small' is first-person, while 'He's trying to dominate me' is third-person.

Maslow says that experiential knowledge is *sine qua non* but not all. It is necessary but not sufficient. He does not want to separate it from conceptual knowledge. He says that experiential knowledge is prior to verbal-conceptual knowledge but that they are hierarchically-integrated and need each other (Maslow 1969, pp. 46–47).

And he says that there are ways of checking out subjective knowledge, by comparing it with other people's subjective knowledge. This is where we should usually start:

This is why I can think that (1) most psychological problems do and should begin with phenomenology rather than with objective, behavioural laboratory techniques, and also (2) that we must usually press on from phenomenological beginnings *toward* objective, experimental, behavioural laboratory methods. This is I think a normal and usual path from a less reliable beginning toward a more reliable level of knowledge.

(Maslow 1969, p. 47)

But the phenomenological approach – the use of subjective and first-person experience as a source of knowledge – requires high standards of the knower. Carl Rogers, as we shall see in a moment, also makes the same point. The injunction might read, says Maslow, 'make yourself into a good instrument of knowledge. Cleanse yourself as you would the lenses of your microscope. Become as fearless as you can, as honest, authentic and ego-transcending as you can' (Maslow 1969, p. 48). And he notes that if this were taken seriously, the education of scientists would be very different from what it is now. One might cultivate peak experiences, or Zen Buddhism; one would explore altered states of consciousness; one would work in therapy to dispose of one's neuroses. We have to learn how to know the world by setting aside our supposed knowledge of it. (Mitroff and Kilmann (1978) speak of 'authenticity' in relation to the kind of scientist we are talking about here.)

(7) *The comprehensive vs. the simple*. Scientific work has two directions or poles or goals: one is towards simplicity and condensation, the other towards total comprehensiveness and inclusiveness. Both of these are necessary, but we should distrust simplicity as we seek it. We should also not value simplicity and elegance to the exclusion of richness and experiential truth. We should accept the formula 'First look, and then know', but add to it 'and then look again'. We can then learn that scientific knowledge, no matter how abstract, can enrich our experience rather than impoverishing it, so long as we don't use it as a substitute for experiencing. The movement is from the comprehensive to the simple, and back again to the comprehensive, if we want to make human sense.

(8) *Suchness vs. abstraction*. There are two different kinds of meanings, which are complementary rather than mutually exclusive. Maslow calls one 'Abstractness meaning' (classifications) and the other 'Suchness meaning', having to do with the experiential realm. One tends to reduce things to some unified explanation; the other experiences something in its own right and in its own nature.

This gets us away from the tendency to call anything other than a simple unified explanation 'absurd', 'meaningless', 'ineffable', 'inexplicable', and so on; to do this is 'a failure of nerve'. By talking about 'suchness meaning' we are saying that direct experience can be studied, talked about, deepened and better understood. Such an approach does not have to exclude intuition as a type of knowledge.

There may be two kinds of scientists: the cool, who go most for abstraction and explanation, and the warm, who go for suchness and understanding. But great scientists integrate both.

(9) *Values and value-free science.* If we say that science can tell us nothing about why, only about how; if we say that science cannot help us to choose between good and evil, we are saying that science is only an instrument, only a technology, to be used equally either by good men or by villains. But Maslow believes that science can discover the values by which people should live.

First, the weak instinctoid needs which he discovered and popularized can be thought of as built-in values. And it is these values which are found, uncovered, recovered, perhaps we should say in the course of psychotherapy or self-discovery. Second, science itself has a set of values. (Mitroff (1974) fruitfully explored this idea.) Some scientists actually confess to trying to shape the culture as they would like it to be. Certainly in the human sciences this idea is becoming more popular: a critical approach is more valued now than it has ever been.

(10) *Maturity vs. immaturity.* Science is incredibly 'masculine', in the sense of idealizing the stereotyped image of the male. Maslow sees this as a sign of immaturity, much more to do with the adolescent boy who desperately wants to be accepted as a man, rather than with the mature man, who may have many 'feminine' traits. Ian Mitroff has also written very well about the way in which science habitually falls into a 'masculine' form (Mitroff 1974, Chapter 4).

What we have been looking at in this chapter is a remarkable flight of the human mind. Humanistic psychology is not just psychology. It is indebted to Eastern thought. And it is interested in science – not from the point of view of simply accepting the standard view of science as postulated in a myriad academic texts, but rather of creating a newer view of science as a human endeavour which calls on the whole person rather than just on the intellect.

The paradox here is that although humanistic psychology is and is not psychology, it has some claim to be the only psychology which is a true psychology. Let Ken Wilber explain what we mean by this. Wilber says, following St Bonaventure, that men and women have at least three modes of attaining knowledge – 'three eyes', as he put it. These are: the *eye of flesh*, by which we perceive the external world of space, time and objects; the *eye of reason*, by which we obtain a knowledge of philosophy, logic and the mind itself; and the *eye of contemplation*, by which we rise to a knowledge of transcendent realities.

In mathematics, in logic – and more: in imagination, in conceptual understanding, in psychological insight, in creativity – we see things with the mind's eye which are not fully present to the eye of flesh. Thus we say that the mental field includes but greatly transcends the fleshy field.

The eye of contemplation is to the eye of reason as the eye of reason is to the eye of flesh. Just as reason transcends flesh, so contemplation transcends reason. Just as reason cannot be reduced to, nor derived from, fleshy knowledge, so contemplation cannot be reduced to nor derived from reason.

Wilber then says that, by and large, empiric-analytic science belongs to the eye of flesh, phenomenological philosophy and psychology to the eye of mind, and authentic religion and meditation to the eye of contemplation. What I am saying here is that humanistic psychology is the classic way to use the eye of mind. Most psychology makes the classic mistake of trying to study people by using the eye of flesh. This then isolates their behaviour – the observable actions they pursue in the world – and ignores most of what is actually relevant – their intentions, their meanings, their visions.

Empiric-analytic inquiry is a *monologue* – a symbolizing inquirer looks at a nonsymbolizing occasion; humanistic psychology, however, is a *dialogue* – a symbolizing inquirer looks at other symbolizing occasions. The paradigm of empiric-analytic inquiry is, 'I see the rock'; the paradigm of humanistic inquiry is, 'I talk to you and vice versa'. Empiric-analytic inquiry can proceed *without* talking to the object of its investigation – no empirical scientist talks to electrons, plastic, molecules, protozoa, ferns, or whatever, because he or she is studying preverbal entities. But the very field of humanistic inquiry is *communicative exchange* or intersubjective and intersymbolic relationships (language and logic), and this approach depends in large measure on talking to and with the subject of investigation. We saw this in our examination of Maslow's thinking. And any science that *talks* to its subject of investigation is not empirical but humanistic, not monologic but dialogic.

Wilber has a nice diagram which summarizes this with admirable concision.

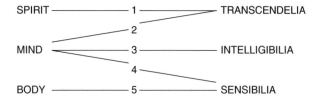

(5 is simple sensorimotor cognition, the eye of flesh. 4 is empiric-analytic thought. 3 is mental-phenomenological thought, the eye of reason. 2 is paradoxical thinking, mind attempting to reason about spirit. 1 is gnosis, the eye of contemplation (Wilber 1983, p. 67).)

What we are saying, then, is that if the humanistic approach both is and is not psychology, the part that is psychology is real psychology, proper psychology, the type of psychology that is genuinely applicable to human beings.

Secular humanism

There have been a number of pronouncements by important people recently about secular humanism, saying that it is a dead end, a spiritual disaster, a false doctrine and the gospel of materialism.

However true or false these accusations may be – and others like them – our withers are unwrung. We do not have to concern ourselves about them one way or another, because humanistic psychologists are not secular humanists. How could they be, if what we have seen in this chapter is true? But it is one of the oldest confusions in the business. I remember when I first went to an AHP event in London, the caretaker told me it was the humanist meeting, and I thought at the time that it was run by some humanist group.

But in fact the two things are like chalk and cheese. The main plank in humanistic psychology is the integration of body, feelings, intellect, soul and spirit, and it says so very clearly in all the introductory leaflets put out by AHP affiliates in various countries around the world. This integration is the key to what we call self-actualization, and all our workshops touch on it in some way. The secular humanists, on the other hand, are often not much interested in the body or in feelings, and actively deny any existence to the spiritual or transpersonal aspects of our life.

I actually joined the British Humanist Association (BHA) at one time, to see whether any links could be made, but I found the people involved in it to be aridly intellectual, unawarely sexist and very narrow, spending a lot of their time and energy knocking Christianity, and some of the rest on issues like abortion and euthanasia. I lasted a year and walked out in protest at the sexism expressed at the Annual General Meeting.

Now it may well be that secular humanism should not be judged by the activities of the BHA (or the National Secular Society, which it much resembles) because humanism is itself a much wider philosophy. Nevertheless, the BHA is trying to represent it, and there must be some connection somewhere. None of these things is humanistic psychology.

2

HUMANISTIC PSYCHOLOGY IS AND IS NOT OPTIMISTIC

When people first come across humanistic psychology, they usually find it presented as full of blue-sky optimism. This is because the presentation is restricted to Abraham Maslow and Carl Rogers. What I want to say here is that humanistic psychology is not restricted to these, but also includes people like James Bugental, Rollo May, Kirk Schneider and Alvin Mahrer who are not particularly optimistic at all.

MASLOW AND MAHRER

Abraham Maslow is a very important pioneer figure in humanistic psychology. His theory of human needs and human development says that there is a normal process of growth which applies to all people (see Table 2.1). We start with purely physiological needs, which have to be satisfied. Once these are satisfied to an acceptable extent, security needs appear, and we want a fixed framework for our world – something firm to hang on to and believe in. Once we have this to an acceptable extent, effectance needs appear (this step was added by David Wright (1973) but I think Maslow would have accepted it), and we want to achieve some kind of mastery of our own bodies and the world around us; at this stage it is seen in rather rigid terms, on a kind of horsetrading, win/lose basis, in the short term. This marks the end of what Alderfer (1972) calls the Existence phase of development.

As with most of these stage theories, it is possible for a person to get stuck at a given stage. If the needs are not satisfied, or if there is something traumatic at the time which cannot be digested for one reason or another, the person can remain at a lower stage of development. We have all come across people who are stuck at the stage of security and safety. They do not dare to move on. To such a person, safety is paramount, and no risks must be taken at all. Similarly, it is possible to get stuck at the stage of mastery. Such a person is only interested in power. In any situation, if I am locked in at this level, I look to see where the power is, and try to get close to that.

24

Table 2.1 Maslow's hierarchy of needs and some collateral research

Level	Maslow	Kohlberg	Loevinger
6	Self-actualization Being that self which I truly am Being all I have it in me to be Fully functioning person Authentic Creative	Individual principles True personal conscience Universal principles fully internalized Genuinely autonomous Selfishness B	Autonomous: integrated Flexible and creative Internal conflicts are faced and recognized Tolerance for ambiguity Respect for autonomy
5	Esteem 2 Goals founded on self-evaluated standards Self-confidence	Social contract Utilitarian law-making Principles of general welfare Long-term goals	Conscientious Bound by self-imposed rules Differentiated thinking Self-aware
		THE GREAT GAP	
4	Esteem 1 Respect from others Social status Recognition	Law and order Authority maintenance Fixed social rules Find duty and do it	Conformist 2 Seeking general rules of social conformity Justifying conformity
3	Love and belongingness Wish for affection Need for acceptance Need for tenderness	Personal concordance Good-boy morality Seeking social approval Liking to be liked	Conformist 1 Going along with the crowd Anxiety about rejection Need for support
2	Effectance Mastery Imposed control Blame and retaliation Domination	Instrumental hedonism Naive egocentrism Horse-trading approach Profit-and-loss calculation Selfishness A	Self-protective Wary and exploitative People are means to ends Competitive stance Fear of being caught
1	Safety Defence against danger Fight or flight Fear: world is a scary place	Obedience/punishment Deference to superior power Rules are external and eternal Musts and shoulds	Impulsive Domination by immediate cue, body feelings No reflection

Note: After David Wright (1973), omitting lowest level of Maslow (physiological) and Loevinger (pre-social, symbiotic) (1976).

continues overleaf

Table 2.1 (cont.)

Level	Piaget	Alderfer	Wilber
6	Dialectical operations (Klaus Riegel 1984) Beyond formal logic Integration of contradictions	Growth	Centaur 2 Vision-logic Bodymind integration Peak experiences Existential self
5	Formal operations Substage 2: Thinking about thinking Forethought, speculation	Growth	Centaur 1 Ecological imagination Awareness of awareness Relative autonomy
		THE GREAT GAP	
4	Formal operations Substage 1: Capacity for hypothetico-deductive thinking	Relatedness	Mental ego Full rationality Syllogistic logic Science/mathematics
3	Concrete operations Ability to take role of other	Relatedness	Mythic-membership Dependent on roles Norm-dominated
2	Preoperational Mastery Incapable of seriation	Existence	Magical Primary process thinking High credulity
1	Sensoriphysical	Existence	Body ego Archaic level of thought

Once we have this feeling of mastery to an acceptable extent, needs for love and belongingness appear, and we seek general social approval – we like to be liked. Once these needs are satisfied to an acceptable extent, we go on to the need to win esteem from others – we want to measure up and be accepted for our performance in some specific role; it becomes very important to know where we stand. This marks the end of what Alderfer (1972) calls the Relatedness phase of development.

Again we can get halted at one of these stages, and fail to move on. The person who stops at the level of love and belongingness wants everyone to love them. Here comes the people pleaser, the archetypal conformist. Such a person is willing to give up everything for the sake of social approval – and this means the approval of all, not just a few. No one must disapprove. Large numbers of people fall into this category. If, on the other hand, we get fixated on the level of getting esteem from others, we become the archetypal bureaucrat. We absolutely need to know our status, our position, our rights and duties. We only want the approval of people we respect and look up to. Other people do not matter.

Once these needs are satisfied to an acceptable extent, our own self-esteem needs begin to appear, but are often suppressed or find the way blocked. However, difficult or not, at this point our own self-respect becomes the most important thing; we set our own standards, rather than taking them from others. And once this need is satisfied to an acceptable extent, the full self-actualization needs appear, and we start to seek to realize our full potential, to raise our sense of what is possible, to explore our own creativity, our need to know and understand, our need for beauty, and so on (see Table 2.1). This marks the end of what Alderfer (1972) calls the Growth phase of development.

This theory of development or maturation became very acceptable to the people in and around humanistic psychology, and it made a lot of sense when applied to the problems found in organizations, as we shall see in later chapters. Later it was strongly supported by quite independent work on moral development (Kohlberg 1981) and ego development (Loevinger 1976) – hard research carried out in several countries. This is a very brief thumbnail sketch. People familiar with the Maslow scale will notice that I have made two amendments to the usual statement of it. I have supplied an extra need between 'Safety' and 'Love and Belongingness' labelled as 'Competence or Mastery'. This makes the scale much more compatible with the other scales already mentioned. And I have separated the two kinds of 'esteem needs', because a need for 'esteem from others' and a need for 'self-esteem' are two quite different things, as Maslow himself observed later.

The difference between the need for esteem (from others) and the need for self-esteem should be made very clear in the final write-up. Make the differentiation sharply, clearly, and unmistakably.

WHAT IS HUMANISTIC PSYCHOLOGY?

> Reputation or prestige or applause are very nice, and are for children and adolescents even absolutely necessary before real self-esteem can be built up. Or to say it the other way about, one of the necessary foundations for self-esteem is respect and applause from other people, especially in the younger years. Ultimately, real self-esteem rests upon all the things mentioned above, on a feeling of dignity, of controlling one's own life, and of being one's own boss. Let's call this dignity.
>
> (Maslow 1965, p. 45)

One of the worst things that has happened to the theory is that it has often been printed in the form of a triangle or pyramid. At the bottom are the physiological needs, and at the top is self-actualization (see Rubin and McNeil 1987, p. 248 or Atkinson et al. 1993, p. 547 for example). I don't recall Maslow ever doing this, but in popular undergraduate texts it is often done. It is much more logical to print it as a simple ladder, which is how it is always treated in any case. I have expanded a good deal on all this recently (Rowan 1998a, Rowan 1999).

It is clear in any case how optimistic the theory is. It is almost as if we are all on an escalator which will take us all the way to the end, if we will just stay on it.

Alvin Mahrer has a very different story to tell. His writings come later than those of Maslow. His big theoretical book, called simply *Experiencing*, came out in 1978, and was reprinted by a different publisher in 1989. He comes from the same humanistic and existential camp as Maslow, but he writes in a different key. For him there is nothing like an escalator. Our relationship with the world comes from our relationship with our own inner figures. These inner figures he labels as 'potentials'. In other theories they are labelled as subpersonalities, ego-states, internal objects, selves, little Is, small minds, agents, complexes and so forth (Rowan 1990). Much of our energy, in many cases, is taken up with internal struggles between our own potentials.

In other words, his theory of personality is not what Maddi (1996) calls a fulfilment theory (like Maslow or Rogers or Allport), it is a conflict theory (like Freud or Jung or Rank or Perls). You could call it a psychodynamic theory, because it is all about the inner dynamics of the personality which lie beneath the surface.

Instead of our early life being a progression from one set of needs to the next, as in Maslow's version, it is a struggle to emerge from the psychological field set up by our parents. In the process of this struggle, we very often acquire inner conflicts, setting up parts of ourselves as enemies who threaten us. A very clear exposition of exactly how and why this happens is to be found in Ken Wilber's chapter 'Where It was, there shall I be' in Volume 1 of the *Collected Works* (1999b). Some of these we may be conscious of, but others we may not be aware of at all. We simply feel driven or compelled to act in certain ways, which may or may not be to our advantage.

One way of escaping from the pain which this gives us is to go into a state of unfeeling. If we choose this defence, we become what Mahrer calls half-persons. Instead of relating to the world directly, we hide behind a wall of safety which prevents us from feeling too much. And we live in a society which favours this. 'The collectivization occurs as a mechanical, techno-logical society doing to us what each individual is busy doing to his deeper potential' (Mahrer 1978, p. 268).

One of the functions of individual therapy is to free us from the internal conflicts which may turn us into half-persons. By opening up the inner world which seems at first so unknown or so threatening to us, we can come to terms with our own potentials, and even transform them into life-enhancing assets. For Mahrer, as for Bugental (1987), therapy is ideally a life-changing process. The person who comes out is not the same person who went in. 'Here is the utter risk. When you emerge from the first internal process after a few minutes of being with your insides, or after a day of intensive self-probing, or after months of good psychotherapy, then you are different – perhaps only slightly, perhaps sharply different – from what you were. Be that new person, whatever that is' (Mahrer 1978, p. 285).

Of course it has to be the right kind of therapy. Any therapy which aims at adjustment, at the cure of symptoms, at the reduction of anxiety and so forth is simply enabling the person to go on functioning at the old level, in the old way. And most therapy is like this. For this reason Mahrer is very critical of most therapy. It seems to him that the goal of such therapy is to avoid change rather than embrace it. For the real transformation that Mahrer is talking about, it has to be a therapy which is prepared to deal with the deepest regions of the personality, and aims at liberation.

So Mahrer is not saying that it is a hopeless case, at all. He is just saying that there is nothing automatic about our healthy development as persons. It has to be chosen and perhaps fought for against odds. If we take that route, and are prepared to do the work, we can emerge healed and whole. And in his later books (e.g. Mahrer 1996) he explains exactly how this may be done.

ROGERS AND MAY

Let us now look at another important and interesting contrast between humanistic writers. This time both are therapists. (Maslow of course was not a therapist.) Again Rogers and his work are very well known, and very well described in recent books such as the scholarly work of Godfrey Barrett-Lennard (1998).

Rogers says that people can develop into 'fully-functioning persons', and that there is really no obstacle to this. There is a natural process of organismic growth which only requires nurturing and enabling. The two processes of unhindering and unfolding are sufficient to facilitate the natural growth of the person.

His approach was essentially based on the idea that the 'neurotic' or 'mentally sick' patient was basically all right, and made sense. By simply paying attention to the patient – or client, as Rogers preferred to say – and taking their speech and actions seriously, the person's own basic health would begin to work and produce a cure.

This brings out one of the thoughts which is very characteristic – people are all right as they are. Remember the transformation of quantity into quality referred to in the Introduction, and the paradoxical theory of change mentioned there. There is nothing extra which they need in order to be whole – all that is necessary is for them to take down the shutters and the blinkers, and let the sun shine in. As Rogers puts it:

> One of the most revolutionary concepts to grow out of our clinical experience is the growing recognition that the innermost core of man's nature, the deepest layers of his personality, the base of his 'animal nature', is positive in nature – is basically socialized, forward-moving, rational and realistic . . . We do not need to ask who will socialize him, for one of his own deepest needs is for affiliation and communication with others . . . He is realistically able to control himself, and he is incorrigibly socialized in his desires. There is no beast in man. There is only man in man . . .
>
> (Rogers 1961, pp. 90–105)

This outlook distinguishes humanistic psychology from the other two main streams in psychology today. Both behaviourism and psychoanalysis have a pessimistic, 'bad-animal' view of human nature, and therefore an exaggerated respect for the needs and powers of society to socialize and tame the child, and to keep the adult socialized and tamed. (Cognitive psychology in its own way betrays a lack of trust in the person, and is no better in this regard.) It is for this reason that humanistic psychology is sometimes called the Third Force. Rogers links with Maslow in that his theory of the person also holds that people tend naturally and of themselves to grow into fully functioning people, though they can hold themselves back from that in many different ways and for many different reasons. There is again one great force which drives through people and pushes them on, though they may resist or be prevented by others from going all the way.

Children are prevented from developing normally by conditions of worth being applied to them. This means that they are not valued for themselves, but only for their ability to conform to the parental needs and wishes. They may then lose their internal locus of evaluation, and with it their ability to trust their own judgement. They have been given a negative self-image, and have lost touch with the real self. To act upon the negative self-image is to increase this separation.

Rogers (1959) laid out his theory with great precision, and there is nothing half-baked about it. He was awarded both scientific and professional accolades, and certainly deserves to be listened to. But his optimism is clear and undeniable.

Rollo May found this inadequate as a total view of the person. He wanted to say that people were more complex than Rogers made out. In particular, he wanted to say that Rogers did not do justice to the *daimon* in people. This idea of the *daimon* is not an easy one to grasp. In Ancient Greek mythology, it is a spirit which can be good or bad, but which is essentially divine. It speaks of the energy or activity of a god or goddess, which may be favourable or unfavourable. It could also be something like a guardian angel, also known as the genius of a person. May is saying, then, that there is a whole dimension that Rogers is missing: a vast energy which can be used for good or ill. May also found Rogers lacking in an appreciation of the negative. He felt that negativity, destruction, evil, were all essential parts of good literature and meaningful life. The struggle, May felt, was strengthening. 'Damn braces: Bless relaxes', as William Blake used to say. May spells this out very clearly in one of his books:

> We need, therefore, to put the question, Does not Rogers' emphasis on rationality, and his belief that the individual will simply choose what is rational for him, leave out a large section of the spectrum of human experience, namely, all the irrational feelings? Granted that it is not 'exquisitely rational' to bite the hand that feeds you, yet that is just what clients and patients do – which is one reason they need therapy. And furthermore, this anger, aggressiveness and hostility, often express the patient's most precious effort toward autonomy, his way of trying to find some point at which he can stand against the authorities who have always suffocated his life – suffocated it by 'kindness' as well as by exploitation.
>
> (May 1980, p. 18)

This appreciation of anger comes up again and again in May's work, and he says that it is a valuable emotion, and needs to be cultivated when oppressive forces are at work. Where Rogers sees growth, May sees paradox. One of his most eloquest sentences comes out of this belief: 'Growth is always within a dialectical relationship in a dilemma which is never fully resolved' (May 1980, p. 19). In other words, struggle is an essential part of life. To wish it away is to wish life itself away. Jung said something similar.

May returns later to the question of Rogers and his attitude to therapy in a critical way. He asks whether one of the weaknesses of the Rogerian approach is his 'underplaying of the negative aspects of will'. He detects a tendency to cover over the emotional differences between patient and therapist. And he continues:

> Rogers has, of course, been in the forefront of those insisting on respect for the patient. But is not respect best and most profoundly shown by openly admitting anger, hostility and conflict with another, but at the same time not withdrawing one whit from the relationship? Indeed, such 'inclusion of the negative' normally can make a relationship, and the mutual respect in it, more solid and trustworthy.
>
> (May 1980, p. 216)

It can easily be seen that there are real differences here, and that May emphasizes paradox and the negative in a way that Rogers does not.

Humanistic psychology embraces both Maslow and Mahrer, Rogers and May. It does not have to decide between them. It does not have to accept one and reject the other. It also embraces James Bugental, who was the first President of the Association for Humanistic Psychology. Here is what he says:

> When I am most able to attend to my patient in the way that is creative, I listen to him and experience his total presentation of himself in a fashion which subjectively gives me the experience of participation with him in his telling of himself. Then it is almost as though I can feel his words flowing from my own awareness concurrently as I hear them from him. From time to time my immersion in this stream of his talk and all that goes with it will be intruded upon by awarenesses from within myself which may either be disruptions due to my inauthenticity (incongruity) or may be my sensing of the patient's incongruity or inauthenticity. This is not an intellective or rational or deductive matching of what the patient is presenting with what I deem to be the reality. It is a wholistic response of my subjective awareness to the experience of being immersed in the patient's presentation of himself.
>
> (Bugental 1981, pp. 110–111)

This is not optimistic or pessimistic, it is just human. And ultimately that is all that humanistic psychology is about: being human. It is not about being right or wrong.

CENTAUR CONSCIOUSNESS

It is important to say, I believe, that the only way that humanistic psychology can hold together the contradictions is through its penetration of the secrets of Centaur consciousness. It is only in recent years that this understanding has dawned. The person who has led the way in pointing this out is Ken Wilber, who at first called it the Existential level of psychospiritual development (Wilber 1975). By 1977 he was also calling it the Centaur level (Wilber 1977). By 1980 he was preferring to refer to the Centauric realms (Wilber 1980). It was not until 1996 that anyone else independently mapped Centauric consciousness, Jenny Wade (1996) doing it in one way (calling it Authentic consciousness), and Beck and Cowan (1996) in another (calling different aspects of it Green, Yellow and Turquoise consciousness), both making use of the little-known research of Clare Graves. Centaur consciousness makes use of dialectical thinking and what Wilber calls vision-logic. Now that this work has been done, it is easy for anyone to see that what we have here is a crucially important field for exploration and further work. And already it is clear that Centaur consciousness is not the end of the road, as so many of us thought it was when Maslow wrote. It is a necessary moment in the process of psychospiritual development: and it has produced humanistic psychology. We shall see more about this in the next chapter. This means that we do not have to be perfect or have all the answers. It also means that we can claim to be self-actualized without being too proud or too assertive. The self we are actualizing is only the Centaur self, not anything more or less.

Similarly if someone at the Centaur level claims to be authentic, this is not an overweening or suspect claim – it is just part of being human. In the early days of my acquaintance with humanistic psychology, I wondered what a fully functioning person would look like. I soon discovered Barry Stevens (1970), who in her writing shows what it means to be authentic, open, perceptive and all the other things which Maslow (1987) says are the characteristics of the self-actualized person. I am not saying she is a perfect person, just that in that book she is a good example of a human being.

3

HOW HUMANISTIC PSYCHOLOGY
HOLDS THE CONTRADICTIONS

If humanistic psychology is so full of contradictions – and there are others we have yet to meet in later chapters – how is it that it hangs together at all? In this chapter we shall examine one way in which this might happen, without at any point saying that this is the only possible story.

Suppose that there were a level of consciousness, historically developed, which had as essential features such central values as those put forward by Maslow, Mahrer, Rogers, May and Bugental. Suppose that in the process of such development it became very clear that this level of consciousness had boundaries at both ends, so to speak, and could be very well outlined in terms of such boundaries. And suppose that all the features we have been noticing were essentially characteristic of this level of consciousness.

THE WILBER MODEL

Such a theory has been put forward by Ken Wilber (1996a, 1996b) both on an individual and on a social level. He has used the work of Gebser (1985) and Habermas (1979) in a creative way to make a very solid account of how this level arose and where its boundaries lie.

What he says is that there is a process of psychospiritual development which we are all going through, both as individuals and as members of a historically located culture. He has outlined this process, and shows that we are very familiar with its early stages. The later stages are much more controversial, but follow the same form.

The easiest way to describe this model seems to be by going through Figure 3.1. It can be seen from this that there are three broad sections, labelled as pre-personal, personal and transpersonal. One of Wilber's most insistent themes is that we tend to suffer from the pre/trans fallacy – that is, we confuse what is pre-personal with what is transpersonal. Some do it (like Freud) by saying that the transpersonal does not really exist – it is just a projection from the pre-personal; others do it (like Jung) by saying that the

34

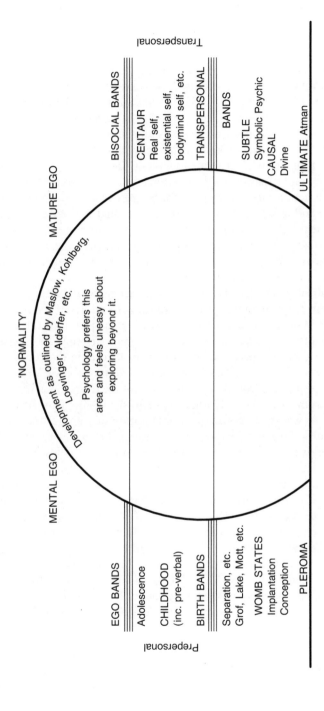

Figure 3.1 Ken Wilber's map.

Source: Rowan (1983b, p. 102). Revised and consolidated by John Rowan in April 1982 and approved by Ken Wilber in May 1982.

pre-personal does not really exist – anything beyond the personal must be transpersonal.

The term 'transpersonal' is still unfamiliar enough that it needs some explanation. I like Grof's succinct description, where he says it is concerned essentially with 'experiences involving an expansion or extension of consciousness beyond the usual ego boundaries and beyond the limitations of time and/or space' (Grof 1979, p. 155).[1] Many of us have had moments at least of this kind of experience – surveys show that something like a third of the population have had peak experiences at one time or another (Hay 1990). These can be experiences where, as Maslow says, 'the whole universe is perceived as an integrated and unified whole' (Maslow 1970, p. 59) and where the ego boundaries seem to be stretched or removed. Such an experience can sometimes be remembered for the rest of a person's life, and can have a profound effect on how the person lives that life. Many people working in this field feel that the proportion of the population experiencing such events is probably much higher, except that people push the experience away as too disconcerting, and do not like the idea of changes in consciousness which go this far (Davis et al. 1991).

Now what Wilber says is that these experiences are really intimations of a possible transition from one level of consciousness to another. What is so reassuring about Wilber is that he says this is no great leap into the deep waters of spirituality (or religion, or occultism), but a change no greater than that which we have experienced several times before, in the course of our development so far. We have already gone from symbiosis with the mother to separation, and from body-self as an infant to membership-self as a child, and from there through adolescence to the mental ego. At each of these transitions we had to revise our whole notion of who we were, and even what kind of self we were. So we know what it is like to revise our self-definition. The move from mental ego to the Centaur stage is just another such change, and peak experiences are a very common harbinger of this particular transition. Incidentally, the name Centaur was chosen not to suggest something mythological, but just to mark the contrast with the Mental Ego stage, where the basic image is of a controlling rider (the intellect) on a controlled horse (the emotions and body), separate and distinct. At the Centaur stage we think in terms of bodymind unity instead. Jenny Wade (1996) calls this the Authentic stage of development.

Now the movement from the Mental Ego to the Centaur (sometimes called Real Self), can be quite a wrenching move. It usually happens as a result of some crisis, such as a partner leaving, loss of a valued job, death of

---

1 This statement of Grof's is not formal or adequate enough to be a complete definition. In fact, it leads him to count some experiences as transpersonal which are clearly not. I have spelt this out at some length on pages 42–45 of my book on the transpersonal (Rowan 1993).

a loved one, and so forth, which brings us into therapy. It is the stage where we say in effect 'I know how to play my roles very well, and to get esteem from others to quite a reasonable extent, but it all seems to be about them: how about me? How about the person behind all the roles? I know all about playing parts in other people's dramas: how about writing my own dramas?' Usually this thought does not occur at the beginning – at the start we are very often lost in some problem which seems overwhelming – but it starts to dawn as the journey progresses.

But the movement does not have to start like that. Nowadays it can start in a much more positive way, where we say in effect 'I know I can do my stuff adequately, but maybe I can do more than that. I am able, but maybe I can be more able.' This is the line of personal growth, rather than of problem-solving. It can also be linked with starting to take a training in counselling or psychotherapy, and finding that one's own therapy is obligatory. But however it starts, the movement is away from role-playing and towards authenticity.

It is very important to note, however, that this Centaur, this Real Self, is still regarded as single and bounded. It has definite limits, a habitation and a name. People at this level often talk about community, as Beck and Cowan (1996) have pointed out at some length, but their actions are in fact very individualistic. Wallis (1985) in a sociological analysis, describes this whole way of looking at the world as epistemological individualism.

The actual experience of the real self is, I have argued, a mystical experience. This is the feeling of being in touch with my own centre, my inner identity, my true self, my authenticity – that self which lies behind or beyond all self-images or self-concepts or subpersonalities. It is what Assagioli (1975) calls the 'I' – the centre point of the whole personality. It is what Wilber (1996a) calls the complete bodymind unity. It is a developmental step, principally discontinuous, involving step-jump rather than gradual form (Boydell and Pedler 1981). We can now say 'I am I', and it means something to us.

The existential tradition has a great deal to say about how it works. Martin Buber quotes from the tales of the Hasidim: Before his death, Rabbi Zusya said: 'In the coming world, they will not ask me: "Why were you not Moses?" They will ask me: "Why were you not Zusya?"' (Buber 1975, p. 251). This is the classic existential insight, that we are responsible for being ourselves, and this is a high and deep responsibility indeed. If we take responsibility for ourselves, we are fully human. This seems to me a very important step in psychospiritual development, because it is a gateway to the realization that we *must have spiritual experiences for ourselves*, we cannot get them from someone else. This is the basic attitude of the mystic in all religious traditions – to get inside one's own experience, to commit oneself to one's own experience, to trust one's own experience. Everything now seems clear and true, and there is no fear any more.

Now it seems to me that the person who has had most to say about the actual content of this level of consciousness is Abraham Maslow. In his book *Motivation and Personality* (1987) he has in Chapter Eleven a list of 19 characteristics of the self-actualized person. In parentheses, let me say that we all – including Maslow – used to be a bit shy of talking about a self-actualized person. We often retreated to talking instead about a self-actualizing person. To claim to be self-actualized seemed to be claiming to have reached the ultimate, and this seemed to be arrogant pride indeed. But what Wilber makes clear – and this seems to me one of his great achievements – is that there are levels beyond self-actualization. This is not the place to go into them, because they are outside the range of humanistic psychology, but Wilber names them as the Psychic, the Subtle, the Causal and the Nondual. They are the transpersonal levels of consciousness, and we shall be meeting them in Chapter 10.

So the level of self-actualization is a relatively modest one, and to say that one is self-actualized is not such a great matter after all. It is certainly beyond the level of the Mental Ego, and therefore beyond the majority of people (as Kohlberg's research in particular clearly shows), but it is by no means unreachable by people who are prepared to do their own growth work by whatever means.

As has just been noted, Maslow stated 19 characteristics of people who had reached such a state of consciousness. By dint of study and self-study, I have added 11 more, with the results to be found in Box 3.1. There can be disagreements as to which of these is more important, central or essential. It has been argued, for example, that openness is the key concept (Mittelman 1991, 1992, 1994, 1995). But I would like to look particularly at autonomy and authenticity. On autonomy I just want to make one point, based on my own experience.

One of my most interesting discoveries was about the pathology of autonomy. At first, one of the attractions of the humanistic approach for me was its emphasis on autonomy. I was already very good, I thought, on autonomy, so maybe I was self-actualized already. I felt quite superior on that score. But the truth of the matter was that I did not have autonomy at all. What I had was what Reich, and Lowen, and Fairbairn and Lake call a schizoid defence system. In other words, I was rather distant and private and emotionally shut down. This was partly, and perhaps mainly, because in my first 30 years I had lived in 30 different places, and to avoid feeling upset at leaving people, places, pets and toys I had developed a protective defence of not getting attached to them. It was this enforced and pathological independence that I had mistaken for autonomy. Faced with a problem, my tendency was to withdraw. And it was only by being challenged about this in encounter group after group that I began to see through it. And this confirmed for me that I was in the right place – that the humanistic approach offered the best way for me to develop as a human

Box 3.1 Characteristics of the self-actualized person, or Centaur consciousness

1. **Perception of reality**   An unusual ability to detect the spurious, the fake and the dishonest in personality, and in art. Maslow reports research finding that people at this level 'distinguished far more easily than most the fresh, concrete, and idiographic from the generic, abstract and categorised' (Maslow 1987, p. 128). But also they are not frightened by the unknown. They have a tolerance for ambiguity.

2. **Acceptance**   This includes self-acceptance as well as the acceptance of others. A relative lack of overriding guilt, of crippling shame and of extreme or crippling anxiety. Lack of defensiveness. This quality was of course emphasized by Carl Rogers in his work, too, at about the same time (Rogers 1942, p. 113).

3. **Spontaneity**   Simplicity and naturalness, lack of artificiality or straining for effect. A superior awareness of their own desires, opinions and subjective reactions in general. One of the key ideas is that spontaneity is not the same as impulsiveness, and Moreno was the person who spelt this out most firmly.

4. **Problem centring**   Not ego centred. They usually have some mission in life, some task to fulfil, some problem outside themselves which enlists much of their energies.

5. **Solitude**   They like solitude and privacy to a definitely greater degree than the average. Self-actualizing people do not need others in the ordinary sense, though many of them like to be with others. They have a real choice.

6. **Autonomy**   These people can maintain a relative serenity in the midst of circumstances that would drive other people to suicide; they are self-contained. They are self-movers, origins rather than pawns.

7. **Fresh appreciation**   They have the capacity to appreciate again and again, freshly and naively, the basic goods of life, with awe, pleasure, wonder and even ecstasy. They can often see 'with the eyes of a child'.

8. **Peak experiences**   Spontaneous mystical experiences are common. Those who have them may be called peakers, and contrasted with non-peakers. Such experiences are mostly what Horne (1978) has called 'casual extraverted mysticism'.

9. **Human kinship**   They have a deep feeling of identification, sympathy and affection. They feel kinship and connection, as if all people were members of a single family.

10. **Humility and respect**   They have a democratic character structure in the deepest sense. They are able to learn from anybody who has something to teach them.

11. **Interpersonal relationships**   They can have deep and profound interpersonal relations. The other person in the relationship is often also close to self-actualization. Alvin Mahrer has written about this:

continues overleaf

Box 3.1 (*cont.*)

'When relationships are of this order, they define the highest and most valued interpersonal relations available to human beings' (Mahrer 1978, p. 579).

12. **Ethics**   These individuals are strongly ethical, they have definite moral standards, they do right and do not do wrong. Needless to say, their notions of right and wrong and of good and evil are often not the conventional ones.

13. **Means and ends**   They often regard as ends in themselves many experiences and activities that are, for other people, only means. They appreciate the doing itself.

14. **Humour**   They laugh at the ridiculous, but there is no hostility in their humour, and no rebellion. They don't make jokes that hurt someone else.

15. **Creativity**   They are creative in a special way; their creativity touches whatever activity they are engaged in. They don't have creativity, they are creative. They even see creatively.

16. **Resistance to enculturation**   They maintain a certain detachment from the culture in which they are immersed. They do not suffer from what Moreno called 'normosis' – the struggle to be normal.

17. **Imperfections**   They can be ruthless; they may be absent-minded; they may shock by lack of politeness; they may be too involved with sick people; they may have internal strife and conflicts; they can be stubborn and irritating. There are no perfect people.

18. **Values**   The topmost portion of the value system of the self-actualizing person is entirely unique. This must be true by definition, for self-actualization is actualization of a self, and no two selves are alike.

19. **Resolution of dichotomies**   The age-old opposition between head and heart, reason and instinct, thought and will disappears in healthy people; they become synergistic rather than antagonistic. Desires are in excellent accord with reason. Be healthy and then you may trust your impulses.

20. **Authenticity**   Combination of self-respect and self-enactment. 'Walks the talk.' No gap between intentions and actions. Can relate to people directly and uniquely. 'I and you' rather than 'I and it'. Coming from the centre, not from a role.

21. **Integration**   There is no split between thinking and feeling, mind and body, left brain and right brain, masculine and feminine, persona and shadow (Jung), operating potentials and deeper potentials (Mahrer), conscious and unconscious, and so on. If new conflicts are discovered, there is no resistence to working through them.

22. **Non-defensiveness**   More inclined to find the truth within what the other person is saying than to defend against it or try to prove it wrong. May defend own right to be different, but still not in terms of right and wrong.

continues

Box 3.1 (cont.)

23. **Vision-logic** Not constrained by the rules of formal logic. May be interested in alternative logics, such as fuzzy logic, many-valued logic or dialectical logic. 'Never let yourself be bullied by an either-or.' Wilber (1995) has written at length about this.

24. **Paradoxical theory of change** Beisser (1972) in the Gestalt school developed a set of ideas which have been found to make a lot of sense by Gestaltists. Also found in focusing, experiential psychotherapy, psychodrama, person-centred work and so on. Change occurs not by trying to go somewhere you are not, but by staying with what is. This is very different from the common idea of self-mastery.

25. **The real self** The chart in *The Reality Game* (Rowan 1998b, p. 74) shows that the idea that there is a centre and a periphery to the personality, and that the centre is true and the periphery false, is popular in the Centaur stage. The real self seems to me a crucial part of Centaur thinking, because without a real self the notion of authenticity collapses.

    It is a skin-encapsulated self. It is the ultimate, pure sense of 'I', considered as a separate being. That is its essence. It is quite different from the Mental Ego, however. It does not need all the props, the support, the boosting, the confirmation that the Mental Ego needs. It is a centred gyroscope with its own power supply.

26. **'I create my world'** One of the great discoveries of the Centaur stage is that it makes sense to take responsibility to the limit, and to say that we are responsible for everything. People like Will Schutz and Alvin Mahrer have spelt this out in great detail. There are some common misunderstandings of this view, but this is not the place to go into them. (See Rowan 1998b, pp. 110–112.)

27. **Intentionality** At the Centaur stage, just because we take responsibility for our actions, we are fully behind what we do. This enables real commitment. Intentionality and commitment go very closely together.

28. **Intimacy** Intimacy between two people is made possible only at the Centaur stage because it is only then that roles can be laid aside. You can't be intimate and playing a role at the same time.

29. **Presence** To be genuinely present with another person is a rare ability. Ronnie Laing could do it. Carl Rogers could do it. Again it cannot be done through role-playing. To try to portray presence is not to be present.

30. **Openness** It has been suggested (Mittelman 1991) that openness is in fact the key element in the Centaur experience. It is certainly important in humanistic management theory.

Source: First 19 items come from: Maslow, A. H. (1987) *Motivation and Personality* (3rd edn), New York: Harper & Row, abbreviated by John Rowan 1999. Items 20–30 by John Rowan.

being. This was a slow process – it did not happen at once. It was painful for me to realize that I had been kidding myself all these years, and I resisted this knowledge for as long as I could.

So autonomy is a tricky concept, but it is certainly possible to tell the difference between genuine autonomy and a schizoid defensive system. Let us now go on to look more closely at authenticity.

AUTHENTICITY

Existential principles are fully embodied in most of the forms of humanistic psychotherapy, including person-centred, Gestalt, psychodrama, experiential therapies, Primal Integration, radical therapy, feminist therapy, several body therapies, dream work and so forth. They are very much at home there, contributing essentially to the humanistic emphasis on the whole person and the authentic relationship. The humanistic view of authenticity is broader and more inclusive than that to be found in existential analysis, and this seems to be because those who hold hard to existentialism in an exclusive way are much too wedded to Heidegger's notions. Emmy van Deurzen, for example, says this: 'Being anxious because of our acute awareness of our human limitations and mortality is therefore the key to authenticity and with it the key to true humanity' (van Deurzen-Smith 1997, p. 39). This one-sided emphasis on death and destruction is just what is wrong with existential analysis in its understanding of authenticity. Compare it with the formulations of Jim Bugental, who has written two books about authenticity. He says that authenticity is a combination of self-respect (we are not just part of an undifferentiated world) and self-enactment – we express our care or involvement in the world in a visible way. Here is a key quotation:

> By authenticity I mean a central genuineness and awareness of being. Authenticity is that presence of an individual in his living in which he is fully aware in the present moment, in the present situation. Authenticity is difficult to convey in words, but experientially it is readily perceived in ourselves or in others. Authenticity has three functional characteristics: 1. The authentic person is broadly aware of himself, his relationships, and his world in all dimensions. 2. The authentic person accepts and seems to go to meet the fact that he is constantly in the process of making choices, that decisions are the very stuff of living. 3. The authentic person takes responsibility for his decisions, including full recognition of their consequences. It is here that the terrible threat of authenticity resides.
>
> (Bugental 1981, pp. 102–3)

In other words, what we in humanistic psychology are saying is that auth-enticity is an experience. People who deny the existence or importance of the real self are, I believe, people who have never had an experience of the real self. This means that they can talk about freedom, but they cannot act freedom. As Rollo May has said so well: 'Freedom is a quality of action of the centred self' (May 1980, p. 176). The humanistic view is that action is the acid test of experience.

What it seems so hard to convey to existential writers is that the real self, the self which is to be actualized in self-actualization, is not a concept but an experience. It is not something to be argued at a philosophical level, it is something to be encountered at an experiential level. If existentialists say that authenticity is merely 'an openness to existence, an acceptance of what is given as well as our freedom to respond to it' (Cohn 1997, p. 127) then there is no way of perceiving authenticity. It becomes an abstract and useless concept. Other existentialists have gone much further, as for example here:

> Authenticity consists in having a true and lucid consciousness of the situation, in assuming the responsibilities and risks that it involves, in accepting it in pride or humiliation, sometimes in horror and hate. There is no doubt that authenticity demands much courage and more than courage. Thus it is not surprising that one finds it so rarely.
>
> (Sartre 1948, p. 90)

It demands so much because it involves moving beyond the confines of the familiar mental ego; but this is what Heidegger never envisaged. To get away from the abstract argument, let us take a concrete example. It comes from a book by Allen Wheelis called *The Desert*, and it goes like this:

> Look at the wretched people huddled in line for the gas chambers at Auschwitz. If they do anything other than move on quietly, they will be clubbed down. Where is freedom? . . . But wait. Go back in time, enter the actual event, the very moment: they are thin and weak, and they smell; hear the weary shuffling steps, the anguished catch of breath, the clutch of hand. Enter now the head of one hunched and limping man. The line moves slowly; a few yards ahead begin the steps down. He sees the sign, someone whispers 'showers', but he knows what happens here. He is struggling with a choice: to shout 'Comrades! They will kill you! Run!' – or to say nothing. This option, in the few moments remaining, is his whole life. If he shouts he dies now, painfully; if he moves on silently he dies but minutes later. Looking back on him in time and memory, we find the moment poignant but the freedom negligible. It makes

no difference in that situation, his election of daring or of inhibi-
tion. Both are futile, without consequence. History sees no freedom
for him, notes only constraint, labels him victim. But in the consciousness of that one man it makes great difference whether or not
he experiences the choice. For if he knows the constraint and
nothing else, if he thinks 'Nothing is possible', then he is living his
necessity; but if, perceiving the constraint, he turns from it to a
choice between two possible courses of action, then – however he
chooses – he is living his freedom. This commitment to freedom
can extend to the last breath.

(Wheelis 1972, pp. 286–287)

For humanistic psychotherapy, authenticity is a direct experience of the real
self. It is unmistakable, it is self-authenticating. It is a true experience of
freedom, of liberation. We have already heard what Bugental says about it.
And that is not all.

There is an important link between authenticity and genuineness as
described by Carl Rogers. 'It is my feeling that congruence is a part of
existential authenticity, that the person who is genuinely authentic in his
being-in-the-world is congruent within himself; and to the extent that one
attains authentic being in his life, to that extent is he congruent' (Bugental
1981, p. 108). Again it takes Bugental to draw our attention to the heartland of the humanistic approach, which is also the heartland of the existential approach. Both Bugental and Rogers are clear that congruence is
difficult and demanding, and recent writers like Dave Mearns (1994, 1996,
1997) have made it clear that it cannot be taught as a skill. It is really very
curious to see how someone like Spinelli can go along with all this, and then
somehow draw back at the last moment. Consider this quote:

As **authentic** beings, we recognise our individuality. Further, we
recognise that this individuality is not a static quality but is, rather,
a set of (possibly infinite) potentialities. As such, while in the
authentic mode, we maintain an independence of thought and
action, and subsequently feel 'in charge' of the way our life is
experienced. Rather than reacting as victims to the vicissitudes of
being, we, as authentic beings, acknowledge our role in determining our actions, thought and beliefs, and thereby experience a
stronger and fuller sense of integration, acceptance, 'openness' and
'aliveness' to the potentialities of being-in-the-world.

(Spinelli 1989, p. 109)

I couldn't have put it better myself. It is difficult for me to see how he can
go along with so much of the humanistic view of the matter and yet not
quite be able to adopt the label of 'humanistic'. It may have something to

do with his adherence to Heidegger. It has been clear to me for some time that there is something wrong with Heidegger's view of authenticity. He was perhaps the first to talk about it, yet it was always strange that he talked so much about inauthenticity, and had so little to say about authenticity itself.

Later people such as James Bugental had a lot more to say about authenticity, but people who study Heidegger very often do not know much about Bugental, and may even not have heard of him.

A DIGRESSION: CHARLES HAMPDEN-TURNER

I want to digress for a moment here, to look at the question of how we move from the Mental Ego to the Centaur. One of the clearest stories about this comes from Charles Hampden-Turner, an Englishman who trained at the Harvard Business School. He takes as his focus the application of the principles of humanistic psychology throughout the whole society.

In his first major work (Hampden-Turner 1971) he starts by making very explicit the point which Maslow starts from – that there is a process of human development which moves from a position of alienation or anomie to a position of creativity and spontaneity. At one end of the scale we have human diminution, where people use each other as means, put each other down, score points off each other and so on, while at the other end of the scale we have full humanness, where people treat each other as ends in themselves.

What Hampden-Turner says is that this can be seen as a spiral of experience, such that at any one time we are either moving up the spiral toward full humanness or down the spiral towards alienation and anomie. The assumptions we make, the relationships we set up, the organizations we produce, all help in some way to move us up or move us down the spiral. And the one thing which is most important in enabling us to move up the spiral is authentic human interaction. Hampden-Turner is very much in the existentialist tradition. He would agree with Ronnie Laing, another person working in this tradition, that:

> Personal action can either open out possibilities of enriched experience or it can shut off possibilities. Personal action is either predominantly validating, confirming, encouraging, supporting, enhancing, or it is invalidating, disconfirming, undermining and constricting. It can be creative or destructive. In a world where the normal condition is one of alienation, most personal action must be destructive both of one's own experience and of that of the other.
>
> (Laing 1967, p. 29)

But what Hampden-Turner does is to document this with a mass of evidence, marshalled with immense care and thoroughness, and applied to every aspect of our society. For example, he shows that most of our organizations (whether industrial, governmental or whatever), most of the time, are driving people down the spiral into anomie and alienation, rather than up the spiral into autonomy and moral insight. Such organizations act as if it is good for people to be put down, because that way they learn to be tough and impervious, and that is necessary in a tough world. But this is just the kind of action to create the horror world it purports to deal with. The other way, where we open up to the other person, treating him or her as an equal suffering human being, helps to create instead someone who is strong and vulnerable at the same time. And this is a partial description of full humanness. The areas which Hampden-Turner shows to be most important, and which recur over and over again in his analysis, are these:

Existence   People exist freely. The further up the spiral an individual is, the more he or she acknowledges this. On a good day, we may be aware of this. We can then move on to clearer perception.

Perception   The world has contradictions in every area, and clear perception sees this. We also become clearer in our perception of ourselves, and our identity.

Identity   Awareness of one's own body, one's own experience, one's own self – a refusal to cut out or block off any of these things. Self-acceptance follows, to some degree. We see ourselves as more competent.

Competence   Owning and allowing one's own ability. Refusal to cripple oneself. We become more happy in our own skin, not rejecting our own abilities. Because of our clearer perception, we can be more authentic.

Authentic   Investing oneself intensely in human relationships, not holding back or seeing things in terms of the past or future. Acting as a whole person. Taking responsibility for the risks we take in living.

Risk   A willingness to suspend one's existing understanding, and open up to a new possibility. Flexibility involves constant self-questioning, and ultimately taking nothing for granted. We can then reach out to the world and to other people.

Bridging distance   The higher up the spiral, the bigger the gap which can be bridged between oneself and another person. This distance may be physical, psychological or social. On bridging such distances, we allow ourselves to meet the other person and make an impact upon them.

Impact   One can meet another person in such a way that it is at the same time self-confirming and self-transcending. This is particularly important when meeting people in authority. It is as if we could see through the authority to the person behind it.

Dialectic   If a meeting is genuine, a higher synergy can come out of it. A real meeting of differences is creative. But this means not suppressing the differences, and doing justice to them. The paradox of integration emerging from differences can then be experienced.

Integration By taking real notice of the feedback from one's encounters, one's own mental structures become richer and more complex, thus enabling a deeper understanding to take place. This is an expansion of consciousness. Our existence is now richer, and we can move on up the spiral. (Hampden-Turner 1971, Chapter 3)

Obviously a great deal could be written about each of these points, and this is just what Hampden-Turner has done in his book. They are mentioned here merely in order to suggest that these are all points which are within the scope of each one of us. What Hampden-Turner says is that working on each of these helps each of the others – they are connected in a very precise way, such that each one on the list facilitates the one following, and the last one on the list facilitates the first.

What Hampden-Turner has given us, then, is a well worked-out theory of human development in the social field, which can be used for our own personal growth, or to change the organizations we work in, or to change the way our whole society works. It enables us to see through the pretensions of most of the psychology that is taught in our universities and other halls of learning, which merely serves to uphold the existing order for the benefit of those who run it.

Since *Radical Man* was written, David Wright has written a number of papers which seem to show that Hampden-Turner's general case makes a lot of sense from a sociological point of view. The many research studies by Lawrence Kohlberg (1981) and Jane Loevinger (1976) are brought together and shown to be consistent with Maslow's theory. David Wright (1974) points to a gap between the lower levels and the higher levels on the spiral (see Maslow's chart, Table 2.1, this volume, pp. 25–6), and says 'The transition between [these] levels [4 and 5] marks a significant watershed in terms of the nature of the possible bases of social order . . . [After it] people can consciously and intentionally construct and maintain a social order of their own choice.' In other words, so long as we are operating at low levels of development we are liable to be pushed around by external forces or our own internal rigidities, or to find ourselves competing with others for scarce resources. At the higher levels, the possibilities open out, and we no longer see problems in the same way. We start to see how to cooperate with others in a non-exploitative way, a way of using power in such a fashion that the more power we give away, the more we have. This is called synergy, which is sometimes referred to as the 2 + 2 = 5 principle.

This makes it possible to believe that our present time of troubles is actually a transition period to a person-centred society, where the industrial system would be subservient to, and responsible to, the larger purposes of the society. The overall goal would be the cultivation and enrichment of all human beings, in all their diversity, complexity and depth. Nowadays more and more people are saying the same thing, notably Marilyn Ferguson (1982), Fritjof Capra (1983) and Murray Bookchin (1986). Riane Eisler (1995) and Scilla Elworthy (1996) have shown how this applies to women in particular.

The more recent work of Hampden-Turner (1981, 1983) shows how important dialectical thinking is for humanistic psychology. In the first of these two books he shows it can link many separate fields of psychology and philosophy together and illuminate them all. And in the second, he also shows how helpful catastrophe theory is as an adjunct to this. My own essay (Rowan 1992) on Hegel makes the links between pure dialectical thinking and what Hampden-Turner calls being fully human. Hegel (1971) says that there are three levels of mind – the Primary level, the Social level and the Self-actualizing level (actually he says Soul, Consciousness and Mind, but I prefer my version). Self-development consists in moving up the levels from the Primary level, through the Social level, to the Self-actualizing level. And each of these three levels contradicts the previous one, so that we have to reject one to go on to the next. The Primary level has to do with one-sided subjectivity, the Social level is to do with one-sided objectivity, and the Self-actualizing level is subjectivity on a higher level – a new kind of subjectivity which includes but surpasses one-sided objectivity – an objective sub-jectivity, in fact. Rationality (as redefined by Hegel) runs through all the levels. My own view is that most people involved in humanistic psychology do not realize how much they need and use and depend on dialectical thinking in their work (see Rowan 2000 for more on this).

HOW HEIDEGGER GOT IT WRONG

Returning now from our digression, in this section I want to look carefully at the curious story of how Heidegger missed all this. I want to show that the facts can be accounted for by Heidegger's (quite understandable) failure to distinguish between two kinds of consciousness. These two kinds of con-sciousness, representing two different notions of the self, were first clearly described and distinguished by Ken Wilber. As we have already seen, Wilber makes a clear distinction between the different levels of consciousness, and in particular between the Mental Ego (locked in to Maslow's middle layers) and the Centaur, which we have been looking at in detail.

Mental ego   One of the important stages in psychospiritual development is named by Wilber as the Mental Ego stage. At this stage we are dominated by our roles. We get our esteem from other people. We need to be respected by people we respect. We have no centre of our own, but rely on the social consensus to know how things are. We split the mind from the body, and want the mind to be in charge of the body. At this stage we are, in a word, inauthentic. This way of being in the world, as Heidegger well says, restricts 'the possible options of choice to what lies within the range of the familiar, the attainable, the respectable – that which is fitting and proper' (Heidegger 1962, p. 239).

Everyone seems to be agreed that there is such a state of consciousness, and that it can be described as inauthentic. Eric Berne (1973) describes it well as 'script-bound'. Other writers describe it as a fraudulent self-concept, an idealized self (Horney 1968), a self-image (Perls 1969) or a persona (Jung 1966). Wilber says that wherever there is a persona there is also a shadow, and that for him the ego is actually made up of persona plus shadow. Wilber goes further, however, and distinguishes between the immature ego, which is raw and easily pushed around, and the mature ego, which can play with roles and is not so fully identified with them. The inauthentic realm, the realm of Das Man, the realm of the 'they', is thus pretty well charted. Charles Tart (1986) has called it the 'consensus trance'.

Centaur If we move on in our psychospiritual development (and this is by no means inevitable, according to Wilber) the next way-station we come to is the Centaur. Do not be confused about the word 'centaur'. It is not intended to say that this realm has anything to do with mythology. It is just an indication of one of the main features of this stage of development – the person acquires a sense of bodymind unity. At the Mental Ego stage the model of the person is that of a rider on a horse. The rider is the intellect, which ought to be in charge and in control, and the horse is the emotions and the body, which ought to submit and keep in order. At the Centaur stage the horse and rider become one.

With all of Wilber's stages, it is true that the process of moving from one to the other is not smooth. It is more like a step-jump, and there is often a feeling of breakthrough going with it. It is a dialectical movement, full of energy and force, rather than one which is peaceful and gradual. Hence the move from the Mental Ego to the Centaur is often a dramatic one: the person suddenly wakes up and says – 'I am me!' – or some such. As one of Rogers' clients said at the end of his therapy – 'I don't know what I'm going to do, but I know it is I who will do it!'

Wilber also calls this the existential self.

> Notions of authenticity, of concrete-being-in-the-world, of pure experiencing and true seeing, of Dasein, of intentionality, autonomy, meaning and the centred self – I am sorry to just toss out these terms, but the existential literature is so vast and so profound, that I can only hint at its essence by throwing out phrases and urging the reader to consult the original works.
>
> (Wilber 1996a, p. 46)

This is my first step, then, to recapitulate the differences we have observed between the Mental Ego and the Centaur. A process of transformation has enabled the person to move from inauthenticity to authenticity. This is a change of consciousness and a change of the person's notion of the self.

We can now go on to delineate the fault which Heidegger perpetrated in not making this distinction. Because he could not see that inauthenticity represented one stage of development and authenticity another, his version of authenticity is restricted to what the Mental Ego could understand and cope with. It seems that when he talks about authenticity he is really talking about the mature ego – the ego which is not so restricted by roles and can even play with them to some degree. But the mature ego can never be fully or truly authentic, because it is still fitting in with the world of Das Man. This is what the ego does. So when Heidegger says: 'Being free for one's ownmost potentiality-for-Being, and therewith for the possibility of authenticity and inauthenticity is shown with a primordial elemental concreteness in anxiety' (Heidegger 1962, p. 236), we can only say no, no and no. It is the mature ego who is based in anxiety. The Centaur is not based in anxiety at all. Emmy van Deurzen makes it clear that this is not a misunderstanding

> Anxiety is always an anxiety about ourselves. It is generated out of our awareness that existence involved projection and possibility and makes demands on us to become ourselves. In anxiety the structures of the They-world fade away and we come face to face with ourselves. In anxiety it is disclosed what we are free to become. As such anxiety takes us from inauthenticity to authenticity.
>
> (van Deurzen 1999, p. 119)

This is all ego-talk. The Centaur is not about anxiety, but the mature ego is. To talk in the way that both Heidegger and van Deurzen do restricts authenticity to the realm of the inauthentic. No wonder that they get so confused and so confusing. Here is an example of confusing talk: 'Even when Dasein is inauthentic it is still reaching out of itself, remaining ahead of itself. It is this always being beyond oneself that makes it possible, probable and necessary for Dasein to be both inauthentic and authentic' (van Deurzen 1999, p. 120). If this is not confusing, I do not know what is. And the reason for it is that the whole statement stays within the realm of the Mental Ego.

We have already seen that James Bugental is one of the clearest writers on authenticity, and this is because he writes from the Centaur position. His humanistic-existential approach, as he has sometimes labelled it, exemplifies Centaur consciousness very well.

Charles Guignon criticizes such versions of Heidegger in these words: 'The ideal of authenticity is pictured as the stance of the rugged individualist who, upon experiencing anxiety in the face of the ultimate absurdity of life, lives intensely in the present and creates his or her own world through leaps of radical freedom' (Guignon 1993, p. 215). This is a frequent misunderstanding of the Bugental position. There is nothing about leaps of radical freedom, and we have already seen that it is also not about anxiety in any way. Guignon goes on to repeat another canard often put about, when he speaks about 'the romantic faith that we have something deep within us, a "child within", who is truer, purer and somehow "better" than the dreary, rigid, duty-bound self imposed on us by our socialization' (Guignon 1993, p. 222). He quotes the name of John Bradshaw, among others, in support of this notion. Bugental is not speaking about a child within, and nor is Ken Wilber. We are speaking, at the Centaur stage, of someone who has gone beyond the Mental Ego, not someone who is regressing to a mythical childhood. As Wilber puts it very clearly: 'The centauric level is *the* great level of the human potential movement, of existentialism, of humanistic therapy, all of which take as their basic assumption the integration of mind, body, and emotions into a higher-order unity, a "deeper totality"' (Wilber 1979, pp. 118–119). There is nothing here about inner children, or romanticism, or radical leaps, or any other of the flummery of which humanistic-existential thinkers like Bugental have been accused. In the two great chapters which Alvin Mahrer (1978) wrote about integration and actualization, which state very clearly the means by which the Centaur stage emerges, there is nothing about Guignon's concerns.

It does seem to me that we can see through Heidegger's confusion much better if we see that inauthenticity belongs to the Mental Ego stage of development, where we *must* look to others for our validation. Authenticity cannot belong to this realm, but has to be found in the next stage of development, the Centaur stage. As Wilber, Mahrer, Bugental and May all make clear, we only get there by a process of re-owning our own split-off parts – all that we have disowned in ourselves. Authenticity is about the hard-won self which emerges from the flames of destruction of the falsity within us. If we do not have the courage to go through that process, we shall never be authentic. If we do, we can. As Maslow used to say, at every point we have the choice between safety and growth. It is all about real change, real transformation of the self. Heidegger could never see that, because he did not have such a notion. For him, Das Man was omnipresent and inescapable. For us it does not have to be.

What we are now seeing, then, is that Centaur consciousness is the answer to the question as to how we hold together the contradictions which seem so important in the understanding of humanistic psychology.

Part 2

APPLICATIONS OF
HUMANISTIC PSYCHOLOGY

4

COUNSELLING

There are many varieties of counselling, and it is a term which is used rather loosely. One recent book distinguished counselling from psychotherapy by saying: 'Again this usually involves a one-to-one relationship of professional worker and client. Here the aim is usually to give a more practical kind of advice about personal, work or emotional problems.' But humanistic psychology has quite a different view of counselling, derived partly from the ideas of Rollo May, and partly from the work of Carl Rogers and others in the person-centred tradition. And in recent years this has been added to by the quite different work of Harvey Jackins and the people who have followed him.

ROLLO MAY'S CONTRIBUTION

In the early 1930s, Rollo May visited Europe and attended seminars given by Alfred Adler. When he returned to the USA and started work at Michigan State University, he found Adler's ideas entirely relevant to his work there with students. He started giving lectures on his approach, and in 1939 these were published under the title of *The Art of Counselling*. It turned out that he had invented humanistic counselling. Of course May was one of the founders of the Association for Humanistic Psychology, and remained a member until his death. And in the late 1980s he was invited to revise this book for republication in a very different, and much more accepting, climate. The result was a new edition of the book (May 1989) which was not so much a complete revision as a return to the roots.

It turns out that not only Alfred Adler, but also Otto Rank and C. G. Jung, were powerful influences on May's integrative position. May's powerful statement – 'It is the function of the counsellor to lead the counsellee to an acceptance of responsibility for the conduct and outcome of his or her life' – comes almost directly from Rank (May 1989, p. 21). It is a bolder statement than most would make today, but it speaks very directly from the humanistic position, as we saw in the previous chapter.

From Jung came an emphasis on individuation. May quotes Jung as saying: 'Each of us carries his own life-form, an indeterminable form which cannot be superseded by another' (Jung 1933, p. 69). May describes this life-form as the real self (May 1989, p. 24). And he sums up by saying: 'It is the function of the counsellor to assist the counsellee to find his true self, and then to help him or her to have courage to be this self' (May 1989, p. 28). We are clearly here not in the realm of cure and adjustment. May's approach is all about personal growth and freedom.

But in order to clarify that he is not advocating atomistic individualism, May is concerned to emphasize that he is devoted to social integration. This comes directly from Adler. 'Adler observed, too, that no one can separate oneself from one's social group and remain healthy, as the very structure of one's personality is dependent upon the community' (May 1989, p. 30). This is to see the basic humanistic point that we are inescapably social, and that our self is a social self. That is why social psychology continually veers toward the humanistic, even when it does not want to do so. But of course in counselling there is no such conflict, and May sums up by saying: 'It is the counsellor's function to assist the counsellee to a cheerful acceptance of social responsibility, to give courage which will release the counsellee from the compulsion of inferiority feeling, and to help the counsellee to direct his or her striving toward socially constructive ends' (May 1989, p. 34). Again this is a bolder statement than many would want to make today, and again it is right in line with humanistic values.

May was of course a great exponent and explorer of Centaur consciousness, as is pointed out very tellingly by Wilber (1983).

Rollo May was, therefore, a pioneer of the humanistic approach to counselling, and is named by DeCarvalho (1991) as one of the founders of humanistic psychology. It is strange to me, therefore, to see no reference to the work of May in the work of Carl Rogers, who was developing his own ideas at about the same time.

And what a time it was! It is only in recent years that historical work has been published showing that the spirit of the time, as exemplified for example by Franklin and Eleanor Roosevelt, was full of the pioneering élan also found in May and Rogers. Godfrey Barrett-Lennard (1998) outlines ten points of similarity (pp. 40–45) between Rogers and Roosevelt between 1935 and 1945, which are striking and illuminating.

PERSON-CENTRED COUNSELLING

It was in the early 1940s that Rogers (1942) started to put forward his ideas about counselling, and in the next 10 to 15 years his views became very widely accepted (Rogers 1951). In 1946 he was elected as President of the American Psychological Association (Cohen 1997). Nowadays probably most of the courses on counselling in this country, and in many other countries (Thorne 1992), are based on Rogerian principles – or as he preferred to have them known, person-centred principles. He said in conversation in 1981 that he hoped the name 'Rogerian' would go down the drain.

People come for counselling – whether to school counsellors, marriage guidance counsellors or whatever – with a variety of problems. Usually the problem has to do with a conflict of some kind. And resolving the conflict is not easy; if it were easy, one would not consult a counsellor. And usually the reason it is not easy is that the person's rigidities or fixed patterns of behaviour have become involved, either with each other or with another person. So working on this one problem may mean working on these long-standing patterns, or at least giving the person some space and time to see what is really involved.

Perhaps the essence of the matter is that the humanistic counsellor genuinely believes that the client has the answer, and can find the answer given the time and space to do so. And so if I am a person-centred counsellor, I refuse to help, and do not see my role as one of taking any kind of responsibility for the client's problems. What the counsellor does instead is to facilitate the client's own self-searching, in such a way that the client feels understood, and believed-in, and basically capable. As Rogers (1961) says:

> One brief way of describing the change which has taken place in me is to say that in my early professional years I was asking the question, How can I treat, or cure, or change this person? Now I would phrase the question in this way: How can I provide a relationship which this person may use for his own personal growth? It is as I have come to put the question in this second way that I realize that whatever I have learned is applicable to all of my relationships, not just to working with clients with problems.
>
> (Rogers 1961, p. 32)

This is one of the things which people coming to humanistic psychology are most struck by: it is not only a field of study, it makes ethical and personal demands on those who get into it. So what is the secret of this relationship which Rogers tried to build up, and which he found to be so fruitful and healing?

A few years ago, you might have read that Rogers' technique was one of reflection – mirroring the client's responses back. This was never, in fact, true. And in his later years Rogers took great pains to make it clear that this is not what he was saying at all. What he was trying to say was that insofar as I as the counsellor can be genuinely there in the relationship, you as the client will feel genuinely listened to and taken seriously; and will start to take yourself seriously. Now it is surprisingly difficult to be genuinely there; listening is a hard task, for reasons which John Enright outlines very clearly:

> I am quite serious in asserting that most of us . . . are . . . not fully aware of our actual present. Much of the content of our consciousness is remembering, speculating, planning ('rehearsing' for our next interpersonal performance), or carrying on a busy inner dialogue (or monologue). More specifically, we professionals sitting with a patient may be diagnosing, 'prognosing', planning our next intervention, wondering what time it's getting to be, etc. – we are only too rarely being really open to our experience of self and other.
>
> (Enright 1970, pp. 300–301)

So asking the counsellor to be genuine, and to be there, and to be listening, is asking a lot. It seems clear that I as the counsellor cannot in fact do this unless I have done some work on my own personal growth, sufficient to open up perception to the point where the outer world is let in rather than kept out. Enright continues:

> Those of us who are not seriously mentally ill remain sufficiently in touch with the actual environment to move through it reasonably effectively . . . but miss so many nuances that our experience of the world and the other is often pale and our memories of it, therefore, weak. Engaged as we are with our own phantoms, we attend only sketchily to the other. Since he then seems rather pale and incomplete, we fill him out with our own projections and react vigorously to these. The resulting encounter often gives a convincing show of life and involvement where, in fact, there is little.
>
> (Enright 1970, p. 301)

So person-centred counselling always implies that I as the counsellor am willing to undergo the same discipline which I am urging on the client. If I am a person-centred counsellor, I am not someone who has undergone training and is now an expert – I am someone who is continually working on myself to be more aware of potential sources of bias, partiality and general inattention. Let us then look, with this much understood, at the three conditions which we touched on briefly before, which Rogers says are necessary to his kind of counselling. (It is often pointed out that Rogers actually laid down six conditions, not three, but we can pass over that issue here, because the other three conditions are of a different order.)

The first is genuineness. At times Rogers has used the term 'congruence' to clarify what he means by this. As a counsellor I am, as near as possible, completely open to my own feelings – I am able to live these feelings, be them, and be able to communicate them if appropriate. Note that Rogers, like Schutz, is not advocating that I as the counsellor should blurt out my feelings at all times, but simply that I should be aware of them, and allow the whole situation to determine whether they are uttered or not, and if so, how. The important thing, Rogers says, is to be real. 'The more genuine and congruent the therapist in the relationship, the more probability there is that change in personality in the client will occur' (Rogers 1961, p. 62). In case that quote causes some raised eyebrows, it may be worth noting here that Rogers distinguishes between: (1) the personality of a person, as something on the surface, something that the person presents to the world; (2) the self, which is more basic; and (3) the organism, which is more basic still. What Rogers is aiming at is the ultimate integration of the organism, with all its sensory and visceral experiences, with the self, in a consistent and harmonious way.

For this to happen, the second requirement of the counselling relationship is non-possessive warmth. This has sometimes been put by Rogers as a demand for 'unconditional positive regard', which seems hard to achieve. But like genuineness, this is a limiting case, something to aim at. It is easier if I as the counsellor accept myself first – again it cuts both ways, and again it is not easy.

> It involves the therapist's genuine willingness for the client to be whatever feeling is going on in him at that moment – fear, confusion, pain, pride, anger, hatred, love, courage or awe. It means that the therapist cares for the client, in a non-possessive way. It means that he prizes the client in a total rather than a conditional way. By this I mean that he does not simply accept the client when he is behaving in certain ways, and disapprove of him when he behaves in other ways.
>
> (Rogers 1961, p. 62)

This attitude by the counsellor was phrased by someone else as 'I care, but I don't mind'. That is, 'I care about you, but when you do something bad, wrong, or stupid, it doesn't hurt me, it doesn't make me suffer – I won't add my evaluations to your burdens'. This is of course a powerfully paradoxical point of view; usually we think of caring and not caring as opposites, but here is a dialectical position which unites caring and not caring. And this comes out of the basic outlook we found in Chapter 2 – that each human being, deep down underneath it all, is all right. There is a basic lively health and intelligence there which we can believe in and rely on.

The third requirement is empathic understanding. It is not enough for the counsellor to be genuine and accepting and warm – there must be some demonstration that this is all working. And if it is working, the client will feel understood. When someone understands how it feels and seems to be me, without wanting to analyse me or judge me, than I can blossom and grow in that climate. Carl Rogers puts it like this:

> Acceptance does not mean much until it involves understanding. It is only as I understand the feelings and thoughts which seem so horrible to you, or so weak, or so sentimental, or so bizarre – it is only as I see them as you see them, and accept them and you, that you feel really free to explore all the hidden nooks and frightening crannies of your inner and often buried experience
>
> (Rogers 1961, p. 34)

But it seems to Rogers that empathy can never actually put ourselves into someone else's world. Only you as that person can really experience your own world. So all we can do is continually check it out with the person – 'I heard you say you felt left out. Does that mean you felt weak and helpless, or was it something a bit different from that?' If we keep doing this in the early stages, we may eventually get on to the person's wavelength, and be able to sense things which are just beneath the surface. It means cultivating our intuition, and helping our intuition by giving it good materials to work on. But ultimately we can never be as empathic with another person as we can be congruent with ourself, according to Rogers.

Let us just digress for a moment to point out that Martin Buber never really understood the concept of empathy as described by Roger, nor as described by Heinz Kohut (1984). And because Buber never understood it, and thought it meant some kind of merging with the client or patient, he always wanted to replace it with his term *inclusion*. The fact is that Buber's inclusion simply is empathy as described by Rogers and Kohut.

Now Rogers does not simply say that these three requirements are good – he has undertaken and stimulated a great deal of research to check them out empirically. The book which he co-edited with Rosalind Dymond (Rogers and Dymond 1954) is a superb example of how research can be used to discover a great deal about what actually goes on in the process of counselling. And later much more research was done by Rogers and by those who followed him, as has been described in detail by Barrett-Lennard (1998).

Three years later, Rogers (1961, pp. 132-158) outlined a seven-stage process which has been used in subsequent research, and which I think helps a great deal in understanding what his form of counselling is all about. It is based on analysis of many recorded interviews, and details seven stages which you as a client may go through in sorting out your problems.

First stage: Communication is only about externals. There is no apparent desire to change. Much blockage of internal communication. Sees the present in terms of the past.

Second stage: Feelings may be shown, but are apparently not recognized as such or owned. No sense of responsibility in problems. Experience is held at arm's length.

Third stage: Some talk about the self, but only as an object. Description of past feelings. But very little acceptance of feelings – they are usually seen as unacceptable.

Fourth stage: More intense feelings may be described from the past. Some recognition that there may be more than one way of looking at things. Some awareness of contradictions in self.

Fifth stage: Feelings are expressed freely in the present. More differentiation of experience – more precision, more self-responsibility. But some fear of what bubbles up through.

Sixth stage: A breakthrough stage, where feelings come through, are experienced now, and accepted. More awareness now of the body, and also a mental loosening of previous ways of seeing the world and self.

Seventh stage: New feelings are experienced and accepted. You as a person trust your own process. No need to pin things down finally. Strong feelings of being able to choose and be self-responsible.

Rogers says that any change down this list is desirable and worth working for. A full traverse from beginning to end would probably take years rather than weeks or months. Later Godfrey Barrett-Lennard in Australia spelled out in a rather different way the stages which people went through in person-centred therapy, and his account (Barrett-Lennard 1998, pp. 106–122) is well worth attention.

One of the great strengths of Rogers' approach has always been his interest in research, and the standard Bergin and Garfield (1994) handbook gives much of it, showing that his approach does actually bring people along the path which he has set. A particularly interesting book came out in 1996, giving actual transcripts of a number of Rogers' own interviews, together with sophisticated commentaries on them from younger experts. This book (Farber et al. 1996) clarifies many of the questions which you may have about the person-centred approach.

One question of terminology may not be out of place here. We have talked about personal growth, and about counselling, and in the next chapter we talk about psychotherapy. In my view these are all the same thing – and indeed some forms of learning and some forms of attitude change are the same thing too. In all these cases we are referring to movement up Hampden-Turner's spiral, or through Rogers' stages, or up Maslow's levels, away from alienation and anomie towards full humanness. But the great advantage of Rogers' approach is that it does not push the client into any special techniques or assumptions. It takes you as the client right where you are, and takes that seriously. And so it is an approach which has very wide application – we can even use it informally in our ordinary social contacts and personal relationships. But if we do, it is important to do it our own way, and not to think to ourselves 'How would Carl Rogers do it?' You can't be genuine, and be Carl Rogers, at the same time – unless, of course, you actually are Carl Rogers.

Someone who has taken Rogers' ideas further in his own way is Eugene Gendlin, who we shall meet again in the next chapter. Gendlin (1981) has emphasized the importance of listening, and again has used research to show how important it is to pay attention to the whole felt experience of the client and not just the words. More recently, Gendlin (1996) has developed his ideas much more generally and has a great deal to say of importance.

Counselling of this and closely allied types is now very common in Britain, and there is an organization, the British Association for Counselling (BACP), which brings together the various approaches and organizations offering counselling under one umbrella. There are other organizations in the field of counselling too, but the BAC is the largest.

Recent developments

In recent years some important developments have taken place within the field of person-centred counselling. We can look at these under three main headings: work with individuals; configurations of self; and research.

Individuals

In recent articles, Dave Mearns, a Scottish professor, has been writing about working at relational depth with clients in person-centred therapy. (As usual, I use the word 'therapy' to cover counselling, therapeutic counselling, counselling psychology and psychotherapy.) He starts by asking 'Is it relational depth which is the special issue, or should we be turning the coin over and asking serious theoretical questions on why this phenomenon is so rare? Is it, for example, because we are too afraid of others or perhaps of our Selves, or both, to risk meeting each other at relational depth?' (Mearns 1996, p. 306). He describes what he means by relational depth and gives these examples from clients:

> It felt as though he was right there, in the garden, with me – like he could see it as well.
>
> It felt as though she was right *inside me* – feeling *me* in the same moment that I was feeling myself.
>
> I knew he felt my terror. But it wasn't just that – it was one of those *I knew he knew I knew* things – like we were communicating at a lot of different levels at the same time.

62

He also gives examples of what therapists say about the experience – here is just one of these:

> I had not been *in* that far with a client before . . . I think it happened by accident really . . . I felt so relaxed and at ease with myself. Instead of thinking one step ahead, I just found myself responding to him in the moment – sometimes in ways which were unusual for me. It was amazing how powerful, yet simple, the process was.

Mearns makes the point that he is not saying that working at relational depth means that this sort of thing is happening at every moment. 'The interaction between therapist and client will move around the contact spectrum, at times engaging very deeply and on other occasions much more superficially' (Mearns 1996, p. 308). He also says that the idea of *presence* is very important for the whole process:

> the counsellor is able to be truly *still* within herself, allowing her person fully to resonate with the client's experiencing. In a sense, the counsellor has allowed her person to step right into the client's experiencing without needing to do anything to establish her separateness. This second circumstance is made much easier for the counsellor if she is not self-conscious.
>
> (Mearns 1994, p. 8)

This quality has of course been remarked on many times. For example, Laing, Bion, Hillman and many others have talked about presence in this sort of way. 'Perhaps we might add a little to the theory by suggesting that a prerequisite to achieving this personal 'stillness' in relationship with the client is not merely 'unselfconsciousness', but also that the therapist is not *afraid*' (Mearns 1996, p. 309).

And if this can happen, then 'the therapist who is willing to work with the client at relational depth tries to leave aside conventional ways of responding and projects himself or herself fully into the client's experiencing' (Mearns 1996, p. 310). This is not easy to do or even (for many) to imagine, because it is not a skill, it is not something to be learned. It is more like all sorts of things to be unlearned. For a trainee it may be a source of puzzlement, of helplessness, even of despair. 'The student might feel somewhat despairing . . . but their trainer would be delighted that the student was coming to the point where they realised that a simple portrayal of therapeutic qualities which were not fully integrated into the Self and in that sense congruent, could no longer be sustained' (Mearns 1996, p. 310).

This interest in and concern for the trainee is carried through in a later article (Mearns 1997) in which the author speaks in more detail about the challenge these ideas offer both to the student and to the training centre. He says:

> There is a tendency for person-centred therapists, early in training, to endeavour to portray therapeutic conditions such as empathy and unconditional positive regard in the vain hope that they can show how good they are as person-centred therapists even without the training. In an intensive and extensive training course the student will find that he or she cannot meet clients or fellow course members at relational depth through mere portrayal but that the development of congruent functioning poses many challenges to his or her personal development. Congruent functioning requires a *stillness* and *fearlessness* within the person of the therapist. Achieving that personal stillness and fearlessness demands extensive personal development helping the trainee first to become *aware* of the fears, second to come to *understand* the fears and thirdly to *experiment* with increasingly fearless relating.
>
> (Mearns 1996, p. 113)

All this has to do, of course, with personal work in individual therapy and in group work. It is here that the student can explore the basic structure of that which holds him or her back in many areas of life, not only in the therapeutic relationship. A lot of this is about awareness – awareness of self, awareness of the other, awareness of the between and the social context. But as well as these general matters, a good training course can also offer workshops on specific areas, such as abuse, spirituality, sexuality, cultural issues and so forth. All these things can help in reducing the barriers which make it difficult to engage with a client at relational depth.

This seems to be an important issue which Dave Mearns has raised in a very specific way, and which seems well worth our attention. I have suggested elsewhere (Rowan 1998a) that there is a link here with the transpersonal.

Other developments have been taking place in Europe. Jochen Eckert and Eva-Maria Biermann-Ratjen in Hamburg have been writing about the treatment of borderline personality disorder from a person-centred standpoint. This is a departure from the usual position in that it expressly allows a medical diagnosis to take the stage. These authors take developmental issues into account in a way that is uncommon in person-centred circles. This enables them to say things like this: 'So here is a rule to stick to: as a client-centred therapist treating a borderline patient, hang on to your unconditional positive regard for all you are worth' (Eckert and Biermann-Ratjen 1998, p. 357). It can be seen here how there is no abandonment of person-centred principles, but rather a much more pointed use of them.

Also in Germany, at Bochum, Rainer Sachse has been working on what he calls goal-oriented client-centred therapy of psychosomatic disorders. Again he is willing to use diagnostic categories taken from the medical model. All these people are doing research as well as conducting therapy sessions themselves.

In Canada Leslie Greenberg has been developing what he calls process-experiential psychotherapy, which has as one of its components client-centred psychotherapy. This is a fascinating development, which can be followed very well in Greenberg et al. (1998).

Configurations of self

Another contribution from Dave Mearns has been the discussion of what he calls configurations of self. These are very close to what I have been calling subpersonalities (Rowan 1990), and what others have called parts. Mearns says: 'For my own understanding I use the term "configuration" instead of "part", because each "part" is itself made up of a number of elements which form a coherent pattern generally reflective of a dimension of existence within the Self' (Mearns 1999, p. 126). Mearns recognizes that this conception has parallels with internal objects, internal voices, sub-personalities, ego states, intrapsychic families and so forth. He says that person-centred therapists often play favourites among such configurations, paying most attention to those which are most hopeful and positive: 'Person-centred therapists are particularly prone to pay attention to these 'growthful' members of the family but are not so good at offering an equally full therapeutic relationship to 'not for growth' configurations' (Mearns 1999, p. 127). It has long been recognized that very often there is a part of the client who does not want to be there, and does not want to change. Now here is a person-centred therapist saying the same thing.

Mearns recognizes that some of these configurations are of the nature of introjects. They have been swallowed whole, so to speak, from the parents or other influential figures. Once installed, they tend to attract the 'self-fulfilling prophecy' effect, those which are positive attracting good vibrations, those which are negative calling out the very responses which they most fear. If we work at a truly existential level, Mearns says, we can recognize each of these for what they are and work appropriately with them.

Research

Research from a humanistic point of view is an activity which is not unlike therapy. In both cases people need to be met as human beings and as equals, not as subjects or objects. Again Dave Mearns has a contribution to make here:

This notion of meeting the participant as an equal is not new to social research: the 'participant observer' approach emphasizes the relevance of the researcher's involvement in the process under investigation. But while many workers in action research have found it to be a more viable procedure than detached observation, it has never attained theoretical respectability. There has always been a tendency to view such involvement as a 'necessary evil'. However, in the context of the person-centred approach, this involvement is an important part of a practical and theoretical framework, from which can develop such processes as acceptance, congruence, and empathic understanding.

(Mearns and McLeod 1984, p. 376)

There is a growing interest in research, as humanistic psychology seeks to come nearer to centre stage, rather than being out on the periphery of psychology.

CO-COUNSELLING

It would be a mistake, however, to think that this is the only way of carrying out the process of counselling. One of the most powerful influences of recent years has been the rise of co-counselling networks quite outside the orbit of the growth centres, and outside the practice of professional counselling.

The basic idea of co-counselling is this: after proper training, which ensures the presence of shared assumptions and techniques, two people meet once a week (or as often as suits them) for two hours (or whatever time suits them). Then for one hour the first person is the client and the second the counsellor; and for the second hour they swap roles. Thus each person gets counselling and gives counselling equally. The role relationship is quite formal: the counsellor is not to comment, or give advice, or sympathize, or share experiences, but only to pay attention (to notice everything about the client – posture, tone of voice, as well as the words he or she is saying) to assist the client to get to emotional discharge, and to allow the client to direct the process. Experiences leading to the theory and practice of co-counselling began in the early 1950s in Seattle, Washington, USA, with the work of Harvey Jackins. His work led to the development of a substantial body of theory and practice known as Re-evaluation Counselling.

The word 'discharge' is precisely defined in co-counselling. It refers to a set of inherent, physiological processes that, when pursued to completion, lead to spontaneous 're-evaluation' – that is, the making sense of experiences that were up until then 'mis-stored' as a result of the hurts connected with them. These discharge processes are crying, shaking and trembling with cold or warm perspiration, laughing, raging, talking and yawning. All humans begin life with these recovery processes intact. However, by the time we are adults most of us have been hurt in connection with these processes and are inhibited from using them as much as we would have naturally if they hadn't been interfered with.

The counsellor's role is to help the client discharge so that the client can access his or her own thinking and solve his or her own problems. When adequate emotional discharge can take place, the person is freed from the rigid pattern of feeling and behaviour left by the hurt. The basic loving, cooperative, intelligent and zestful nature is then free to operate.

No limits are put on the degree to which the client can reclaim his or her original genius-sized ability to think, to interact well with others, and to enjoy life. The goal is to fully 're-emerge'. This goal of complete re-emergence profoundly shapes the co-counselling process. One can aspire to a life that goes far beyond coping. One can go far beyond 'reaching one's potential' in any limited, societally-defined way. In assisting the client to re-emerge from distress, the counsellor is far from passive. The counsellor's role is, in essence, to provide 'contradictions' to a client's distresses. A contradiction is defined in co-counselling as anything that allows the client to see that his or her distress recordings do not represent present-time reality. When the client's distress is contradicted sufficiently, he or she will always discharge.

The most basic contradiction to any human's distresses is the aware, caring presence of another person – in this case, the counsellor. The counsellor must also be able to manifest his or her own inherent human attitudes of respect for, delight in, and confidence in the client in order to be very effective. Next in importance is to pay such careful, thoughtful attention to the client that one can offer specific contradictions to that client's distress. Offering such contradictions is especially important when the client is tackling chronic distresses (those hurts that have been so heavily reinforced that the client has identified with them, sees them as reality, and therefore has difficulty viewing them as 'a problem').

A large number of more general contradictions have also proven very useful in enabling the client to discharge. These include: closeness with the counsellor; complete self-appreciation; taking a powerful stance in relation to the content and 'characters' of the original hurtful experience rather than a passive stance; contradiction of self-deprecatory statements; role-playing with the client taking the more powerful role; 'scorning' fear; and many others. In the recent period (late 1990s) Jackins speculated that deliberately focusing all of one's attention on positive reality was the most efficient way to discharge many distresses.

None of this is elaborate or mystifying because the client knows and can use all the same approaches and techniques, too. In most forms of therapy, what is mystified and may take years to discover is that it is the client who has to do the work. In fact, only I as a client know what I am ready to work on and how deeply. So in co-counselling the client remains in charge of the healing process from the beginning to the end. As a person continues with co-counselling, what may happen is that, after having started on a superficial level, each person starts to access deeper distresses which usually involve childhood incidents and relationships. Ongoing use of the process results in profound changes in one's life, as rigid patterns of behaviour are discharged and replaced by fresh thinking, appropriate to each new situation.

Co-counselling is also very cheap. The 40-hour course costs between £40 and £115 at 2000 prices, depending on where you do it, which includes the necessary literature. After taking a course (unless you go for extra training courses or want to become a teacher of the method) it is free.

The training for teachers of the method takes somewhat longer, and some care is taken to ensure that no one teaches co-counselling without formal approval from the Community, except on a one-to-one basis. One-to-one teaching – sharing your skills with another person – is very much encouraged for all co-counsellors. And so it spreads.

Up until recently, co-counsellors were discouraged from widely publicizing the method. One reason is that large numbers of interested people might have overwhelmed the resources available at the time. Also, by reaching out one-to-one, co-counsellors could selectively invite into co-counselling those people who were able to listen back. To be accepted into co-counselling classes one must, in general, be able to give as well as receive counselling. Peerness is an important tenet. By mutual 'boot-strapping' between peers, the resource could eventually be gathered to assist people who needed some one-way counselling before they were able to exchange counselling. However, in 1997, the World Conference of the Re-evaluation Counseling Communities concluded that present conditions made 'going public' both workable and desirable. Co-counsellors are now making the process known in the media and in a wide variety of other ways.

By the time we are adults, we have accumulated many rigid patterns of behaviour and feeling. Jackins speculated that the typical adult is left with only about ten percent of his or her original ability to be intelligent, loving and zestful. He estimated that much of our distress has been accumulated because of the systematic oppression in our current societies – we are oppressed as young people, as women, as black people, as men, and in many, many other groupings.

Unless we have the chance to discharge our hurts, we operate within the limitations of our chronic distress patterns. It is as if we function within a 'portable prison cage' or under a 'lead ceiling'. We tend to take these limitations for granted, viewing them as 'who we are'. We no longer have a clear awareness of the patterns or of their origins. However, once we understand (at least theoretically) that we are saddled with such distress recordings, we can begin the process of dismantling them. We can, in effect, go back, discharge the painful feelings that were installed at the time we were hurt, and re-evaluate the rigidities that stemmed from them. We can also more easily protect ourselves from additional hurtful experiences. As this process goes on, one generally feels better, functions more flexibly, and recovers many 'lost' abilities. One also tends to take increasing and broader responsibility for making things go well.

This obviously gets the benefit of the findings of Sidney Jourard on self-disclosure. And consequently, it does appear to be a particularly effective technique for fostering personal growth. It has an additional benefit: an extensive world-wide network of co-counsellors, teachers, Reference Persons, and Communities has been systematically organized and exists in more than 85 countries. Each person who is trained in the method has access to the names, addresses, and phone numbers of hundreds of others who have been on similar training courses.

In the 1960s co-counselling spread to Britain, largely through the efforts of Tom Scheff. The network expanded quickly, but friction started to grow over the amount of control exercised from Seattle and the amount of autonomy wanted in Britain. This led to the British representative, John Heron, seceding from the main body and starting up his own organization, which became part of Co-Counselling International, a rival group. And John Southgate started up his Dialectical Peer Counselling network, later better known as the Barefoot Psychoanalyst group (Southgate and Randall 1989), bringing in a heady mixture of Marxism, Karen Horney and other approaches. The late Glyn Seaborn Jones started his own system, called Reciport, mainly for people already in his network of therapy and group work. In spite of all this variation, the basic principles have remained the same, and this seems to be a very stable and well-organized area of work.

The basic theory of co-counselling has points of similarity with Carl Rogers' ideas. Deep down, people are OK: they are possessed of an enormous amount of creative and flexible intelligence, as well as a caring, cooperative and zestful nature. Rogers talks of 'conditions of worth' as essentially traumatic impositions of alien values. A point which Rogers does not make, and Jackins does, is that such traumatic situations leave a residue of hurt. This seeks discharge and the whole set of associated feelings will tend to be evoked by new situations bearing some similarity to the original distressing events. This 'triggering' phenomenon was termed 'restimulation' by Harvey Jackins. When we are 'cut to the quick' by a remark which may seem quite innocent to everybody else, we may suspect the presence of restimulation. Madison (1969) has some very interesting examples of this, under the heading of what he calls 're-integration' in his book on student personality. Stanislav Grof (1979) also refers to it in his account of the COEX system.

The Guidelines for the Re-evaluation Counseling Communities state that co-counselling is a 'one-point programme' – that is, the only agreement necessary to participate is to work 'to recover one's occluded intelligence and to assist others to do the same'. This can only be done, of course, assuming this analysis, by breaking down or loosening the blocks or 'patterns' that were set up by the hurtful experiences. And since the patterns exist only because of not being allowed to discharge the painful emotion, the answer is to 'go back', as it were, recall the situation, and discharge the grief, fear, rage, embarrassment and physical distress that were contained in it. 'Re-evaluation' follows spontaneously after sufficient discharge, and the situation is seen in a new light. The previously mis-stored data from the hurtful experience is freed by the release of tension to be available as discrete bits of information rather than all tied together.

What this means, in effect, is that Jackins is aiming directly at what Carl Rogers has described as the sixth stage of therapy. He is aiming very directly at emotional discharge and catharsis. Thus, in his form of counselling, the client is made aware of the primary importance of emotional discharge.

The process does seem to work. One can get to the real work on a problem much more quickly using these methods than by sticking to the more naturalistic Rogerian conversation. The client can still spend time walking all around the problem if he or she wants to, but there is no longer any need to disguise, mystify, or ignore the real aim of the counselling session, which is to get into this opened-up state which Rogers describes as his sixth stage, where the real work of breaking down the bodymind patterns can take place most effectively.

One of the key differences between the co-counselling approach and the Rogerian approach comes in the treatment of self-denigration – the times when a client starts labelling him or herself as bad or inadequate or dangerous, or when a client goes in for a great deal of self-blame. The Rogerian approach is well-stated by Audrey Newsome and her colleagues at Keele.

> Clearly it is often painful to listen to a person denigrating himself or spelling out in detail the extent of his anguish or self-rejection, but in Rogers' view this must be endured if authentic growth is to take place later. It is usually the case that only when negative feelings have been fully explored can faint and hesitant expressions of positive impulses be voiced.
>
> (Newsome et al. 1973, p. 62)

Jackins' view, however, is that putting oneself down is a distress pattern in itself and that reviewing the negative feelings is only useful if the client is discharging. A pattern of putting oneself down will have been reinforced over the years by parents, teachers, peers and others. It tends to be self-perpetuating and addictive in its effect; it has come to feel natural and is therefore difficult to break out of. Furthermore, while one is 'sunk in the depths' of one's bad feelings, one has very little free attention available to see what is actually going on and use one's intelligence to change it.

In Jackins' early writings (Jackins 1965), he describes the key essential to good counselling as achieving a 'balance of attention' on the part of the client such that he or she is poised between early distress and the real situation (the presence of the counsellor, the outside realities and so on). Jackins later found the concept of 'contradiction' more useful. A client will discharge whenever sufficient 'contradiction' to the distress allows him or her to notice that the distress is not present-time reality. So what the counsellor must do, on this reasoning, is lighten the darkness of self-criticism by contradiction (caring, validation, etc.).

The central importance of contradiction and examples of it have been mentioned earlier. As an additional example, the counsellor may ask the client to try saying the exact opposite of a negative statement just made, or sometimes to say the same thing but in an expansive way, or a cute way, or a silly way – anything to break the pattern and let in an altered perspective. A contradiction may often come out as a self-validating statement – a statement about how good or right or marvellous one is. What happens after this is interesting and often very valuable; the client may begin laughing, for example. If you as the counsellor can look a bit quizzical (or in some other way indicate that you are 'outside of' the client's distress) the laughter can go on and on for quite a while, or it may then switch into tears because the self-invalidation is noticed to be so untrue after all; then fear may come, then anger at the unfairness of it all. I found one of my own fears to be a very deep and primitive fear about my own OK-ness. It is as if somehow it was wrong or dangerous to be healthy and happy and strong and good. I went through the whole sequence of discharges (grief, fear, etc.) using the phrase – 'I just want my own real strength'. After the fear, when I had discharged some of that, came laughter, the laughter which says, 'Yes! It is true!' (Jackins 1970).

There is, of course, no guarantee that any particular sequence will follow predictably, but almost always some change comes in the way the problem is seen. Somehow the breaking of the pattern and resulting discharge allows some chink of light into a dark situation and enables one to be less identified with that problem. These assertions of one's own OK-ness are called 'positive directions' and are a sub-set of a whole range of possible ways to 'contradict' one's distress.

In addition to one-on-one sessions, the multiplied attention available in group meetings is often powerful in enabling the client to discharge while contradicting his or her distresses.

An inherently positive human nature, discharge, spontaneous re-evaluation following discharge and contradiction are all key concepts. Also key is the total distinction made between the intact human and the distresses which plague him or her; the human is always regarded and treated with complete respect even as the pattern is being 'attacked'.

Another useful tool is goal-setting. Goal-setting is a way to contradict the discouragement-producing effects of distress patterns in addition to helping the client take charge of his or her environment. Jackins devised a 'chart' to facilitate goal-setting. You write down specific goals for yourself, then what you would like to see happen for your closest associates, then for your circle of acquaintances, and on in a wider circle, eventually encompassing the universe as a whole. An ongoing commitment to social change follows logically: one must take charge of the broader society if only to make the events in that sphere enhance rather than obstruct (or put an end to!) the reaching of one's more personal goals. Goals are set in each of these spheres – goals that are to be accomplished today, next week, next month, next year, in five years, in ten years and in a lifetime. Being able to formulate what one wants to accomplish in a lifetime guides one in determining the more immediate steps (Jackins 1973).

The group associated with John Heron (Evison and Horobin 1983) has added such techniques as non-verbal interaction; guided fantasy; good parent and bad parent; regression techniques, possibly leading into a primal (briefly described as a deliberate regression to an early stage where one re-experiences the intense pain of the infant); and transpersonal directions. All these will be described later on – they come from a variety of disciplines, and some of them depart from the principle that the client shall be in charge. There is no way, for example, in which the client can be in charge during a primal (Janov 1990), or even a 'mini-primal', as Heron reassuringly but perhaps misleadingly calls it. As Rose Evison and Richard Horobin say:

> [When working in the primal area] it is also a good idea to work with an experienced counsellor, since you are bypassing the usual safeguards which in co-counselling usually ensure that you do not get any further into distress than you can handle. You need to know that your counsellor can fish you out of deep distress if you get caught in it.
>
> (Evison and Horobin 1983, p. 53)

The addition of the transpersonal is also perhaps worth a word. Transpersonal psychology deals with altered states of consciousness-meditation, trance states, expanded awareness and transcendence generally (see Rowan 1993). It says that these things can be studied and understood in the same way as any other aspect of human experience.

Now if anything like this is true, the methods of co-counselling are well designed for dealing with such matters. As Heron (1974) has suggested, the 'positive directions' could now include things like – 'I am'; or 'I am one with all things'; or 'I am one with creation'. Not all people's problems are mundane – some of them have to do with the orientation of one's whole life and one's relation to spiritual realities. Why should counselling not deal with these areas too?

Another set of additions to the basic co-counselling armoury come from the other breakaway group, associated with John Southgate (Southgate and Randall 1989). They have added Gestalt therapy, guided fantasy, some ideas from Karen Horney (1942), and again regression leading to primals in the Janov (1990) manner. There is also a whole new theoretical rationale, based on the dialectical thinking of Marx and Hegel, which in my own view is very interesting, and I became a teacher of this method for a year or two. But today the group exists no more, and the book (Southgate and Randall 1989) remains on its own as a still valuable monument which can be used by people who want to work on themselves without spending more than the price of the book itself.

Some of the same reservations obviously apply as in the case of the Heron additions – the client not being in charge during regression, and so on. Gestalt therapy can, it seems to me, be either compatible or incompatible, depending on how much it is used.

An issue which is raised by John Southgate, however, is the question of how self-improvement or self-development relates to the wider society. By adopting a dialectical point of view, he makes it clear that there is a historical element which most approaches (although not Jackins') ignore. Our counselling or other practices have effects which depend not only on what they intend to be or do, but also on the part they play in the social change processes which are going on in contradictory ways. In other words, co-counselling is on someone's side, whether it intends to be or not. This is an important point to be aware of: it is not for nothing that people in Left groups often call social workers (who use counselling techniques a great deal) the 'soft cops'. In the past, social workers have often played the role of controlling by helping. So it seems that John Southgate is raising very real issues here.

Both Jackins and Heron have stressed that co-counselling does not begin and end with the individual client. Not only does co-counselling tend to produce more autonomous people who can say 'No!' to the injustices and unfairnesses they find around them and inside themselves. They also come to see the wider community as very much a part of the whole operation. Both groups are concerned about relationships between the sexes, treatment of disabled people, the problems of teachers in schools and other organizations, etc. They are also consistent in urging that co-counselling should carry over into the way relationships are conducted generally – for example, that we could be much more aware of the way we invalidate others, especially children and those 'weaker' than ourselves.

73

During the 1980s and 1990s the relationship between individual counselling and social change became increasingly clear within the Re-evaluation Counseling Communities.

In the early 1970s, women who were becoming aware of women's less-than-equal treatment in the wider society and glimpsing their possible liberation from these limitations were also showing up in co-counselling classes. Sexist attitudes were being questioned and discharged on. The same sequence of events occurred with racism, as more and more African-heritage, Asian-heritage, and Native American people found their way into classes and questioned racist behaviours and assumptions. In the same way, blue-collar workers, disabled people, Jews, older people, young people – and gradually others of the many groups singled out for particular brands of oppressive treatment in society – were encouraged in co-counselling to speak up about the hurtful attitudes and practices they had been subject to and to heal from these hurts.

The above experiences greatly broadened the scope of Re-evaluation Counseling. A whole theory and practice for eliminating oppression began to be worked out. 'Oppression' is defined by Jackins as the systematic mistreatment of a group of people by the society and/or by another group of people who serve as agents of the society, with the mistreatment encouraged and enforced by the society and its culture. A related key concept is that of 'internalized oppression'. Here, the oppression that has been directed at targeted persons is internalized in such a way that they continue to oppress themselves, as well as members of their own group and members of other groups who have been oppressed in a similar way. As much (or more) damage is done to the lives of oppressed people by the internalized form of the oppression as by the external oppression.

Formats were created in which persons in the oppressed role in the oppressor–oppressed dynamic could speak out, be heard without argument, and discharge experiences of being discriminated against, put down and denied resources. It became standard practice in classes and workshops to include work on oppression. Increasingly, workshops were held that focused on the liberation of a particular group. Leaders for these constituencies have emerged and been designated, and 24 journals provide a forum for particular groups to share their experiences using co-counselling to free themselves from their held-in-common distresses and to devise strategies for making broader change.

It soon became clear that a theory and practice was also needed to help those in the oppressor role (which includes all of us, in one grouping or another) to discharge the early experiences that, in effect, forced us into these roles. A recently-published pamphlet (*The Human Male*) explains how men are oppressed as men as well as set up to play an oppressor role and also names and describes the institutions of society that oppress men and force them to act as oppressors. There has also been progress in revealing and discharging the systematic hurts that are inflicted on owning-class children in order to prepare them for their role as oppressors. As of the year 2000, the Re-evaluation Counseling Communities have made the elimination of racism a top priority.

Harvey Jackins was a labour union organizer prior to founding Re-evaluation Counseling, and he never stopped writing about the implications of Re-evaluation Counseling for societal transformation. One such publication is *Logical Thinking About A Future Society*, published in 1990. Most co-counsellors become eager to help build a just society in which the flourishing of all humans is the first priority.

More information about Re-evaluation Counseling can be found on its web site: www.rc.org

DREAMS

One area which is not given much direct attention either in personal growth work or in counselling, yet which really belongs there very firmly, is the realm of dreams.

The great thing about working with dreams is that we can do it at many different levels and in many different ways (Wilber 1986a, pp. 151–153). Hence almost any approach to therapy or counselling can gain from working with dreams.

There are four main ways of working with dreams. One is to treat them as information about the past (Freud 1975). They can be looked at for clues about internal conflicts stemming from childhood traumas or decisions. They can give a great deal of news about the unconscious mind and what is going on there. And obviously this will be helpful in analysing one's life and one's problems.

The second way is to treat them as information about the present. We can see a dream, as Perls (1969) used to say, as an existential message from you to you. One way of using this approach is to take up the role of each person and each thing in the dream, to find out what it is trying to say. This, too, can be productive and useful. The existential way of working with dreams is well exemplified in the work of Ernesto Spinelli (1997, pp. 63–75). The work of Alvin Mahrer (1994) also belongs here.

A third way is to treat them as information about the future (Mahoney 1972). Not simply as precognition though this can certainly happen – but more as information about where you need to go next. This kind of prospective approach, pioneered by Jung, is very popular in the transpersonal approaches (see Glouberman 1995, Chapter 13).

And the fourth way is not to interpret the dream at all, but to let it be a guide to the inner world. This is the approach of Hillman (1979), who says that the dream world is a world of its own, needing to be understood on its own terms, and not needing to be translated into some other terms.

All these approaches are possible because dreams are symbolic and, like all symbols, can be taken in various ways (Faraday 1976). For example, a cross is a symbol which, in various contexts, can mean a crossroad, a kiss, a Christian emblem, an addition, a hospital or ambulance, a flag of St George and so on. It is hopeless to say that a pistol always stands for this, or an oven for that, as old-fashioned dream books try to do.

Most forms of therapy encourage people to remember and work with dreams (Garfield 1976), and it is worthwhile to keep a dream diary. To remember a dream, write it down in the same position as that in which you dream it, preferably without putting on the light. Then change position and see if more details come. Write down the specifics as much as possible, including any unusual words or phrases that seem to be remembered.

It is possible to set up informal dream-sharing groups, and this can be very interesting, even if you are not in any process of therapy or counselling (Shohet 1985). There is a saying that an unremembered dream is like an unopened letter. We owe it to ourselves to get access to the whole dream country in our minds. And this peer-counselling approach is a good way of doing it.

For more information on all these matters, see the following websites:

Rollo May
www.ship.edu/~cgboeree/may.html

Person-centred counselling
www.adpca.org

Re-Evaluation Counseling
www.rc.org

Co-Counselling International
www.dpets.demon.co.uk/cciuk/index.html

5

PSYCHOTHERAPY 1

GESTALT THERAPY

Humanistic psychotherapy is a rich field, and we shall need two chapters to
deal with it. Within this field there are several named specialities, each of
which deserves separate treatment. The first of these is Gestalt therapy. It
should really perhaps, as some have argued, be called Gestalt awareness
practice, because it is much more than just a therapy, but since it is usually
called Gestalt therapy, we may as well give in to this usage. Gestalt is used
possibly more than any other method in psychotherapy, either on its own
or in combination with other approaches. It originated in the work of Fritz
Perls, who was one of the most creative therapists of the Esalen era. He was
always at the centre of controversy, and as Gaines (1979) has shown, was a
very interesting, if often infuriating, man.

Gestalt therapy can be carried out on a one-to-one basis, or in a group.
But even in a group, it is usually one person who is the focus of attention,
and the therapist is usually working with one person at a time. The attempt
is made to get the person to be aware and in contact with the world, instead
of suppressing most of what is going on. Perls says that rather than try to
change, stop, or avoid something that you don't like in yourself, it is much
more effective to experience it fully and become more deeply aware of it.
You can't improve on your own functioning, you can only interfere with it,
distort it and disguise it. When you really get in touch with your own
experiencing, you will find that change takes place by itself, without your
effort or planning. In recent years people seem to refer a lot to Beisser
(1972), who labelled this as 'the paradoxical theory of change', but of
course he simply took it from Perls.

There are two things which Perls warns against, and two which he
favours. He warns against 'shouldism' and 'aboutism', and is in favour of
the 'how' and the 'now'. 'Shouldism' he calls 'the self-torture game':

I'm sure that you are very familiar with this game. One part of you
talks to the other part and says, 'You should be better, you should

77

not be this way, you should not do that, you shouldn't be what you
are, you should be what you are not.'

(Perls 1970, p. 17)

He says that we grow up completely surrounded by demands of this kind,
and that we spend much of our time playing this game in adult life. But it is
a non-productive game – it does not actually produce any action – and in
Gestalt therapy one learns how to give it up. One simple hint is to use the
word 'could' every time one would normally use the word 'should'. This is
an interesting experiment which can be tried at any time.

'Aboutism' is the attempt to keep any real awareness or contact at arm's
length by an intellectual process which is often called scientific, though as
many people have pointed out (Reason and Rowan 1981), this is actually a
mistaken understanding of science. It produces the kind of reification which,
as we have already seen, is not countenanced by humanistic psychology:

Talking about things, or ourselves and others as though we were
things, keeps out any emotional responses or other genuine involvement. In therapy, aboutism is found in rationalization and intellec-
tualization, and in the 'interpretation game' where the therapist says,
'This is what your difficulties are about.' This approach is based on
noninvolvement.

(Perls 1970, p. 17)

In relation to people, Perls sometimes calls this 'gossip'. When we talk
about someone's problem, even if the person is there, and even if we are
highly trained professionals, and call it a 'case conference', it is still gossip.

The 'how' is what Perls invites the people involved in therapy to attend
to. How are you stopping yourself doing what you really want and need to
do? 'Gestalt therapy is being in touch with the obvious.' How are you
sitting, how are you breathing, what are your hands doing, where are your
eyes looking – all these things are part of who you are and how you are
living your life. By becoming aware of these things, and enabling them to
speak to us, Gestalt therapy opens up a whole wide window on our functioning, and starts off a process of change towards greater integration of
mind and body:

So if you find out how you prevent yourself from growing, from
using your potential, you have a way of increasing this, making life
richer, making you more and more capable of mobilizing yourself.
And our potential is based upon a very peculiar attitude: to live
and review every second afresh.

(Perls 1969, p. 29)

78

And this brings us to the second positive principle, the 'now'. The 'now' is both very easy and very difficult to grasp, as we have already seen. It can only be fully understood in or after a peak experience. But one of the things which Gestalt therapy aims at is just this peak experience. As Perls says:

> The task of all deep religions – especially Zen Buddhism or of really good therapy, is the *satori*, the great awakening, the coming to one's senses, waking up from one's dream . . . When we come to our senses, we start to see, to feel, to experience our needs and satisfactions, instead of playing roles and needing such a lot of props for that – houses, motor cars, dozens and dozens of costumes. . . .
>
> (Perls 1970, p. 248)

So by trying to assume that we are in the now already, we may actually get there. Many of the techniques of Gestalt therapy – the role reversal, the turning of questions into statements, the importance of saying 'I' instead of 'it', the use of fantasy and present-tense dreams – stem from this resolve to act as if we were fully in the now.

There is a superb book of readings on Gestalt therapy, which covers many aspects of this approach and the various ways and contexts in which it can be used, edited by Fagan and Shepherd (1970). The work of Barry Stevens (1970) shows what it would be like to live this way all the time, instead of just using it during therapy sessions. And if you want to see Fritz Perls in action, there are several films, a book called *Gestalt Therapy Verbatim* (1969), and another one called *The Gestalt Approach and Eye Witness to Therapy* (1976).

In recent years, however, a number of people from different angles have said that Perls should not be taken as the best exemplar of Gestalt therapy. The most prominent of these is Gary Yontef. He has made a radical distinction between two ways of acting in a Gestalt context, one of which he does not label, and the other of which he labels as the boom-boom-boom. This first came to my notice in a paper of 1991, but this piece also appears in his book of collected papers (Yontef 1993) and so I shall use the page numbers from the latter. They are described in the following ways:

Yontef approach
Hard-working, person-to-person, contact-oriented. (p. 8)
Centres on the paradoxical theory of change. (p. 12)
Supports the patient growing and the next step emerging, rather than a next
    step being aimed at by the therapist. (p. 12)
Boom-boom-boom
Technique is accentuated. (p. 8)
Arrogant, dramatic, simplistic, promising quick change. (p. 11)

Replaced careful therapeutic exploration with gimmicks. (p. 11)

The results were often unintegrated, inauthentic and inflexible. (p. 11)

A behaviour-modification approach: getting the patient to take the next step. (p. 12)

Resistance is broken down. (p. 12)

Met narcissistic needs of the therapist, not therapeutic needs of the patient. (p. 13)

People were injured in obvious and subtle ways. (p. 14)

It seems quite clear to me that the boom-boom-boom description is a caricature. It is not at all clear who exactly it is a caricature of. Yontef says that it is not Perls, yet Perls is the only name mentioned. My own view is that Perls cannot be accused of these things. So it is anonymous people with no record, no references, no identity, no evidence. In the next few years, others have taken up the cudgels.

John Wheway (1997) wants to say that there is a great gulf fixed between the old, bad type of Gestalt therapy which believed in the real self, and the new, good type of Gestalt therapy which adopts the position of inter-subjectivity. 'When we focus primarily on the intrapsychic – or take the essential criterion of maturity to be that of becoming autonomous to the extent of not needing others – we conform with the conventional emphasis. Perls's Gestalt Prayer encapsulates and represents this attitude in pre-dialogical Gestalt' (Wheway 1997, p. 18) And he speaks on the same page of 'the myth of the isolated mind'. I want to argue here that it is right to emphasize intersubjectivity, but wrong to try to lose the concept of the real self.

Lolita Sapriel (1998) is also concerned to rescue Gestalt therapy from the threat of the real self, and to replace all such talk with the idea of dialogue. She takes up an either-or position, contrasting the idea of an autonomous self with intersubjectivity theory, which 'posits that one's sense of self is an emergent phenomenon of intersubjective relatedness' (Sapriel 1998, p. 42). What I want to argue here is that the idea of dialogue is a good one, full of useful meanings and important to therapists of all persuasions. I then want to add that the idea of the self is a good one too, full of useful meanings and important to therapists – perhaps particularly to Gestalt therapists.

Gordon Wheeler (1998) contrasts 'developmentalism' and 'contextualism' and again wants to say that the former is wrong and the latter is right. He too embraces the either-or, saying for example 'Adapting Goodman, we do better to picture self-process not in *the hidden centre of the person*, but *"at the boundary" between me and my environment*, actively poised to resolve the worlds I think of as "outer" and "inner" into some workable, liveable whole' (Wheeler 1998, pp. 116–117). It seems rather obvious that we do not need to dump the one in order to believe in the other. To do so is profoundly undialectical, and therefore unhumanistic.

The whole idea of a dialogical relationship is relatively new, and entirely valid and important. Where I think its proponents go wrong is when they think they somehow have to give up the idea of a central self in order to pursue the idea of dialogue. I am not quite sure why this is.

What we are faced with in our life as human beings is not a comfortable resting place either in a separate self or in a social field. I think Maurice Friedman put it quite well when he said: 'The self experiences the vertigo of being a free and directing consciousness, on the one hand, and an 'eddy in the social current' – to use George Herbert Mead's phrase – on the other' (Friedman 1964, p. 169). To take just one horn of this dilemma and make it the whole, as some of these intersubjective enthusiasts seem to do, is not on in my view. It is not right, it is not existential and it is not Gestalt.

Another new development in Gestalt is the acceptance of the need for diagnosis, together with the continuing belief in the centrality of aware process. Joseph Melnick and Sonia Nevis argue that instead of rejecting the whole idea of diagnosis, it should be accepted, with the following provisos:

> Consistent with the here-and-now focus on change is the Gestalt tendency to diagnose with verbs and not nouns. Seeing the world in an active and therefore potentially changing way, the clinician chooses words that emphasize behavior. Thus, the description is of 'obsessing' rather than 'obsessive'.
>
> (Melnick and Nevis 1998, p. 430)

They go on to say that diagnosis is not something which is done on one occasion and never revised, so far as they are concerned. It is quite a different model, which retains the emphasis on process:

> Traditionally, Gestalt therapists have diagnosed by paying attention to the phenomenon in the moment. At some point an aspect of behavior becomes interesting, something stands out, and a pattern emerges. The pattern might lead to a diagnostic statement such as, 'The patient appears to be retroflecting' (constricting his or her emotions). The remaining therapeutic work in that session might be focused on that retroflection.
>
> (Melnick and Nevis 1998, p. 431)

They then point out that the behaviour is readily observable, that the method of working with it is clearly articulated, and that the piece of work can often be completed within the one session. The next session will be new and fresh, starting again from scratch.

This is an interesting subversion of the ordinary meaning of the term 'diagnosis', and it is also used by some of the other contributors to the same volume (Greenberg et al 1998). It reminds me of the approach to diagnosis of Diana Whitmore, when she says that she is always paying attention to the emerging working hypothesis: 'it is both wise and practical for the working hypothesis to be consciously created, loosely held and eventually verified or adjusted' (Whitmore 1991, p. 62). This seems a much safer form of diagnosis (or assessment, as it is usually called nowadays) than that assumed in most accounts.

Gestalt does seem to lend itself to splits in the profession. We have already seen how some people are setting up an 'either-or' position in regard to the real self on the one hand and intersubjectivity on the other. Some Gestaltists (like Isadore From) adopt the whole Freudian apparatus of Ego, Id and Superego, which seems extraordinary (From 1984, Müller 1996). And a recent chapter on Gestalt therapy in an otherwise excellent edited book on aspects of humanistic and transpersonal psychology (Shane 1999) manages to give a complete rundown without mentioning the name of Yontef at all!

EXPERIENTIAL PSYCHOTHERAPY

Experiential psychotherapy is a strange label in a way. It would be hard to find any version of psychotherapy which was not experiential. But what is now called experiential psychotherapy is quite central to humanistic psychology. Perhaps the best-known exponent of it is Eugene Gendlin.

He has long been known for his excellent work on focusing (Gendlin 1981). This is a method by which the person, either in company with another person or persons, or on their own, gets in touch with their own felt experience in a therapeutic way. This is not only very good in itself, it also enables the person who has done it to work more effectively in any of the other forms of therapy. Gendlin (1981) makes it clear that the felt experience of the client is central to all forms of therapy, no matter what the labels, and uses research very well to point this up.

In more recent times, Gendlin (1996) has been developing a focusing-oriented psychotherapy which pays a lot of attention to the body, and using the basic idea of bodymind unity. He calls his approach 'the experiential method', and it does genuinely integrate bodily experience with mental experience. He gives many practical hints and tips as to exactly what to do and how to do it, and the more he does this the more centrally humanistic he gets. He is obviously one of the driving forces in the new movement to get experiential therapy on to the map as an integrating force in the humanistic field.

But perhaps the best expression of the new experiential ideas is the book edited by Leslie Greenberg and others (1998) which offers a new look at the whole field. This is one of the most interesting, and most useful books to illuminate the lives of humanistic practitioners. It represents a whole new approach to humanistic work in therapy, and is both challenging and helpful.

It consists of 20 chapters by 27 authors, from five countries. They come from Gestalt, psychodrama, person-centred work, experiential psychotherapy, focusing, existential analysis – the whole gamut of humanistic work. Indeed, it seems at times as if the word 'experiential' is being used as a kind of code-word for 'humanistic', in the same sort of way that 'psycho-dynamic' is used as a code-word for 'psychoanalytic'. But this is a new kind of 'humanistic', and so it makes sense to have a new word for it. There is a lot of emphasis on the relationship in therapy. There is an awareness of constructivism. The idea of the 'real self' is questioned. Words like 'empathy' are reexamined and redefined – there is a whole chapter on this. Gary Yontef is here, pushing his version of dialogic and field theory. Kirk Schneider is here, with some updated ideas on the existential approach, saying that for him the therapist is like Virgil in Dante's *The Divine Comedy*.

> Virgil does not advise Dante about going into his hell, nor does he attempt to explain that hell to Dante. Furthermore, he does not talk *about* the hell to Dante. Nor does he rationally restructure, reprogram, tranquilize, or cheer Dante up about his hell. By contrast, Virgil joins, stays present to, and makes himself available for Dante as he proceeds on his labyrinthine journey.
>
> (Schneider 1998, p. 110)

The client is always seen as the active agent in the process of therapy. Art Bohart and Karen Tallman have an excellent chapter on this. They speak of therapy as 'Dialoguing with another creative intelligence' (Bohart and Tallman 1998, p. 197). Al Mahrer provides another of his clear and hard-hitting chapters, this time on 'How can impressive in-session changes become impressive post-session changes?'

So far so predictable, perhaps. This is the humanistic approach we know and love, give or take a few modifications. But now comes a series of chapters which seriously challenge the usual humanistic position. The titles tell you: 'Process-experiential therapy of depression' (Greenberg et al.); 'Process-experiential therapy for post-traumatic stress difficulties' (Elliott et al.); 'Experiential psychotherapy of the anxiety disorders' (Wolfe and Sigl); 'Goal-oriented client-centred psychotherapy of psychosomatic disorders' (Sachse); 'Experiential psychodrama with sexual trauma' (Hudgins); 'The treatment of borderline personality disorder' (Eckert and Biermann-Ratjen); 'A client-centred approach to therapeutic work with dissociated and fragile process' (Warner); 'Experiential approaches to psychotic experience' (Prouty); 'Psychopathology according to the differential incongruence model' (Speierer); and 'Diagnosing in the here and now: A Gestalt therapy approach' (Melnick and Nevis), the chapter we looked at in our discussion of Gestalt. In other words, these people are biting the bullet and using diagnostic labels so that they can communicate better with psychiatrists and other professionals.

This was a great shock for me, because I have long argued against diagnosis (or assessment, as it is now more usually called) on the grounds that the therapist is then likely to treat the diagnosis rather than the person. I have in fact argued this at length in Chapter 2 of my book *The Reality Game* (Rowan 1998b). So I read these chapters very carefully. And what I found was that they had miraculously managed to square the circle and embrace both humanistic values and principles and the medical model of diagnosis. Listen to the authors of the chapter on depression:

> In our approach therapists make tacit moment-by-moment assessments of clients' states and processes that guide their responses. Assessment of different types of clients' momentary processing leads to different momentary interventions that facilitate different types of exploratory processes. Process diagnoses of this type, in our treatment of depression, involve discriminating such things as whether the client is processing predominantly in an internal experiential manner, or in a conceptual and externally focused manner.
>
> (Greenberg et al. 1998, p. 236)

You can see what is happening here. Diagnosis, instead of being done once at the beginning of the treatment, is being done on the hoof or on the wing, over and over again. This is of course what we also saw in the work of Melnick and Nevis a few pages back. This was all new stuff for me, and I found it enthralling. These people write much more precisely, much more carefully, than anyone I have come across before in the humanistic world. They have then been able to think about difficult questions like – what is the difference between a depressed person and an anxious person? And they have come up with answers. By doing so they have been able to go further, and make real arguments for the proposal that the humanistic approaches to therapy are good and effective not only for neurotic problems, but also for borderline and psychotic types of distress.

Here is a new breed. These are people who are not afraid to look at patterns and constellations within people, and describe them in detail. As the final chapter states:

> This type of process-sensitive approach provides a process-diagnostic and process-directive form of treatment that will become the hallmark of a modern experiential psychotherapeutic

methodology. In this approach the therapist uses process diagnosis as a key tool and is seen as an expert not on *what* a client experiences but on *how* to differentially facilitate optimal client processes at particular times.

(Greenberg et al. 1998, p. 456)

These people want to know what they are doing, and why they are doing it, in great detail. They speak much less about intuition, about emotional feeling, about the whole. They want to use the whole gamut of the humanistic instruments, not as serving a single purpose, the same for all clients, but in a differential way:

No longer is experiential therapy to be seen as a uniform therapy without differential interventions for different disorders. Rather, it should be seen as having a variety of methods, ranging from empathic responding to feeling, through talking about the relationship, to the use of enactments, and a specific set of relational stances ranging from supportive, through disclosing, to confrontational that are differentially applied to different experiential states on the basis of what is most likely to promote particular kinds of processes most helpful at that time. These processes range from awareness of current processing activities, through symbolizing affect, to making sensory contact with reality and doing homework.

(Greenberg et al. 1998, p. 461)

This is not the language we are used to. In a way it is shocking. But I do not see how any humanistic practitioner could not be interested in it. To me it is exciting beyond measure. It is not only interesting at the level of practice, it is challenging at the level of political and economic realities. There is a lot of politics in psychotherapy, often denied by the idealist. We do live in the marketplace. We do compete. And the vision of this book, and it is a vision that certainly interests me, is that we can have a tough humanistic psychotherapy fit to hold its own and take on all comers. I want to end with a long quote from the very end of the last chapter, because it sums up this whole enterprise in what I find an inspiring way:

Finally, integration of various approaches under an umbrella identity of experiential therapy will be necessary to create a new third force. This will include the major approaches identified here, client-centred, existential, and Gestalt, and other experiential approaches such as focusing-oriented therapy, the body therapies, bioenergetics, feeling-expressive therapy, feminist therapy, logotherapy, psychodrama, and reevaluation therapy. This integrated force will then be strong enough to stand alongside cognitive and dynamic approaches as a recognized alternative. Once an experiential therapy identity has been established by an integration of diverse subgroups under a common framework, the task of exploring commonalities and differences with cognitive and dynamic therapies can begin. Then, from a strong base and with a secure identity, experiential therapy will be able to enter a dialogue with other orientations. Experiential therapy will be able to make a stronger contribution to these other approaches and will be more able to learn from them, aiding in the quest for an ultimately unified, non-school-based approach to treatment. Until the time of an integrated approach to the treatment of psychological problems has been developed, experiential therapists need a strong identity based on the study of good practice. We have attempted, in this book, to lay the groundwork for this.

(Greenberg et al. 1998, p. 465)

This should certainly be on the shelf of any library concerned with psychotherapy. It makes a real contribution, and each chapter contains much to think about. We have come back to paradox again. Humanistic psychotherapy does and does not adopt a medical model.

ALVIN MAHRER

One of the names in the book just mentioned is particularly noteworthy. This is a therapist, theorist and researcher named Alvin Mahrer, born in the US and working in Canada. In my opinion he has made the greatest contribution to theory in humanistic psychology since Maslow died. He had been writing for years about research in psychotherapy, but in 1978 he produced a remarkable book called *Experiencing*, which was in effect a manifesto for a whole new look at psychology and psychotherapy. In it he says that we have to talk, if we want to make sense of human beings, in terms of their deeper potentials. These deeper potentials are always OK, but they may be defined by the person who has them as bad or dangerous, for reasons which may be very complex and under many influences. All the psychopathology of the person can be traced to the nature of his or her relationship (integrative or disintegrative) with these deeper potentials; and all therapy must be essentially concerned with enabling the person to meet and to come to terms with them.

He went on to write several books about the actual practice of psychotherapy, culminating in his biggest work on the subject (Mahrer 1996), exposing the very central nerve of what goes on in the process of therapy between the two parties involved, and showing that most of what is done in the name of therapy is anything but therapeutic. He is indignantly critical of many different approaches:

> Virtually every helping approach assists the person in achieving the above goals [of avoiding real change] by shifting to another operating potential, and thereby helping the person maintain his self, reduce the burgeoning bad feelings, and push back down the rising deeper potential. These are the aims of supportive therapies, crisis therapies, suicide prevention centres, and the whole enterprise of chemotherapeutic drugs and pills. These are the aims of custodial treatment, behaviour therapies, ego therapies, milieu therapies and social therapies. Nearly every approach which aims for insight and understanding joins the person in achieving these goals. Programs of desensitization and token economy and deconditioning are the allies of the person in working effectively toward these goals. The war cry of all these approaches is the same: control those impulses, push down the insides, reduce the bad feelings, stop the threat, maintain the ego, push away the threat to the self, deaden the tension, guard against the instincts.
>
> (Mahrer 1978, p. 367)

In his more recent work he has mellowed a great deal, finding something good even in behaviour therapy, but the contrast still remains between therapy which fulfils the humanistic paradigm, as we have seen it so far, and other therapies which do not. So his work on psychotherapy is radical and challenging, no matter how mellow the manner of its presentation.

A very similar critique has been put forward by Gendlin (1981) who also calls what he does experiential psychotherapy. Gendlin makes it clear that the felt experience of the client is central to all forms of psychotherapy, no matter what the labels. And he uses research very well to point this up.

Mahrer (1985) has actually written a complete book on research in psychotherapy, saying radical and far-reaching things such as that all the existing research on outcomes is misconceived and illusory. But this is not a negative statement for him, merely the obvious implication of his strongly argued view that the only legitimate way of doing research in psychotherapy is to examine the outcomes which take place in each individual therapy session. Some of the vignettes he uses to illustrate this are some of the most moving and highly charged incidents that I have ever seen in a book on therapy. Such moments are visible and can be examined in minute detail through the use of recordings, and analysis of them can lead to actual improvements in therapeutic practice. Such research is of real use to practitioners. It is an extraordinary but little-known fact that the existing research, massive though it is (Garfield and Bergin 1978, Brown and Lent 1984), has never been of the slightest use to practitioners.

We shall come back to the question of research in a later chapter, but enough has been said to show what a unique and massive contribution has been made by Mahrer over the past few years, in the mainstream of the development of humanistic psychology.

6

PSYCHOTHERAPY 2

BODY WORK

The humanistic view is that psychotherapy is about bodymind unity. Instead of the dualism of the Mental Ego, where the intellect is seen as a rider on an unruly horse, we have a monistic view. One of the pioneers of this new way of looking at the body was Wilhelm Reich, and we may lead into it by considering his approach. Many people know that Reich was originally a student of Ferenczi, and later led Freud's seminar group on resistance. What Reich said was that a natural energy normally flowed through the body. This energy could be blocked at various points, usually where the segments of the body (he distinguished seven segments) joined on to one another. These blocks might have been set up originally as defences to some forbidden impulse or some painful trauma, and might be maintained as part of the person's character structure. By working on these blocks and releasing the energy, the person might be made more healthy and happy.

> Bodywork, involving the client's body and their awareness of their body as part of the therapy, was a crucial contribution by Reich to modern psychotherapy. This can include awareness held by the therapist, enhancing the client's awareness of their body, actually changing posture or using bioenergetic exercises (Lowen and Lowen 1977), Reichian massage by the therapist on the client's body and encouraging the client to use their body in movement, voice work and emotional expression.
>
> (West 1994, p. 139)

If removing fixedness in this way is important, this makes it sound as if fixedness of character, which we usually admire, were highly suspect, and Reich actually said that character is neurosis. In other words, we are responding to the world and acting in it either in an appropriate way, which stays in close contact with reality, or in a more rigid or floppy or otherwise inappropriate way. To the extent that it is the latter, Reich would see the undue rigidity or floppiness as neurosis, and would seek to undo the blocks responsible. Reich was a very interesting character himself, and biographies of him have been written by David Boadella (1985) and Myron Sharaf (1983).

This view of the person as a bodymind unity is very useful to the therapist, and of course the field of body psychotherapy has burgeoned, particularly in Europe. One of the main approaches within the Humanistic and Integrative Section of the UK Council for Psychotherapy is Body Work, and two or three of the training organizations within it are devoted mainly to such work. This comprises a number of approaches: bioenergetics, vegetotherapy, biosynthesis, biodynamic psychology, neo-Reichian work, Radix education, Hakomi therapy, Hellerwork, rolfing, postural integration, Tragering, Feldenkrais method, bio-release, Alexander technique and so on.

David Boadella has developed a particular approach within the field, called biosynthesis, and has written about it many times (e.g. Boadella 1988). He also edits the prime journal in the field, *Energy and Character*. He delivered the main speech at the First Congress of the World Council of Psychotherapy in Vienna (Boadella 1997a). More recently, he has submitted a position paper to the Subcommittee for Scientific Validation within the WCP in Rome, which sets out in detail the scientific claims of bodywork in general and biosynthesis in particular (Boadella 1997b). There is a whole somatopsychic tradition in Europe, and regular conferences are held in the area.

This general approach has been adapted and extended in a number of ways by humanistic practitioners. One of the main schools where this has been done is in bioenergetics, led by Alexander Lowen (1976), who has been to the UK a number of times. Bioenergetics lays particular emphasis on grounding, and has many exercises concerned with making better contact with our legs and feet and what they mean to us. Stress positions are used to stir up valuable material which may be connected to the person's energy blocks (Lowen and Lowen 1977).

Both Reich and Lowen think it worthwhile to say that certain patterns of blockages, certain systems of holding energy back, are very common. They draw attention to the existence of certain character types – the schizoid, the masochistic, and so on – and go into much detail as to the way of standing, the body posture and attitude, the type of breathing, the cognitive and affective patterns and contents and so on which belong to each type. One can actually do a body reading which amounts to a character reading, simply by getting the person to stand up and move about, so that one can see how the body is set in particular patterns of action (Kurtz and Prestera 1977). This gives some very clear ideas as to how to work with such a person in therapy.

One of the methods of working is to touch the body itself. The touch may be very light, as in Gerda Boyesen's biodynamic massage (Southwell 1988), or may involve pressure on tense parts, as in Lowen's bioenergetics, or may involve deep restructuring of the muscles, as in rolfing or postural integration (Painter 1986). This means that therapists in the area of body work must know the body very well, and many of them take massage qualifications, both because of the excellent education it gives on the whole body, and because of the legal requirements in certain countries. So in much body work some of the clothing is removed to give access to the muscles and also to enable the therapist to see any changes in colour of the skin as therapy progresses – these may be very important (Whitfield 1988). Not all body therapists use massage tables, but it is quite common for them to do so.

Because of this emphasis on the body, and the possible sexual implications of this, it is particularly important for body therapists to have gone through their own therapy in this way. They can then work through sexual and other feelings which may arise in them when in contact with another person's skin, before ever meeting a client (Emerson and Shorr-Kon 1994). Good supervision is also particularly important in this form of therapy, and very often the therapist will have a supervisor who will help in resolving any distress which occurs as a result of the therapist making any mistakes in this sensitive area. The supervisor can also keep an eye open for any infringement of the rather stringent ethical requirements of this discipline. It is extremely important that no one does this kind of work without adequate training and supervision.

For a wide-ranging run-down on a whole host of approaches to the body it is worth looking at Nicholas Albery's (1983) book. One of the problems with the body therapies is that they seem to lead to a proliferation of individual practitioners each with a method about which he or she is completely dogmatic. For some reason, this seems to be much more the case in the body therapies than in any of the other approaches. It is quite a relief to come across someone like Boadella, who has a lot of knowledge and quite wide-ranging sympathies. He now lives and works in Switzerland.

Anyone who goes in for body work should be aware that it can get into very deep material quite quickly. If the client is ready for that, having done a good deal of more conventional therapy already, and feeling a bit impatient with it, this may be fine. But it is in any case important for any client to make sure that the therapist is a well trained and well practised person, who has worked on themselves for at least five years. It is also advisable to check that the therapist is in supervision. Most good body practitioners recognize the need for supervision in their work. This is, of course, desirable for all therapists and compulsory for members of the Association for Humanistic Psychology Practitioners, and also for the other Humanistic and Integrative practitioners who are recognized by the UK Council for Psychotherapy, and to be found on their National Register.

The body therapy techniques developed by Reich and Lowen and their followers, and described above, involve much stressful and often painful work, such as hitting, kicking, screaming, intense breathing, stress-inducing positions and movements, and deep pressure applied to tight musculature, referred to as one's body armour. The need for this is well described by Stanley Keleman (1985), one of the people who has done most to make explicit the underlying emotional structures in the body.

In contrast to this approach is the body work developed by a few German women, including Elsa Gindler, Magda Proskauer, Marion Rosen, Ilse Middendorf and Doris Breyer (Moss 1981). Their work promotes mind/body awareness and integration using such techniques as movement, touch, natural breathing, sensory awareness and voice work. These are much more nonstressful and nonpainful practices, as Kogan (1980) and Rush (1973) also make clear. Also in this bracket comes Sensory Awareness, pioneered by Charlotte Selver and Charles Brooks (1974) at Esalen in the early 1960s and popularized by Bernard Gunther (1969). This is a very beautiful approach, with a lot of emphasis on breathing and naturalness and the wisdom of the body.

All these methods of body work emphasize therapeutic regression, catharsis and integration. Catharsis is well understood in body work:

> Reich therefore laboured, not so much to produce catharsis, as to reduce the defensiveness that prevents it. Furthermore, he helped his patients to learn about their armouring, so that defences could be less readily reconstituted after therapy. Catharsis combined with insight into the nature of defences helps patients to counteract repression long after therapy is over.
>
> (Nichols and Zax 1977, p. 114)

In recent years there has been less emphasis on catharsis amongst most therapists, because of the dangers which Alice Miller (1985) pointed out of the psychotherapist becoming unconsciously abusive. But of all the approaches to psychotherapy, it is body work which uses catharsis the most, for example by encouraging loud sounds:

> Often the person isn't immediately in touch with the feeling that is being held in. If we persuade them to make a sound, it will start as a flat, toneless 'Aaaaa', then begin to take on emotional colouring . . . it may become a yell of anger, a scream of fear, a cry of pain or grief . . . the whole sense of stuck tension in the body suddenly turns over. The energy has peaked in this act of ex-pression and re-membering – the bodymind has become whole again. As the storm passes there will generally be a sense of release, relaxation and spaciousness.
>
> (Totton and Edmondson 1988, p. 96)

Sometimes direct touch is used to produce the same kind of result. The therapist may press on tense muscles, for example. This usually hurts, and provokes strong reactions which release the held emotions. Group work is used a good deal. The therapist gets involved very directly at times, encouraging the client to shout at him or her, or even lash out at a cushion held in front of the therapist. There is a good discussion of all this in Totton and Edmondson (1988). There is typically a good deal of risk-taking in a body work group, and the group leader has to be well trained and experienced to handle these very direct interactions.

But it is possible to work with the body without touching it. An interesting version of this is to be found in the work of David Grove (Grove and Panzer 1989). He will take a bodily sensation such as tightness in the chest and work with it on a metaphorical level.

CLIENT: I have a tightness in my chest.
THERAPIST: And you have a tightness in your chest. And when you have tightness in your chest, that's tightness like what?
CLIENT: Like a rock.
THERAPIST: And a rock. And when it's like a rock, what kind of rock is that rock?
CLIENT: A hard rock.
THERAPIST: And a hard rock. And when it is a hard rock is there anything else about that hard rock?
CLIENT: Nothing can break it.

(Tompkins and Lawley 1997)

The therapist then continues to explore the symbol of the hard rock by asking further questions, until some kind of transformation takes place. This is a surprisingly effective way of working, and works simply by taking the bodily sensation seriously and working very directly with it, taking it where it needs to go. The repetition of words which may have been noticed above has to do with Grove's view that the child within the client must not be left out, and such language is inclusive of the child mind.

The work of Arnold Mindell also works without necessarily touching the body, but just following the promptings of the physical sensations experienced by the client. His excellent and very helpful book *Working with the Dreaming Body* (Mindell 1985) is packed with examples of how he works on this level. His wife Amy is also now doing interesting work which moves into the transpersonal (Mindell 1995).

Of course, not all the work at this level is body work. The same emphasis on bodymind unity is to be found in existentialism:

I am not just a body or a combination of body and soul. I am rather this process of embodied consciousness which reflects on

93

itself. There is no dualism: I am body consciousness, it is through my body that my consciousness exists. My consciousness is my body.

(Barnes 1990)

It is also to be found in the neighbouring field of phenomenology, as we can see from the following quotation:

It is through my body that I understand other people, just as it is through my body that I perceive 'things' . . . Man taken as a concrete being is not a psyche joined to an organism, but the movement to and fro of existence which at one time allows itself to take corporeal form and at others moves towards personal acts.

(Merleau-Ponty 1962, pp. 186–188)

There is a discussion of the whole question of mind and body in Chapter 6 of the book *Existential Thought and Therapeutic Practice* (Cohn 1997), which relates the whole matter to the practice of existential analysis.

The humanistic tradition takes bodymind unity for granted as the basis of its work. This includes Gestalt therapy, psychodrama, person-centred therapy, focusing, experiential therapy and so forth. The work of Alvin Mahrer in Canada is perhaps particularly notable in this regard. In a 22-page chapter, he hammers home the point again and again that body and mind are not two separate things. He consistently refuses to accept the language of 'biological foundations' which is still so popular in British psychology.

From a biological perspective, *physiological* needs are basic in understanding the body; from a totally different perspective of humanistic theory, *potentials* for *experiencing* are basic in understanding the human body. Physiological and humanistic constructs bear no hierarchical relationship toward one another; each set enjoys independent integrity.

(Mahrer 1978, p. 152)

More recently, Eugene Gendlin has been saying some very good things about the body, based on his long experience with focusing. Gendlin is of course a philosopher as well as a psychologist and psychotherapist. One quote from him may suffice:

This body is not one thing while you are another, a second thing. Your body enacts your situations and constitutes them largely before you can think how. When your attention joins this living,

94

you can pursue many more possibilities and choices than when you merely drive the body as if it were a machine like the car. It lives inherently with others. It is born into interaction and physically implies moves toward and with people. When it first arrives, it implies nursing and being held, and after it absorbs all the complex human circumstances, it can imply an intricate new move in an unheard-of predicament.

(Gendlin 1996, p. 304)

Perhaps enough has been said to indicate that this approach is important and widespread in the world today. Some of the points are well summed up in Box 6.1.

These methods can produce the most beautiful sensations if they are carried out to the end. The strong and frightening emotions are genuinely dealt with and worked through, and then what Reich calls the 'streamings' may be felt – pleasurable sensations running through the body, like a continuous orgasm. This is the natural energy of the body, flowing without blocks or hindrances.

It will be clear by now that all these forms of body work involve catharsis – the process by which emotional discharge leads to a sequence of changes ending in peace, joy or even ecstasy. As John Heider puts it:

Frequently in the course of an encounter group, participants experience a cathartic release of pent-up emotions or tension followed by an unusual, even ecstatic, sense of well-being – a feeling of having been cleansed or reborn. In this postcathartic state, conditions for healing, growth and transcendence exist to an unusual degree: psychosomatic symptoms fall away, insights into personal behaviour come easily and naturally, and a transcendent sense of union with cosmic order is common.

(Heider 1974, p. 32)

In his early days, Freud noticed the value of catharsis, and used it; but later gave it up, because it did not last, and seemed to him illusory for that reason. The symptoms returned, and the amazing experience seemed less amazing because of this. But this need cause disappointment only if we over-value catharsis in the first place. It is beautiful, and so is the cherry-blossom. We can learn from all these things, and the insight from a peak experience is no less real because we remain the person we always were. The moral which Heider draws from this is that catharsis needs to be integrated into an ongoing experience if it is to have the maximum effect.

But body work is not just about bioenergetics or biosynthesis (Boadella 1988) – it is also about touch. One of the distinctive features of the

95

Box 6.1 The body

My body is me

One of the key insights of the Centaur phase is that the self is one with the body. This represents a healing of the split between mind and body which is so common in Western experience and theory.

My body is a map of my past

We respond to life events with our whole bodies, and if the events are traumatic the body often records those events by certain patterns of tension, held by tightness or flaccidity in certain parts of our bodies. This results in extra sensitivity or extra insensitivity in those parts.

My body is a map of my limitations

Moreover, this can also result in a whole pattern of holding, which becomes a character type. There are eight basic character types in this sense.

My body is a map of my potentials

My deeper potentials, which are the key to my development, are registered in my body. Working on my body inevitably puts me in touch with these potentials.

My body is a map of my universe

If I am in contact with myself, I am in contact with my world. The relationship I have with myself is the same as I have with the world. It starts with me. By paying attention to this, transcendental experiences will also come to me.

WAYS PEOPLE GROW

Unhindering

Here we are working with the person's hangups and problems. The body may be badly aligned and in chronic tension. Or it may simply be that there is a lot of blocked energy of one kind or another, which needs to be released.

Unfolding

The natural potentials of the person will come forth as a growth work progresses. Awareness is one of the most important things here. And nurturing relationships are also important.

DANGERS AND TRAPS

The destroy-and-defence game

Keep in touch with what the client is really ready for, and don't push at a pace which is fine for you but too much for the client. Don't pull green apples.

continues

Box 6.1 (cont.)

The flying chair
Be careful that you only use techniques you are familiar with yourself, or you may release more energy than you expect, frightening yourself and the client.

Flying high without ground control
It is important to be grounded when working with high energy techniques. One good rule, for example, is to keep eye contact at all times, and not to let the client go off into unknown spaces.

Liberated soul for a day
Pushing for peak experiences without working through all the problems and impasses of ordinary therapy can produce experiences which do not last. It is better to work gradually, arriving at peak experiences in their natural order.

The laying on of the trip
Don't get too enthusiastic about a method which works well with one person. It is not necessarily the best thing for the next person. Take your cue from the client, not from the last workshop you went to.

My guru is better than your guru
Don't be intolerant of other systems than the one you learned first or best. Every approach is good for some people and not for others.

John Rowan

humanistic approach is its friendliness to human touch. Ashley Montagu wrote a marvellous book entirely devoted to the sense of touch, and as he points out:

> In the evolution of the senses the sense of touch was undoubtedly the first to come into being. Touch is the parent of our eyes, ears, nose and mouth. It is the sense which became differentiated into the others, a fact that seems to be recognised in the age-old evaluation of touch as 'the mother of the senses'.
>
> (Montagu 1986, p. 3)

In a humanistic group there will almost always be some touch, for reassurance, for sensual pleasure, for parental comforting, for support, as a form of meditation, or in any other of the many ways in which touch is used in normal human interaction.

We used to be very unaware about this politically, but since Nancy Henley opened our eyes through her striking book on body politics, we realize that touch can represent power. In her research she showed that people of higher status can touch people of lower status, but people of lower status cannot touch people of higher status. She has some suggestions for women which are well worth mentioning here:

> Women can stop: smiling unless they are happy; lowering or averting their eyes when stared at; getting out of men's way in public; allowing interruption; restraining their body postures; accepting unwanted touch.
> Women can start: staring people in the eye; addressing them by first name; being more relaxed in demeanour (seeing it's more related to status than morality); touching when it feels appropriate.
> (Henley 1977, pp. 202–203)

She adds that there is an especially important thing women can do – support other women nonverbally. She also has some hints for men along similar lines:

> Men can stop: invading women's personal space; touching them excessively; interrupting; taking up extra space; sending dominance signals to each other; staring.
> Men can start: smiling; losing their cool, displaying emotion; sending gestures of support; being honest when they are unsure of something; condensing their bodies.
> (Henley 1977, p. 203)

By becoming more aware of such matters, people in groups can avoid unnecessary dominance and submission, and relate more as equal members of the group. So the whole question of touch and body language has many different aspects to it. We need to work at a number of different levels at the same time if we are to get the most out of our own personal development.

PSYCHODRAMA

One of the most powerful, and also one of the most characteristic, approaches within the humanistic boundary is psychodrama. This was developed by Moreno (1964, 1966, 1969). He studied psychiatry at the University of Vienna at the same time Sigmund Freud was there. In the early 1920s he built a Theatre of Spontaneity in Vienna, and worked on group therapy. He invented psychodrama, and called it the theatre of truth. He was interested in politics, and created the Living Newspaper – a theatre group which portrayed current events in satirical terms. In 1925 he came to the United States. In the years between 1920 and 1940 Moreno invented almost all the techniques which are used today in encounter groups and in

Gestalt therapy. He believed in play, laughter, spontaneity and action, and laid a great deal of stress on non-verbal communication.

Moreno was a big, outgoing, red-headed man, with a charismatic personality and an oversized ego. Everything about him was larger than life size. He found it impossible to cooperate with anyone else, and got very upset when people took his ideas without acknowledgement. One of his friends, in a drunken moment, is reported to have said 'You and Freud are both full of shit: with him it's constipation; with you it's diarrhoea.' And this does express something quite pertinent about the difference between his approach and Freud's.

In psychodrama you take a life situation which is loaded with feeling for you – a row with the boss, being ill-treated as a child, a parting from a spouse, anything at all – and act it out, using people from the group as characters in your play. The group leader is called a director, and facilitates the action by suggesting ways of making it more direct and more intense. The director will usually set up the scene in a concrete way 'so the door is over here, the window is here, and there is a table', to make the scene as evocative as possible.

After the scene has been going for a while the director may suggest role reversal; that is, the person who has initiated the piece of work (the protagonist) changes places with the person who was being talked to. This is sometimes quite revelatory in itself.

Something else that may happen is that a member of the group may feel that the protagonist is not saying what she really means. The group member may then go up behind the protagonist and talk on her behalf. The protagonist, if agreeing, repeats it; or has the option of saying 'No, that's not right.'

There are over 200 different techniques which may be used in psychodrama, and it is difficult to invent a new technique which Moreno did not think of first. Moreno's 'multiple double' technique, for example, where different inner parts of the person all interact with one another, is a direct precursor of Gestalt cushion work on the one hand, and work with sub-personalities on the other.

The aim of the whole thing is spontaneity and creativity. And humanistic psychology has been in the forefront of attempts to consider creativity as a normal attribute of ordinary people. As far back as Schachtel, the great German psychologist who was a precursor of humanistic psychology, it seemed important to point out how everyone had access to creativity, if only they would allow themselves to know it and to do it.

Important blocks to creativity are fear of failure, reluctance to play, over-certainty, frustration avoidance, excessive need for balance, sensory dullness, impoverished fantasy and emotional lives, reluctance to exert influence and so on. If we can outwit these blocks – and Liam Hudson among others showed how this could be done – we can release the creativity which was there all the time. All of these things seem to emerge spontaneously in a good psychodrama group, and this is perhaps why psychodrama is so relevant to creativity.

Moreno's method (as also that of Carl Rogers) is to go indirectly towards creativity by affecting the innermost self of the person, as contrasted with the approach of people like Koberg and Bagnall, who go more directly by directing the person into profitable patterns of external behaviour. Stein (1974) has a good discussion of all this.

My own belief is that there are several different things all going under the name of creativity, and that much of the disagreement in this field stems from this fact.

First of all there is *child self* creativity, which is all about letting go of the adult constraints, and allowing ourselves to be truly playful. This is a delightful form of creativity, free from inhibitions about what is known to be possible.

Second, there is *magical* creativity, based on the needs of a particular group, and using the rituals peculiar to that group. This kind of creativity hits the nerve of the group in some way, and can produce the craze or fashion that sweeps the group for a time.

Third, there is *role-playing* creativity, which is like a commodity served up for the benefit of some paymaster. This is where problem-solving types of creativity are most popular. It can result in a sort of technology of creativity.

Fourth, there is *autonomous* creativity, which springs from the individual's own personal awareness. This can sometimes be rebellious, but it is essentially independent. The person can respond with fresh, brand-new responses to events, and can also create events.

Fifth, there is *surrendered* creativity, which comes from a source outside the self. We speak here of inspiration or of being a channel. The person tunes in, rather than acting directly. There is an emphasis on the problem being worthy of being solved.

Sixth, there is *pure* creativity, where we actually become creativity itself. At this stage we may not be interested in solving problems, because we can't see any problems.

If this schema could be accepted, it might save quite a number of arguments and disagreements. Moreno's main interest was in autonomous creativity, and I think it is this that he most often refers to.

The people who have been through such a process, just because they are now more creative and more sure of who they are, are in a better position to decide whether what they now want in social and political terms is conflict or cooperation. It is not a question of having a preconceived commitment to conflict or social harmony; it is a question of getting to a place where we have a real choice. It is not a question of deciding to be in opposition before we start, but of finding out what we really want, and in the process finding out what opposition there is to that both inside and outside ourselves. It is only thus that our spontaneous choices can be genuinely based on reality. Moreno continually talked of the importance of spontaneity as the key to mental health and full human functioning.

In a psychodrama group, the individual piece of work carries on until some resolution, often of a cathartic kind, is carried out. Then the other participants are asked about their reactions to what has been happening: often someone whose feelings have been stirred up will then do her own piece of work. A feeling builds up between the participants which Moreno called 'tele' – a bond of mutual sympathy and understanding. Tele is quite a difficult concept to grasp, but there is now an excellent and very helpful account of it from Adam Blatner (1994) which makes it all clear. A psychodrama group is a very warm place to be.

Psychodrama has been used a great deal in a large number of settings, such as schools, mental hospitals, prisons, management training courses and so forth, and is suitable for everything from deep therapy to a game-playing exercise, depending on the needs of the people involved (Holmes and Karp 1991). For example, someone contemplating changing jobs may be asked to speak to his or her future self, the person who has been in each of the possible jobs for two years.

Traditionally, psychodrama lays a great deal of stress on the 'warm-up' – that is, the process which gets the group started and moving (Blatner 1973, Taylor 1998). Moreno himself seems to have needed a period with the group in which to get himself 'psyched-up' to run the group. In reality, there seems to be no real need to do warming-up, any more than with any of the other types of group considered in this book.

Recently psychoanalysis has been getting interested in psychodrama, as Powell (1986) has shown, particularly in France and Argentina.

It seems that the potential of psychodrama is much greater than has yet been achieved. The research studies, few as they are, are very encouraging, and one would like to see a much more ambitious application of some of the deeper techniques. The book by Greenberg (1974) shows some of the many things which can be done, and there is a good summary in the Badaines chapter in Rowan and Dryden (1988). Inspiring books have come from Holmes and Karp (1991) and from Holmes et al. (1994).

One problem with psychodrama is that in the hands of people like Blatner, it does tend to get over-elaborate, there are so many prescriptions about what kind of rooms to have, and the furniture, and trained auxiliaries and so on. But I have seen very good work carried out without any of that complication, and really much prefer that.

Work has been going on in this area with video recordings. Obviously it is very revealing to see oneself on video, and one can even do things like talk directly to one's own video image, and play back the results afterwards, for some real self-revelation.

This and other questions are well discussed in the many recent books which have been coming out on psychodrama, including the excellent handbook edited by Marcia Karp, Paul Holmes and Kate Bradshaw Tauvon (1998).

PRIMAL INTEGRATION

One of the most interesting recent developments in humanistic psycho-therapy is the advent of primal integration therapy, an approach which was not included at all in the first edition of this book.

Primal integration is a form of therapy brought over to Britain by Bill Swartley, although it was also pioneered here by Frank Lake. It lays the major emphasis upon early trauma as the basic cause of neurosis, and enables people to regress back to the point in time where the trouble began, and to relive it there. This often involves a cathartic experience called 'a primal'. But some people using this approach do not like this language, and instead call what they do regression-integration therapy. It is strongly influenced by the research of Stanislav Grof (1979), who pointed parti-cularly to the deep traumas often associated with the experience of birth.

Catharsis is sometimes referred to as the ventilation of emotion. But in the kind of work which is done in therapy it seems better to be more specific, and to say with Pierce et al. (1983) that catharsis is the vigorous expression of feelings about experiences which had been previously unavailable to con-sciousness. This lays more emphasis upon the necessity for the emergence of unconscious material.

What Swartley, Lake, Grof and others did was to bring together the idea of catharsis and the emphasis on getting down to the origins of disturbance with another very important question – the transpersonal and the whole area of spirituality. (These terms are explained in Chapter 9.) This means that primal integration therapy can deal with the major part of the whole psychospiritual spectrum mapped out by Ken Wilber (1996a). I believe it is unique in this, except possibly for the holonomic approach described by Grof (1988).

It will be clear from what has been said that primal integration is a syncretic approach which brings together the extremes of therapy: it goes far back into what Wilber (1983) calls the pre-personal realm and deeply into the internal conflicts of the individual; and it goes far into the transpersonal realms of symbols, intuition and the deeper self. It is this combination of extremes which makes it so flexible in practice.

In primal integration therapy the practitioner uses techniques taken from body therapies, feeling therapies, analytic therapies and transpersonal therapies in a very imaginative way, because a lot of stress is laid on the unity of body, feelings, thought and spirituality. As Shorr (1983) says, the intensive use of imagery in therapy leads to much more involvement and much more exciting sessions.

Because of the emphasis of primal integration on early trauma, people sometimes think it is going to put all neurosis down to one trauma, happening just once in one's life. But of course traumas are seldom as dramatic as this. The commonest causes of neurosis are simply the common experiences of childhood – all the ways in which our child needs are unmet or frustrated. Bob Hoffman has spoken eloquently about the problem of negative love. Because of the prevalence of neurosis and psychosis vast numbers of parents are unable to give love to their children. Hoffman says:

> When one adopts the negative traits, moods or admonitions (silent or overt) of either or both parents, one relates to them in negative love. It is illogical logic, nonsensical sense and insane sanity, yet the pursuit of the love they never received in childhood is the reason people persist in behaving in these destructive patterns. 'See, Mom and Dad, if I am just like you, will you love me?' is the ongoing subliminal query.
>
> (Hoffman 1979, p. 20)

This is not necessarily a single trauma, in the sense of a one-off event – that is much too simplistic a view. Rather would we say with Balint (1968) that the trauma may come from a situation of some duration, where the same painful lack of 'fit' between needs and supplies is continued.

The goal of primal integration is very simple and straightforward, and can be stated in one sentence. It is to contact and release the real self. Once that has been done, enormously useful work can be done in enabling the person to work through the implications of that, and to support the person through any life-changes that may result. But until the real self has been contacted, the process of working to release it will continue (see Rowan 1998a, Chapter 5).

But there is one aspect which we must not miss out, and which is crucially important. This is that the primal integration therapist feels it very important to be authentic. If the aim of the therapy is that the client should be enabled to contact the real self, as we have said above, then it is important for the therapist to model that, and to be a living example of a real human being.

So this gives us the paradox of primal integration therapy relying at one and the same time on authenticity and tricks. At first sight these two things seem simply contradictory. How can I be real and at the same time be using techniques, which must inevitably be artificial? I think Len Bergantino puts his finger on the answer when he says: 'Being tricky and authentic can be two sides of the same coin. Being an authentic trickster will not destroy the patient's confidence if the therapist's heart is in the right place' (Bergantino

1981, p. 53). A very similar point is made by Alan Watts (1951), who tells us that in Eastern religious disciplines the learner is often tricked by the teacher into some insight or breakthrough or awakening. The tricks (*upaya*) which are used are an expression of spiritual truth. In primal integration, we may use massage, or painting, or guided fantasy, or hitting cushions, or reliving birth, all in the interests of enabling reality to dawn.

Obviously the main technique is regression – that is, taking the person back to the trauma on which their neurosis is based. Laing (1983) has argued that we should also talk about recession – the move from the outer to the inner world. And Mahrer (1986) makes a similar point. Going back is no use unless at the same time we are going deeper in to our own experience. Primal integration finds that recession and regression go very well together. One of the clearest statements of the case for doing this comes from Grof (1979) when he talks about the COEX system. A COEX is a syndrome of trauma-based experiences which hang together emotionally. It is a pattern of feelings, meanings and other mental and physical experiences which fit together and appear or disappear as a whole. It is a Gestalt which keeps on reappearing in the person's life. If we can unlock it, we can unlock a whole big area of that person's experience.

One of the things that happens in primal work, as Adzema (1985) has pointed out, is that the deeper people go in recession and regression, the more likely they are to have spiritual experiences too. However, in this area there is one very common error we have to guard against. Grof (1980) points out that blissful womb states, which primal clients sometimes get into, are very similar to peak experiences (Maslow 1973) and to the cosmic unity which mystics speak of as contact with God. This has led some people – Wasdell for example – into saying that all mystical experiences are nothing but reminiscences of the ideal or idealized womb. This is an example of Wilber's (1983) pre/trans fallacy. Grof himself does not fall for this error, and has a good discussion of some different forms of trans-personal experiences. I have tried to be even more specific in discussing the various types of mystical experiences. The whole point is that we repress not only dark or painful material in the lower unconscious, but also embarrassingly good material in the higher unconscious (Assagioli 1975). More recently, John Firman and Ann Gila have spoken in more detail about the positive shadow:

> In other words, there is always a negative *and* positive shadow . . .
> We would maintain, for example, that if there is an unconscious
> wound from childhood incest, there may perhaps be an uncon-
> scious image of a valiant saviour. Or if there is an unconscious
> trauma of neglect, there may perhaps be an unconscious ideal of
> being seen as the most special. Or if there is an unconscious
> memory of abandonment, there may be an unconscious hope for

perfect union. There is not only a repression of the negative, but a proportional repression of the positive.

(Firman and Gila 1997, p. 111)

And this positive is just as false, just as phony, as the negative kind of subpersonality. All these things can come out in guided fantasies, in drawing or painting, or in dreams. Dreams can be interpreted, understood or simply appreciated on many different levels (Wilber 1986a). If we want to do justice to the whole person, we have to be prepared to deal with the superconscious as well as the lower unconscious. This seems to me part of the four-level listening process (Rowan 1985) which is absolutely basic to all forms of therapy and counselling.

If we believe, as Michael Broder (1976) suggests, that the primal process consists of five phases: Commitment; Abreaction (catharsis); Insight (cognitive-affective restructuring); Counter-action (fresh behaviour in the world); and Pro-action (making real changes); then it must be the case that the later phases are just as important as the earlier ones. In other words, working through is just as significant as breaking through. The glamorous part, and the controversial part, of our work is the 'primal', the cathartic breakthrough; but in reality the process of integration is necessary and equally exciting in its quieter way. For example, it is a great thing to get to the cathartic point of forgiving one's mother; it is another thing to start treating women decently in daily life, as a result of this.

Primal integration pays a lot of attention to the circumstances of people's lives, which have a great deal to do with the progress of their therapy. Sometimes these external factors have as much influence as the therapy itself. It is very important to recognize these factors and the part they play. Therapists sometimes write as if therapy sessions were the whole of life, or at least most of it, and of course this is never so. The everyday life of the client can be immensely influential in helping or hindering the kind of work which a client needs to do in therapy. And it is everyday life which lasts when therapy is over.

There are some good accounts of primal integration available now, as for example the chapter by Juliana Brown and Richard Mowbray (1994) and my own chapter in Palmer and Varma (1997).

PSYCHOSYNTHESIS

We mentioned that one of the techniques used both in Gestalt work and in primal integration is fantasy. For example, in much of the dream work, the therapist asks the other person to relate a dream in the first person, present tense. Say the person says that they are at the top of a chute, and finds a piece of cardboard to slide down on; the therapist might ask the person to

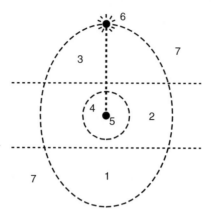

1. The lower unconscious
2. The middle unconscious
3. The higher unconscious or superconscious
4. The field of consciousness
5. The conscious self or "I"
6. The transpersonal self
7. The collective unconscious

Figure 6.1 The Assagioli egg.

play the role of the piece of cardboard – a piece of fantasy where the person is given an opportunity to find out about some (perhaps rejected) part of their own personality.

Now it is possible to take fantasy much further than this. John Stevens (1971) has a whole book which shows how fantasy can be used in Gestalt work. This is exceptional, however, and most Gestalt work only uses fantasy incidentally. There is another discipline, however, which centres itself much more on fantasy, and that is psychosynthesis.

Roberto Assagioli (1975) was an Italian doctor, and one of the first to introduce psychoanalysis into Italy. Around 1910 he began to put forward his own version, somewhat closer to Jung than to Freud, emphasizing that dynamic psychology should not only be concerned with depth (the unconscious) but also with height (the superconscious). And he found that fantasy was very useful in making concrete the difference between therapeutic interventions which went downwards into unconscious material (caves and forests), and those which went upwards into superconscious material (mountain tops and chapels). And instead of waiting for fantasy images to arise spontaneously, one could set up guided fantasies to explore these regions in a systematic way. Assagioli's 'egg diagram' helps to make this clearer (Figure 6.1).

Using his diagram, and taking it quite literally that one is starting from the central point, it is easy to construct fantasies which will explore various parts of one's world. Desoille has constructed several, and Leuner (1984) has added some more (incidentally, many of Leuner's papers were first published in English in Moreno's journal – another instance of where Moreno has helped to pioneer so many of these humanistic methods), which include:

The meadow   Each person's meadow is different, some are green and natural, some are formal gardens, some are even like deserts. Some are actual places, some are imaginary. But often they have something to do with memories with emotional loading from preconscious areas – the middle field of the diagram.

The mountain   This is a climb, and usually has to do with the aspirations of the climber. Sometimes there is a dragon or other opponent near the summit. Kornadt, quoted in Singer (1974), did a research study which found that assessment of striving in such fantasies was associated with achievement motivation and aspiration level.

The dark forest   Here the person is told to go downwards into a deep valley, at the bottom of which there is a dark forest, and to describe what happens when he looks into the forest. The therapist may make helpful suggestions if the scene gets too frightening.

By the use of these and other techniques, the person is encouraged to explore and own the whole of the area open to him or her. Contacting the transpersonal self is one of the final stages of this process.

One of the characteristic methods used in psychosynthesis is the use of a fantasy which leads to the discovery of one or more sub-selves or subpersonalities. It is often found that strange habits or quirks, sometimes quite destructive, make a lot of sense if seen as a kind of sub-system which 'takes over' at certain times and dominates the whole self. And quite often it makes sense to give this sub-system a name, and to concretize it by seeing it in fantasy as a real person, with an appearance and a history of its own. James Vargiu (1974) has written a whole work book about this, where he says that the way to deal with these subpersonalities is in five phases: recognition, acceptance, coordination, integration and synthesis.

I have myself done some research on this, and it does seem as though the idea of subpersonalities makes a lot of sense. There seem to be six main sources of subpersonalities which cannot be reduced to one another:

The collective unconscious   If Jung (1971) is right, this is where the arche-types come from, and the Shadow certainly seems to come out in this type of exercise. Anima figures are also quite common.

The cultural unconscious   This is the internal representation of the external structures of society. In our case, we live in a patriarchal society, and one of the subpersonalities often encountered is the Patripsych. By this we mean all the attitudes, ideas and feelings, usually compulsive and unconscious, that develop in relation to authority and control. As Southgate and Randall (1989) have pointed out, in general, men tend to internalize mastery and control, while on the other hand women tend to internalize self-effacement and morbid dependency. The Patripsych is similar to what Steiner et al. (1975) have called the Pig Parent – an internalized form of cultural oppression. It also seems close to what Doris Lessing (1970) calls the 'self-hater'.

The personal unconscious   The super-egos and ids and complexes and internal objects and ego states and top dogs and underdogs described by Freud, Jung, Guntrip, Berne, Perls and others.

Conflicts or problems   Sometimes the two or more sides of an internal conflict or problem situation may become vivid enough to seem to require an identity each, as is often found in psychodrama or Gestalt therapy, as well as of course in psychosynthesis itself.

Roles   The way we appear to one group may be quite different to the way we appear in another, and each role may bring out a different sub-personality. This may also apply to social frames, as described in Goffman (1974).

Fantasy images   We may identify with a hero or heroine, or with an admired group, and take on some of their characteristics; perhaps sometimes two or more heroes or heroines may merge. And these fantasy figures may come from the past or imagined future, as well as from the present.

The view of psychosynthesis on this is that the subpersonalities must become aware of one another before any integration can take place, so a phase of coordination is necessary where this happens. During this phase, there are inner changes within the subpersonalities – they cease to be so dominant and exclusive, and start to take the others into account. The 'bad' ones are seen to have much positive energy, and the 'weak' ones are seen to be much stronger than they think. And these changes and discoveries make it easier for them to work together. Some more material on sub-personalities may be found in Chapter 13.

At a certain stage, the Transpersonal Self (usually what we have called the Subtle rather than the Causal) tends to be discovered, and this makes the final synthesis a great deal easier. There are various symbols for the

Transpersonal Self – often associated with some kind of experience of ecstasy or insight. Back to satori again!

As a method of therapy, psychosynthesis has much in common with Gestalt therapy, though Perls and Assagioli were very different types of people, and some of the theoretical pronouncements sound very different. Some of the similarities are spelt out by Singer (1974).

It took until 1991 for a training manual to come out, but Diana Whitmore then produced a really excellent book, which is essential for anyone training in psychosynthesis, and has now gone into a second edition (Whitmore 1999) and there are now a number of centres and courses available worldwide.

More recently, John Firman and Ann Gila (1997) have written a remarkable theoretical work, which takes psychosynthesis further in a number of directions. They adopt a much more dialectical approach, introducing for example the idea already mentioned of a positive shadow as well as the usual negative shadow. When this happens after the death of the founder it bespeaks a very healthy school.

7

GROUP WORK

The humanistic approach has always been very interested in group work. We have already referred briefly to the Gestalt group, the psychodrama group and so on. But perhaps the central and most important type of group in this context is the encounter group.

THE ENCOUNTER GROUP

The great authoritative text on groups by Shaffer and Galinsky says that the encounter group proper is 'an outgrowth and compendium of all the group models that preceded it' (Shaffer and Galinsky 1989, p. 201).

This kind of group originated in the 1960s and reached its most classic development in the 1970s. It is now the most general type of group, and someone who has learned how to lead this type of group will find any other type of group relatively easy. But it does require a great deal of skill from the group leader.

It is of course a humanistic group, and shares with other humanistic approaches a belief that the person is basically OK. Consequently it refuses to call people 'patients', and calls them instead participants or group members.

It is also a holistic group, and shares with other holistic approaches the twin slogans – 'Go where the energy is' and 'Move the moment to its crisis'. This energy can be expressed on the physical level, on the emotional level, on the intellectual level or on the spiritual level. The basic rule for the leader of an encounter group is to look for the signs of some kind of energy ready to come out. This can be positive or negative, but it is a fact that negative feelings can often take us further than positive feelings in this kind of work. The ego comes under fire, and in a sense has to be slain so that we can continue on to the next level of development.

My own belief is that the main line of development of ideas about encounter, as worked out in the 1960s and early 1970s, runs through the work of Will Schutz, Jim Elliott and Elizabeth Mintz, and it is their work which lies at the heart of this chapter.

The essential feature of encounter is that it is integrative. What I think is meant by the fullest and most appropriate use of this term is any approach which unifies the three basic legs on which psychotherapy stands: the regressive, the existential and the transpersonal. This is a wholehearted definition which implies a wholehearted approach.

Many of the humanistic groups manage to deal with all three of these areas, but the most coherent version is the encounter group, as developed by the people just mentioned. The encounter group manages it very naturally and with little difficulty. Let us look at each of these areas in turn.

Regression

Will Schutz has probably given the most adequate account of encounter in its full form. His book *Elements of Encounter* (Schutz 1973) gives a succinct account of the history of the development of the encounter group, and also of the principles which emerged from that history. And in his book *Joy: Twenty Years Later* he says: 'I still regard encounter as the queen of the human potential methods; the best method to experience before any other training, so that the person is clear, aware, self-determining, and ready to profit much more from any other training' (Schutz 1989, p. 161). What happens in an encounter group is that the group produces an issue of some kind through one or more of its members, and the leader finds a way of dramatizing that issue so that it can be worked through for the benefit of the individuals who raise the issue, and the group as a whole.

There is an assumption here that this may well lead into something to do with the past, and may also lead the person deeper into their inner world. This is because of the concept of the energy cycle. This is something which gets fairly close to the Gestalt notion of a cycle of awareness (Clarkson 1989). As a need begins to be felt, energy is mobilized to deal with it, and this rises to a peak when the challenge is met; after this there is a relaxation period, when the person winds down. If, on the other hand, the challenge is never met, then the tension of mobilized energy is held in the body, and chronic body structuring may be set up in the worst cases. So in his groups, Schutz looks for the signs of held tension, and seeks to enable the person to complete the energy cycle, by dealing with the real life events which need to be dealt with.

For example a tension between two men may lead to them both carrying out an exercise suggested by the leader, and this may lead to one of them getting in touch with feelings about his father (e.g. Shaffer and Galinsky 1989, p. 207).

Jim Elliott (1976) has given us what is perhaps the most thorough examination of what is actually done in an encounter group, and again made clear that this is a coherent and principled approach, not in any sense a ragbag of different techniques. Its emphases are on interpersonal communication in the here and now; contacting, exploring and expressing feelings; and moving towards self-directedness and self-actualization.

Elliott says that growth is a three-stage process: first destructuring; second the emergence of new noetic material (mental contents such as thoughts, feelings, desires and so forth); and third integration of this material into the person's way of being in the world.

Elliott regards feelings as very important in this. Feelings, he says, are the royal road to the noetic world (the world of mental contents). Feelings are like icebergs, with the most socially acceptable aspects visible, and the more powerful, more primitive aspects submerged out of sight.

> Part of my strategy in working with feelings is to help people get deeper into the feeling iceberg. What I find when I start with a tiny 'insignificant' surface feeling is that it leads to other feelings, deeper down, that seem to occur in layers. The full expression of one layer leaves noetic space for the next layer to emerge. Growth, then, involves work on oneself in the form of uncovering layer after layer of feeling, until one gets to what have been called primal feelings, such as deep rage and pain. That's where the very earliest blocks are released and the most energy becomes liberated.
>
> (Elliott 1976, p. 95)

He goes on to say that it is important in such cases to elicit the complete configuration rather than have a dissociated feeling. This includes the somatic component, the imagery component and the belief component, as well as the feelings themselves. This enables the further processing to take place which leads to real integration with the rest of the person's life.

Regression involves the whole business of delving back into the past, and into the personal unconscious, to find out what went wrong there, and how it can be put right. Certain approaches specialize in this, as for example classical psychoanalysis, Kleinian analysis, the body therapies such as bioenergetics and postural integration, and directly regressive approaches such as primal integration and primal therapy. It seems to me that no therapy can really ignore this area. Even approaches which appear at first to ignore it do actually have to cover it, as we can see from any reasonably extended case history (e.g. Dryden 1987, Kutash and Wolf 1986).

Laing (1983) makes the point that we must also talk about recession, by which he means a move from the outer to the inner world. Going back is no use unless at the same time we are going deeper into our own experience. Regression without recession is of little use or interest. And Mahrer (1986) makes a similar point. Going back is no use unless at the same time we are going deeper in to our own experience. In practice, it seems that recession and regression go very well together. One of the clearest statements of the case for doing this comes from Grof (1979) when he talks about the COEX system, as we saw in the previous chapter. A COEX is a syndrome of experiences which hang together emotionally for a particular person. It is a pattern of feelings, meanings and other mental and physical experiences which keeps on reappearing in the person's life.

This gives us one clear way of working with a client. I might take an experience in the present and say something like

'Get in touch with that whole experience. What does it feel like? How does it affect your body and your breathing? What are the thoughts and meanings tied up with it? (Pause) Now see if you can allow a memory to come up of another time when you had that same sort of experience. Don't search for it, just focus on the feelings and let them float you back down your time track to an earlier time when you had those same feelings.'

When a memory comes up, I encourage the person to go into it and concretize it as much as possible – relive it in some detail, getting right inside it, express whatever needs to be expressed there, deal with any unfinished business from that time. Then we go back further, in the same way, and do the same thing with an earlier memory. Then again, and again, as often as necessary. In this way we descend, as it were, the rungs of the COEX ladder which leads us into deeper and deeper feelings, further down on Elliott's affect tree.

As we do this, we can go into the experience with the client, much in the way which Mahrer (1986) calls 'carrying forward experience' – that is, entering into the experience and co-feeling it with the client. In this way we can say things which make the experience fuller and richer for the client, and which take the client closer to the heart of that experience.

Often it also helps if the client breathes more deeply and more quickly than usual. There is a very good discussion of the whole question of hyperventilation in Albery (1983), where he examines the medical evidence in some detail. It does seem to all of us who work in this area that deep breathing is very helpful in allowing access to deep emotional layers, going deeper both in regression and recession.

Now it is obvious that a procedure like this takes time, and it is really best to go all the way with a particular COEX in one session, rather than trying to take up the tail of one session at the head of the next, which usually doesn't work. This means that the therapist who uses regression tends to prefer long sessions, and also often favours weekend intensive groups, which also enable the client to take a break or breather if need be during the session. I personally conduct some 1-hour sessions, but I also have some 1½-hour, 2-hour and 3-hour sessions; some people working in

113

this area have used up to 10-hour sessions. Grof (1988) describes his large-group sessions in some detail.

In this process people open themselves up to deeper feelings, and thus become more vulnerable, so a high degree of trust has to be built up between client and therapist. But trust isn't a feeling, it's a decision. Nobody can ever prove, in any decisive way, that they are worthy of trust, so the client just has to take the decision at some time, and it may as well be sooner as later.

This represents what Clarkson (1995) calls the reparative or developmentally needed relationship in psychotherapy. It often involves attention being paid to what she calls the transference and countertransference relationship, but this is a matter of degree. A psychoanalytically-trained therapist would use it as a major technique, while a humanistic therapist would merely pay attention to it and deal with it as necessary. A cognitive-behavioural approach might not recognize it at all, and indeed might try to avoid any regression.

It can be seen here how regression and recession are very important, but they are not the end of the road. Work still needs to be done on integrating the insights into the person's ordinary everyday world.

A good example of this kind of work in action is to be found in Gerald Haigh's (1968) article, too long to quote here, where a woman goes into her feelings about her mother and resolves something very important once and for all. So again the regressive content can be very central.

Elizabeth Mintz (1972) has told us particularly about the marathon group, which is in a way the most complete expression of what the encounter group has to offer.

She makes the point that the power of the encounter group is related to its simultaneous functioning as a reality experience and as a symbolic experience. This is more implicit in the work of the other two people we have examined, but of course equally true of their work.

She is also clear that an encounter group is not only a growth group but a therapy group. She denies that there is any real distinction between the two, as if the healthy were healthy and the sick were sick, and a neat line could be drawn between the two. In an encounter group we go down into the neurotic and even psychotic material which we all have within us. This often means regression into the past, and recession into the inner world.

In these ways the Mintz account is complementary to the two accounts already given.

Existential

Let us come on now to how encounter deals with the here-and-now aspects of the matter. Schutz himself lays particular stress upon the existential issue of openness and honesty: 'Honesty and openness are the key to your evolutionary growth. Being honest allows your bodymind to become a clear channel for taking in all the energy of the universe, both inside and outside your body, and to use it profitably' (Schutz 1973, p. 16). This is really the classic existential approach of the encounter group, but it is interesting to see that Schutz says that it only really happens once the other issues are out of the way. In this it is perhaps reminiscent of the point which psycho-analysts sometimes make, that when the client can really free-associate the therapy is over.

Mintz has some points to make about the way the group should be run. At the beginning of the group she lays down certain requirements:

> that the group must function as a group at all times, without one-to-one relationships or subgrouping; that social chatter and history taking are not useful; that after the ending of the group any personal data which have been revealed are to be treated confidentially; and that any reaction which one group member has to another is to be expressed openly and directly.
>
> (Mintz 1972, p. 17)

She goes into the question of what the norms actually are in an encounter group. Her list is so similar to those of Schutz and Elliott that I have taken the liberty of making up my own list which is based on all three. (See Box 7.1.) I sometimes use this as a one-page handout to give to naive groups, especially if they are likely to be rather rigid and intellectual: I first used it with a group of engineering students, who found the whole idea of psychology very difficult, but found these rules quite understandable. It is excellent for groups of men, because it fits in with their typical desire to have things clearly described and laid out.

Will Schutz is particularly keen to emphasize the centrality of the body in all this. Non-verbal methods are used consistently, and body movements and postures are referred to constantly. Stuck feelings are usually held in the body in some quite noticeable way, and it often makes sense to exaggerate some physical action until it reveals what was behind it. Encounter agrees with the body therapies, and with Gestalt, that my body is a map of my experience and my being. Schutz says: 'You are a unified organism. You are at the same time physical, psychological and spiritual. These levels are all manifestations of the same essence. You function best when these aspects are integrated and when you are self-aware' (Schutz 1973, p. 16). This is a good statement of one of the basic beliefs of the humanistic approach which is so fundamentally committed to integration.

Elliott emphasizes more the existential interactions of the group members. He points out that the tangles they get into with each other represent here-and-now material for the leader to work with and untangle: the members then also learn how to deal with such tangles in their everyday lives.

115

Box 7.1 Ground rules for groups

1. **Awareness of the body** Your body is you. It expresses your feelings, if you will let it. If you suppress your own body, you may be willing to suppress other people. In groups like this we often get rid of chairs and tables so that interaction may take place physically as well as verbally. (See also No. 9.)

2. **The here and now** Talk about what you are aware of in this group at this moment. If you want to talk about the past, or about events outside the group, find ways of making them present to the group members. This can often be done by action or role-playing.

3. **Feelings** Let reality have an emotional impact on you, especially the reality of the other group members. Let yourself feel various emotions – but if they are blocked, be aware of that too. Feel what it is like to experience whatever is happening at an emotional level.

4. **Self-disclosure** Be open about your feelings or lack of them. Let people into your world. If you are anxious, let people know about it; if you are bored, it is OK to say so. Be as honest as you can bear to.

5. **Confidentiality** Don't talk about what is said or done in the group outside it.

6. **Taking responsibility** Take responsibility for yourself – do what you want and need to do, not what you think the group wants you to do. If the leader suggests something, it is still your decision whether to go along with it. Be aware of what you are doing to other people by what you say and do: take responsibility for that. Be aware of the 'I and thou' in each statement. You are not an impartial observer.

7. **Risk-taking** If you are torn between expressing something and not expressing it, try taking a risk. Doing the thing you are most afraid of is usually a good idea in this group. You can reduce the danger of hostile statements by saying them nonevaluatively: instead of saying 'You are a cold person', say 'I feel frozen when you talk like that'. This is more likely to be true, and it makes you more real to the others. In a good group, people support risk-takers.

8. **Safety** If at any point you are in danger of going beyond the limits of what you can take, use the code phrase STOP! I MEAN IT! and everything will stop immediately. No physical violence in the group. No physical sex.

9. **Listening** Listening to others lets us in to their worlds. But listening is not just about words – it means being aware of expressions, gestures, body positions, breathing. Allow your intuition to work. Really be there with the other people in the group.

10. **Bridging distances** As relationships in the group become clearer, there may be one or two members you feel very distant from, or want to be distant from. By expressing this, a new kind of relationship may begin to appear. Opposition and distance are just as likely to lead to growth as closeness and support.

continues

Box 7.1 (cont.)

11. **Distress** When someone in the group is distressed, encourage them to stay with that feeling until the distress is fully worked through, or turns into some other emotion. There is a 'Red Cross nurse' in all of us who wants to stop people feeling distressed, and jumps in too soon. A person learns most by staying with the feeling, and going with it to its natural end, which is often a very good place.

12. **Support and confrontation** It is good to support someone who is doing some self-disclosure, some risk-taking, some bridging of distances. It is good to confront someone who is not being honest, who is avoiding all risk-taking, who is diverting energy away from the group's real work. It is possible to do both these things with love and care. A good group is full of mutual support.

13. **Avoidance** Don't ask questions – make the statement which lies behind the question. Address people directly, saying 'I' rather than 'it' or 'you'. Don't say 'I feel' when you mean 'I think'. Ask yourself 'What am I avoiding at this moment?'

14. **The saver** Don't take any of these rules *too* seriously. Any set of rules can be used to put someone down – perhaps yourself. In a good group, you can be who you are, say what you mean, and not have to be some particular way.

John Rowan

Source: Taken from the work of Will Schutz, James Elliott and Elizabeth Mintz, revised 1998.

By using such a format, the encounter group leader can: 1) encourage interpersonal interactions among group members in the here-and-now; 2) elicit the feelings that accompany such interactions; 3) encourage the individual to get deeper into the feelings; 4) help the group deal with the norm-setting attempts that inevitably occur as a reaction to the expression of feelings; 5) help the group create an appropriate climate in which intensive work may be done; 6) train people in more effective ways of communicating and relating; and 7) help people grow by showing them how to disengage themselves from whatever they have become attached to and, from that new, freer position, become involved with whatever aspects of human existence they wish.

(Elliott 1976, p. 32)

So Elliott is stressing here the value of members of the group working with each other, and we shall see later that this is a theme which has become more important as the years have gone by.

Transpersonal

This is a category of working where, as Stan Grof has said, we are involved with 'experiences involving an expansion or extension of consciousness beyond the usual ego boundaries and beyond the limitations of time and/or space' (Grof 1979, p. 155). It takes us into the region of spirituality. We feel we are getting information from we know not where. At first this sounds very unfamiliar and unusual, until we realize that virtually all therapists, counsellors and group leaders rely on their intuition a great deal.

Now according to the psychosynthesis school, which has done a lot of work in this area, intuition is one of the faculties of the higher unconscious. This higher unconscious, or superconscious, is a natural feature of the human mind, which does go beyond the usual ego boundaries. By giving it its proper name, we are able to work with it better and understand it more fully. Intuition, then, may take us into the realm of the transpersonal.

Let us move on to take up another, similar, point about imagination. Encounter group leaders use imagery and fantasy, and these too may take us into the transpersonal realm. When we ask a participant to bring to mind an image of his or her inner conflict, or suggest that they imagine what their opponent might turn into, or invite them to bring to mind a certain scene, we are invoking the imaginal world, which may open the way into the transpersonal.

So when Schutz tells the story of a British woman in one of his groups who was asked to become very small and go inside her own body (Shaffer and Galinsky 1989, p. 218), he was working in a way calculated to enable transpersonal energies to enter in. It is clear that imagery very often involves playing with the normal limitations of time and space. (In his more recent work, Schutz (1981) explicitly uses meditation, prayer, chanting and other spiritual exercises.)

Elliott does not say as much as Schutz about the spiritual aspects of his work, but he does say that human beings are not just physical objects but are best characterized by such words as freedom, choice, growth, autonomy and mystery. These are all characteristics of transpersonal work. He also refers to creativity and liberation (Elliott 1976, p. 58). Creativity, too, is one of the areas which may have to do with the superconscious as described by Assagioli (Ferrucci 1982). A good group leader will not only be creative, but will stimulate the creativity in other people.

Another phenomenon noted by Elliott is the Fusion Experience, which often happens after primals and similar cathartic experiences. The whole person is involved, and seems often taken outside their ordinary world. 'Looking back on the experience, [one has] the feeling that one was outside time and space. Typical comments are "The world fell away" . . .' (Elliott 1976, p. 198). This is the kind of peak experience which is very characteristic of transpersonal work.

Mintz does not say much about spirituality in her 1972 book, but makes up for it by a later book which is all about it. In this book she gives an example where a young man's impotence was cured, not by the usual process of therapy, but by a group ritual in which he symbolically castrated each of the other men in the group. This arose quite spontaneously in the group, and she says of the event: 'It was an enactment of a mythic ritual, a primitive ceremony, which tapped the deep levels of the collective unconscious; it was a transpersonal experience' (Mintz 1983, pp. 153–157). This is not to say that everything describable as mythic must be transpersonal, as Ken Wilber has pointed out at length in his essay on the pre/trans fallacy (Wilber 1983).

In the same book, Mintz talks of countertransference of such a kind that the group leader actually feels inside her own body the next thing which needs to happen for the participant. This links directly with the research on countertransference mentioned by Samuels (1989), which again links this with the transpersonal, and with the Jungian idea of the imaginal world.

It is my strong impression that the climate has changed considerably since the early 1980s, in the direction of more open acknowledgement of the importance of the transpersonal. It was always important in encounter, but it is only more recently that people have said so very much.

In an encounter group it is possible to catch a glimpse of spiritual realities which go beyond ordinary consciousness. In their important book Anthony et al. (1987) have suggested that these glimpses are extremely valuable in opening up a sense of spiritual possibilities. They can show briefly what is possible more permanently if spiritual development is continued. The gibe which is sometimes hurled at encounter groups – that the sense of wonder which they engender is temporary and therefore false – is seen to be a crass misunderstanding of the real meaning of the experience. The breakthrough and peak experiences which come through these means – what Perls calls the mini-Satori – are not illusory, even though they are temporary. They represent what I have argued at length elsewhere are mystical experiences (Rowan 1993).

A good description of the encounter group is given by Shaffer and Galinsky (1989), who put it in the context of other approaches to group work and again make clear that it is a coherent and expressive form of group work, which can stand with any of its competitors in a sturdy and respectable way. They too see Schutz as central in the development of the encounter group model, and some of the comments made on him above are based on their account.

My own work in encounter started in 1970, when I went to groups at the biggest growth centre at the time, *Quaesitor*, which at that time was located at Avenue Road in St Johns Wood, London. It was there that I actually went to a weekend workshop led by Will Schutz, who impressed me very much. Later I also attended groups led by Jim Elliott and Elizabeth Mintz, and met Will Schutz many times in different contexts.

What I like about encounter is the way in which it allows the practitioner to use the whole range of his or her talents, and to explore the gamut of the group's capacity for healing and discovery. I find that I can stretch my capacities to the full in following the energy of the client who is focal at a given moment.

Learning in the group

It may be useful to point out that the kind of learning which tends to happen in an encounter group is of a very special kind. It is what Gregory Bateson called 'Learning III'. Let us examine this for a moment, because it is a point which is not often made. The kinds of learning described by Bateson (1972) are as follows:

Learning I: trial and error processes through which the individual adapts to his or her environments, finding new responses or patterns of response to given situations. Learning practical or communicational skills takes place at this level. Learning at this level has its joys and its miseries, as anyone who has sought to master, say, a musical instrument or a sport will know.

Learning II: processes through which the individual comes to modify the way he or she views (or construes) the context in which the knowledge and skills gained through Learning I are applied. This is sometimes called 'learning to learn'. There are many kinds of experiential groups where this kind of learning can take place. It is generally regarded as valuable when it does so. For example, if a doctor comes to see his role as that of helping a person in physical or mental distress, instead of repairing a faulty biological mechanism, he or she may begin to make use of his or her medical knowledge and skills in different ways. Such a reorientation may be very painful, and/or may be a great release. Once it has taken place, it seems to be self-validating, and is therefore more or less irreversible.

Learning III involves processes through which the individual learns to attend to, and question, and hence bring within conscious control, the habitual ways of construing situations which are the outcomes of Learning II. Learning III entails a much fuller and deeper reflexive awareness. This means a radical questioning of the self. Our imaginary doctor might for example learn to monitor the idea of his or her role which was implicit in the way he or she was dealing with patients, with the possibility of continuing Learning II. In so doing, he or she would find him or herself reflecting upon their deepest beliefs, about themself and their patients and about human life, suffering and death. Thus Learning III involves the whole person, and is likely to initiate change in other areas of their life. Such disturbance is frequently frightening and painful; and once again, it may also be a matter of joy and gratitude.

In saying, therefore, that an encounter group enables Learning III to take place we are maintaining that it is or can be a truly radical experience,

which can lead to real restructuring of a person's belief system. In particular, it can lead to a deep questioning of the self and whatever the self
takes for granted. And ultimately it involves taking nothing for granted.
Barry Palmer, in a very thorough discussion of Bion's group work, says the
same thing about the deepest kind of group in psychoanalysis:

> [This kind of group] even 'proposes' Learning III. It invites parti-
> cipants to become reflexively aware of the person who is committed
> to certain ways of construing his role relationships rather than
> others and who invests them with personal meaning . . . it is
> assumed that people can look after themselves.
>
> (Palmer 1992, pp. 293 and 300)

And it is interesting that Palmer, as a psychoanalytically trained group
leader, sees clearly that it is in this area that encounter is strongest:

> Recognition of this factor may be seen as a major influence in the
> development of all those techniques which attempt to out-
> manoeuvre or dismantle the defences of the ego, such as the
> techniques of the encounter or personal growth movement. Some
> of these are defined as therapeutic, others are derived from 'ways of
> liberation' originating in the East. Their goal, in the terms used
> here, is Learning III.
>
> (Palmer 1979, p. 179)

What we are saying, therefore, is that the integrative nature of the
encounter group makes it particularly suitable for breaking down existing
patterns of relating and patterns of social assumptions. It is therefore very
suitable for the kind of group where men can re-examine their assumptions
about masculinity, and where women can re-examine their assumptions
about femininity. We can see how this works out with women in the
excellent book by Ernst and Goodison (1981).

The advantage of the integrative approach is that it enables the
practitioner to do what is appropriate in a given situation, rather than
sticking to some previously worked out theory. It enables, in particular, the
regressive, the existential and the transpersonal all to be given their due
weight. In this way theory and practice are in a dialectical relationship, each
informing the other. The theory gives rise to the practice, and the practice
in turn enables the theory to be further developed.

THE HUMANISTIC-EXISTENTIAL GROUP

In recent years, the encounter group has diminished in popularity, and what has taken its place has often been the humanistic-existential group. There seem to me to be three main reasons why this has happened. These are the revolutionary turn, the equality turn and the Alice Miller turn.

The revolutionary turn

During the 1970s, people started to come to encounter groups who were already involved in revolutionary politics, sometimes feminism, sometimes Maoism, sometimes anarchism and so forth. These people saw the group as oppressive, led by a leader who hid his or her oppressive power behind a smoke-screen of techniques. And it was true: the leader was very much an autocrat, wielding a great deal of group power, sometimes in a very unaware way. For a time, perhaps five years, this was a valuable corrective and critique of the taken-for-granted position of the leader. It led to a much more aware use of power in the group, and was very valuable in that way.

But as time went on, a new phenomenon began to emerge: the experience of other group members that the challenge to the leader could itself be oppressive. The revolutionary could be just as rigid and heavy as the leader. An acute observer of this scene referred to: 'The peer who, on the one hand confronts that authority, but, on the other hand, makes his or her fellow group members feel just as small, intimidated and vulnerable as they had felt in front of the old, discredited, authority' (Mann 1975, p. 268). Such people were now accused of laying trips on people and putting down everyone who didn't agree with them. This took some time to digest, and when the dust cleared, it was clear that the group scene had shifted considerably in the direction of equality.

The equality turn

During the 1980s, the general tone of the encounter group became more equalitarian. Now it was not a question of a few revolutionaries, but rather of the ethos of the group as a whole. Leaders found they had to become more like members of the group, rather than keeping to the more formal and therapist-like role which they had formerly adopted. This is not a simple matter, however. As has been pointed out by an influential contemporary leader:

There is often ambivalence in the group, with some people wanting the leader to be 'one of us', and at the same time resenting him or her for not being the mythical, perfect authority who knows all the answers and is able to solve all their problems and lead them to Nirvana.

(Wibberley 1988, p. 72)

But certainly my experience is that groups in recent years are much less likely to allow the leader to be very distinct and separate than they used to be. I think this is a permanent change, and that the old group scene can never now return. I feel quite a pang about this, because the old methods, dominant though they often were, did work and did liberate a lot of people. The new ethos seems to me slower and less effective in the short run, though no doubt healthier in the long run.

The Alice Miller turn

Towards the end of the 1980s, the work of Alice Miller and other similar writers became widely known, and it became evident that some of the traditional moves of the encounter group leader were experienced as abusive by those who were particularly sensitive to such issues. These were mostly people who had been sexually abused in childhood, though other forms of abuse could be important too.

Angry confrontation by the leader, so common in the early groups, seems to me now to have almost disappeared because of these influences. Such anger is not perceived now as something freeing albeit painful, but rather as a destructive kind of abuse which repeats early patterns in an anti-therapeutic way. This kind of spontaneity of the leader is now suspect rather than holy.

Some of the issues have been spelt out well by John Southgate and his co-workers at the Institute of Self-Analysis (now known as the Centre for Atttachment-Based Psychoanalytic Psychotherapy), who has taken this material on board in a big way. He says:

In practice there are a number of generally accepted things to say or do in 'therapy' which contradict the Golden Rule [THE CHILD IS INNOCENT]. For example, 'TAKE RESPONSIBILITY FOR YOURSELF'. This contradicts another Golden Rule [NO POISONOUS PEDAGOGY]. The inner child needs to be cared for by a caregiver or advocate and not be responsible for meeting her own needs.

(Southgate 1989, p. 14)

Obviously there is a contradiction here between the Schutz view we noted earlier and the Alice Miller position as spelt out by John Southgate. The

123

resolution is obviously for the leader to be much more sensitive to the actual needs of the real group member, and not to assume that one approach will do for all.

Coming back then to the humanistic-existential group (sometimes known as the existential-experiential group), this is a group where the leader is very much on the same level as the other group members. Shaffer and Galinsky actually call the leader 'the most experienced patient', and say: 'in his search for a more spontaneous and mutual involvement with each patient, the existential therapist is more willing than the psychoanalyst to reveal both his immediate experience in the session and various aspects of his own past' (Shaffer and Galinsky 1989, p. 95). There is much less reliance on techniques and dramatizations and much more on presence and being there. It is still an integrative approach, aiming at 'a symbolic rebirth or a true transformation of character' (Shaffer and Galinsky 1989, p. 95), and so recognizably humanistic.

In all these groups, the self of the group facilitator is explicitly involved. Openness is a prime value. And as Michele Baldwin points out so well: 'Another benefit of openness is that it teaches therapists to take the risks and make the mistakes necessary for becoming an authentic therapist. By disclosing his or her inner process, the therapist helps patients and students to do the same' (Baldwin 2000, p. 4). It is not for nothing that Will Schutz called his version of encounter 'open encounter', as distinct from 'basic encounter' or 'Synanon encounter'.

TRUST, SAFETY AND CONFRONTATION

Three of the most important issues which arise in groups are trust, safety and confrontation.

Trust Trust influences learning, because we have to trust a communication to some degree before we can even hear it, never mind learn from it. Trust influences cooperation, because it is hard to cooperate with someone if we do not trust them. Trust influences getting along with others, establishing friendships and inspiring the confidence of one's peers.

Trust is just as important in a group as it is in individual therapy, but it is actually harder to achieve. It is important in both cases because we cannot open up to another person if we do not trust them. Risking (very necessary in a good group) and trusting go hand in hand.

In a group, if no one takes any risks, stagnation can easily result. But mistrust can get in the way of risking anything. However, there is a paradox here. There is no way of proving that anyone is trustworthy: so we are always going to have to go beyond the evidence if we are going to get anywhere at all. If there is no way of ever proving finally that a person or group is trustworthy, we may as well take a risk and find out that way. So in order to engender trust, we have to act as if we trusted even if we do not trust. We have to risk if we are going to create trust. Then a two-way interaction can start up between trust and cooperation, and the whole group can come alive.

Trusting behaviour influences risk-taking. This is the basic point. To test whether someone is trustworthy involves taking some kind of risk. This testing goes on more at the beginning of a relationship than later on, but it can be renewed at any point where trust wavers. Perceived trustworthiness makes everything easier. Reliance on the words or actions of another is never total, nor should it be, because that way lies disappointment and disillusion. But openness is certainly to be aimed at: partly because it is one of the goals of group work in terms of personal growth. This means the owning of behaviour, and taking responsibility for our own actions. Less important in the end are our expectations of what others will do. The door to cooperation can only be opened from our side. We cannot expect someone else to do it for us.

Safety Often at the beginning of a group people are a little scared of what might happen in the group. The customary reassurance about confidentiality and no violence in the group does not go very far to allay their fears. But really the best answer to this is given by Starhawk (1987), when she says: 'Safety in a group is not a matter of niceness or politeness . . . But a group can establish safety by assuring that risks are shared, that boundaries are clear, and that power structures and hidden agendas are brought out into the open. We cannot eliminate risks, but we can face them with solidarity' (Starhawk 1987, p. 145). It is part of the role of the group leader to hold the boundaries of the group, and to ensure that important issues are not ignored or glossed over.

Confrontation Confrontation (sometimes also called challenging) has to be well handled if it is to be fruitful. It is best done in the spirit of accurate empathy, really trying to get into the other person's shoes before speaking. It should be tentative rather than dogmatic. It should be done with care, meaning that there should be some real involvement with the other person. It should be done with attention to your own motivation: Is it really for the other person's benefit, or for your own benefit? Use real communication so that the message comes from your own self and your own experience, not from some pseudo objectivity. One handy slogan that emphasizes real communication and how to achieve it is: 'Use giraffe language, not jackal language'. Giraffe language is always a description of what is happening inside you: it is a kind of owning up. The giraffe is the animal with the biggest heart in the jungle. Jackal language attacks the other person by labelling, by blaming, by questioning, by preaching – all types of communication which distance us from the other person and makes them defensive.

Also important in a group is the way in which you respond to confrontation: try not to be defensive. Let in the communication, and make sure you understand it – ask questions if necessary to clarify what is being said, and listen to the answers.

NON-HUMANISTIC GROUP WORK

I want to say something about forms of therapy which are non-humanistic, in the sense of not measuring up to the kind of outlook we have been in contact with so far. Some of these are obvious, and hardly need pointing out – drug treatment, electric shock treatment, psychoanalysis, behaviour therapy, behaviour modification – but there is one approach which is genuinely confusing, because it sounds so nice. This is group work, or group therapy, as described by Tom Douglas (1983), an unfortunately popular writer. In this approach everyone sits round on chairs. Most of the groups described in the journal *Groupwork* (published by Whiting and Birch) are like this.

Now one of the things which has been established (Paul Goodman (1962) has in fact an excellent essay on it) is that furniture can have profound effects on human interaction. The way that the furniture is arranged in a room can say 'Keep away from me', or 'Welcome', it can say 'We are equals', or 'You are inferior', it can say 'Pretend you are a brain on a beanstalk', or 'You are here as a whole person'. Now a circle of chairs carries a profound message. It says three main things – first that everyone is on the same level, second that only intellectual interaction is permitted, and third that one mustn't move from one's position. Feelings may be all right so long as they are individual and private feelings, but statements made to another person are expected to be on a head level.

So in a 'therapy group' which is arranged in this way (as in the films *Family Life*, or *One Flew Over the Cuckoo's Nest*, for example), two main lies are being told, before the group ever starts. One is that the therapist is on the same level as anyone else, and the other is that the body is not important. The first of these lies is not so bad, as long as the therapist is not taken in by it, because it helps to reduce the 'transference' element (mistaking the therapist for Mummy or Daddy) to a minimum; but the second is disastrous, because it can prevent any real therapy taking place. People who work in this way are denying themselves the dynamic therapy which is available, and which has been detailed in this and the previous two chapters. We do know how to deal with stuck feelings; we do know how to use the body and its energy; we do know how to cut through the phoney self-dramatizations; we do know how to do therapy without getting caught in the trap of 'helping'; in short, we do know how to do real therapy in a group. And it is not OK to ignore all this.

It is sad to have to say this, because the people I have met who are involved in this kind of approach seem very nice people, and idealistic with it (for example, Mullender and Ward 1991). They are often laying themselves on the line in a very real and honest way. But if I were involved in one of those groups I would want to get the full benefit from whatever skills were available to get me into a better space, and go through whatever was necessary to get there in the least time possible.

SELF-HELP AND THE SYSTEM

There is one danger with humanistic psychotherapy, and that is that it becomes absorbed into the medical system and treated as some kind of auxiliary medical aid. As we have noted already, it is not a medical matter. But there is a temptation, because mental hospitals are run by the National Health Service, to try to get legitimation through those channels. There is a double-bind operating here – if you want to be given working and research facilities, a career structure and all the other normal things, you must do it through medical channels; but if you get it through medical channels, you will be put into the wrong box, have to work under medical supervision, have all your work misunderstood, have to fight to keep your identity, and maybe have your work twisted out of recognition. Back to paradox once again!

But the whole problem of accreditation has been much improved in recent years through the formation of the UKAHPP (Association of Humanistic Psychology Practitioners). No longer is it true that someone who wants to practise an unorthodox speciality must get a qualification in something quite different, to give them the right to do what they wanted to do in the first place. Through the UKAHPP, accreditation can be given to someone who has had a very unorthodox background, so long as that person can demonstrate that they have the requisite training and experience to do what they do, and that they are having supervision and continuing to work on themself. The person must also be willing to sign a statement on ethics and good practice which means that they can be held to account in case of any breaches of the guidelines. Some further details are given in Chapter 12.

There are now more courses and more books (for example the excellent Brammer et al. (1993) which is very nearly complete) in the kinds of therapy we have been describing, and the position is more encouraging than it was ten years ago. Qualifications can now be taken directly, and again we shall see more on this later.

One way of avoiding the whole question of accreditation is to encourage the setting up of self-help centres, where people can practise co-counselling and group therapy of various kinds on each other. There appear to be fewer of these about than there were, which seems a pity. For some other people, Women's Liberation Groups are an answer. These groups do not exist in many areas, however, and it is quite a task to get one started. Also these groups tend to do very well at first, and then get stuck, partly for lack of the techniques and methods which could take them further. But the excellent book by Ernst and Goodison (1981) shows just exactly how a self-help group can use all the methods outlined in the present volume to great advantage, and now that this book is available, self-help methods are much more possible. It really makes a good companion volume to this present one.

Another approach to self-help is the technique of focusing, as outlined by Gendlin (1981) in his book of that name. This is a method by which the person, either in company with another person or persons, or on their own, gets in touch with their own felt experience in a therapeutic way. This is not only very good in itself, but it also enables the person who has done it to work much more effectively in any of the other forms of personal growth, counselling or psychotherapy.

8

EDUCATION AND TRAINING

Humanistic education takes the principles we have been meeting all the way through, and applies them fully in the educational field. This means moving away from the superior–inferior relationship between pupil and teacher, and towards a process in which everyone is learning something. There is a basic trust in the student, as someone who has curiosity about the world, a desire to relate successfully to others, a set of values which are partly fixed and partly changing, a whole lot of feelings which sometimes help and sometimes get in the way, and a real physical body – someone who is a real person with a history, and a number of projects, and who is here now.

However, we also have to recognize that education is a hierarchical world, and that we cannot stand outside it, unless we are Summerhill or some such. We are implicated in all that, if we want to be recognized and have our certificates honoured and valued by the wider society. Again, we are part of the problem as well as part of the solution.

ROGERS

Carl Rogers (Rogers and Freiberg 1994) has said a lot about education, and has been responsible for starting a number of research projects, to find out what works and what does not. His own position is that he finds teaching of little value, and prefers to adopt the role of a facilitator of learning. And it then turns out that the three most important things for a facilitator to do, if he or she is really going to permit learning to take place, are the same three as are needed for a person-centred counsellor or a person-centred encounter group leader. Back to genuineness, non-possessive warmth and empathy!

And it turns out that these things work. Rogers replied to an attack on his methods by two establishment psychologists (Brown and Tedeschi 1972) by quoting research which they had apparently overlooked. In these studies these three qualities of the teacher had actually been measured in the classroom, and the comparative levels of different teachers established:

> It has been shown that they are significantly and positively related
> to a greater gain in reading achievement in third graders (Aspy
> 1965). They are positively related to grade point average (Pierce
> 1966); to cognitive growth (Aspy 1969; Aspy and Hadlock 1967);
> they are related to a diffusion of liking and trust in the classroom
> which in turn is related to better utilization of abilities by the
> student and greater confidence in himself (Schmuck 1966).
>
> (Rogers 1972, p. 19)

In other words, if I as a teacher adopt the person-centred approach, I find
that not only does the class atmosphere improve and become warmer and
more nourishing, but also the children actually do better in terms of marks.
The National Center for Humanizing Education (NCHE) mounted a very
impressive research study (Aspy 1972) which found that 'Students learn
more and behave better when they receive high levels of understanding,
caring and genuineness, than when given low levels of them.' Two decades
of this sort of research was summarized in a book (Aspy and Roebuck
1977) whose title speaks volumes.

Since then, a great deal of further research work has been done, much of
which has been summarized in Rogers (Rogers and Freiberg 1994). Not
only have the findings been supported in different sub-cultures in the USA,
where the work was first done, but also in Germany, which is a very
different culture. It is of course a common form of resistance to any
behavioural-science findings to say 'It wouldn't work here', and nine times
out of ten this turns out to be false. This mass of solid research work must
make us pause and consider the details of this approach to education.

When one walks into such a classroom, it looks different and it sounds
different from a conventional one. Children are working in small groups
rather than sitting in lines, and there is a lively hum or buzz which is
unlike either the silence of a 'good' class (in custodial terms) or the
rowdyness of a 'bad' class. And the basic health of the situation shows
itself when the children are outside the classroom, as David Sturgess
(1972) has noticed.

In the Rogers' (Rogers and Freiberg 1994) book, we find four chapters
by people who have tried out his approach, and from these one can see the
kind of problems which arise when one makes the attempt. One of the
teachers was working with 12-year-olds, one with 16-year-olds, one with a
range of 14- to 17-year-olds, four with undergraduates and one with
teachers. One of the nice things about humanistic teachers is that they are
open to talk about their personal experiences, without a lot of cover-up
and defence. What happens when you let children set their own goals, and
work on them in their own way? What happens when you allow children
to make their own contract as to what they will do today? Barbara Shiel
says:

I must exercise great control when I see a child doing nothing (productive) for most of a day. Providing the opportunity to develop self-discipline is an even greater trial at times. I've come to realise that one must be secure in his own self-concept to undertake such a programme. In order to relinquish the accepted role of the teacher in a teacher-directed programme, one must understand and accept oneself first.

(Shiel 1994, p. 76)

Just like the encounter leader or the counsellor, the person-centred teacher must be prepared to work on him or herself, develop their own self-understanding, deal with their own internal 'shoulds'. But if they do this, the whole job can change. As Barbara Shiel says again:

I have been constantly challenged, 'but how did you teach the facts and new concepts?' The individuals inquiring apparently assume that unless the teacher is dictating, directing or explaining, there can be no learning. My answer is that I did not 'teach'; the children taught themselves and each other.

(Shiel 1994, p. 76)

And the children did teach themselves; the actual results from the class were impressive. Yet they were not exceptional children: there were 36 children in the class, with an IQ range of 82 to 135 – many of them labelled as socially maladjusted, underachievers or emotionally disturbed. There were discipline problems, lack of interest and difficulties with parents.

And it does not appear that Shiel was a charismatic, amazing personality, who would be a success no matter what she did. She comes across as a person who was interested in what she was doing, and was determined to try something properly, and adapt it intelligently – most teachers have all the qualities necessary to do this. One does not have to be a saint, but one does have to be prepared to look at oneself, and drop some of one's own defences against one's own experience.

More recent research has been collected in Rogers and Freiberg (1994) and in Barrett-Lennard (1998). The latter has a great deal to say about the whole research operation in person-centred work, situated historically.

A special issue of *Self and Society* came out (vol. 12, no. 4, Jul/Aug 1984) about self-directed learning, and this gave a good deal of information on how it actually works out in practice in Britain.

Rogers' views and methods are very important, and have been very influential in humanistic education, but as we have seen, his approach is not the only one.

CONFLUENT EDUCATION

Another stream goes by the name of confluent education – the flowing together of intellect, emotions and the body into a single educational experience. The first book in this area was the one by Brown (1971), based on work done under the impetus of a Ford Foundation grant. Here, as in the other areas we have looked at in this book, the way in which people have moved away from Rogers has been in the direction of more intervention. The teacher has a bigger role to play, and also is more conscious of bodily movements and interactions than is Rogers. This is obviously very easy to achieve in a drama class – the body is involved already, and there is little resistance to getting the whole thing moving, either on the part of the students or of the teacher. In an English class, it may be possible to work quite naturally in that direction – after all, drama and English are quite close. But how about science? William Romey (1972) wrote a very interesting book about how he, as a science teacher, went over to humanistic education. One of the key discoveries he made was that he was playing a suspect game with his students; he was asking them questions to which there was only one answer. The result of playing this game was that he was seeing his students in terms of who answers right and who answers wrong, who answers quickly and who answers slowly, who is actively engaged and who is withdrawn and evasive, who disturbs others and prevents them from answering correctly.

Categories soon emerge from this process – 'bright' and 'dull', 'helpful' and 'disruptive', 'earnest' and 'lazy'. The 'bright' are those who like playing the game and have a talent for it; the 'dull' are those who, for one reason or another, are turned off the game of question-and-answer, and have decided it is not for them. The 'helpful' are those who may or may not be much good at the game, but want to be cooperative – they admire or love the teacher, and want to help out. The 'disruptive' are those who actively reject the situation and the game being played. The 'earnest' are those who are not very good at the game, but try extra hard to make up for their difficulties. And the 'lazy' are those who can play the game but often feel insufficiently involved to do so.

All these categories arise from the system of social relations which are set up the moment the teacher stands up in front of a class and begins to play the game. And Romey (1972) decided that these were not very constructive roles for students to play – they narrowed and oppressed the students, whichever way they went in an individual case. And so he made a resolution, which sounds weird but exciting to anyone who went through the orthodox system: 'I will never again ask a learner a question to which I already know the answer, unless he has asked me to play an inquiry game with him.' My experience of science teaching was not like this, and it is quite a shock for someone like me to conceive of a science teacher taking up this way of working.

The very useful book by Elizabeth Hunter (1972) mentions the rule of two-thirds: that in the average classroom someone is talking two-thirds of the time; two-thirds of that time the teacher is doing the talking; and two-thirds of the average teacher's talk is lecture, direction giving and criticism. In many classrooms, as the NCHE project discovered (Rogers 1983), it is 80 per cent teacher talk. All the research ever done, however, says that more productive learning takes place if pupils talk more; if teachers' talk is accepting and encouraging; and if teachers ask questions that go beyond recall and retrieval. So maybe Romey is not so weird after all.

But he goes further again. Hunter says that there are five kinds of questions that teachers ask in the classroom: recall; comprehension; invention; evaluation; and routine management. Romey says he is trying to give up all of these:

> Most of my teaching up until a couple of years ago consisted of trying to think up better, more stimulating questions to ask people. But I don't want learners to be confined by my questions any more. I want to learn what their questions and concerns are. We must trust each other not to pry with questions but to be ready to receive each other's offerings. It's hard for me to do, but it feels very good when people start to talk to me at a deeper level than ever before.
>
> (Romey 1972, p. 72)

If I as a teacher can allow myself to be a whole person in the classroom, the children are more likely to allow themselves to be whole people too. Of course we already are whole people – our bodies, feelings, minds and souls are all there present in the classroom – we just need to give up pretending that we are not.

But of course there is something scary about it. Suddenly to think of oneself as an embodied self in a room with other embodied selves, all trying to make sense of a situation in which no one has a complete picture of what is going on – that sounds difficult and dangerous; much more difficult and dangerous than taking up well-formed roles, which is tidy even if no real learning takes place. It is just a question of what our priorities are. For the humanistic teacher, the priority is testable – just dealing with what is checkably here now, instead of what is supposed to be here now.

In terms of the Maslow levels which we have now looked at, most schools and colleges stop people developing beyond the fourth level – the level of getting esteem from others. This is because of the great emphasis on roles. In a hierarchical organization there is an extreme emphasis on role separation; sometimes, indeed, people are called by the name of the role instead of by their own name, to show that the organization needs that particular role, but does not need that particular person. Now there is a certain deep opposition between playing a role and being oneself. We have been seeing all the way through this book that the aim of humanistic psychology is to explore all the ways in which human beings can be more themselves – more authentic and less phony, more in charge of their own lives and less at the mercy of pressures from outside and from inside. Dorothy Emmet paraphrases Sartre when she says: 'To accept a role is to evade the responsibility of seeing that one is free not so to act, and of freely deciding what one wants to be. It is to evade freedom by sheltering behind one's social function' (Emmet 1966, p. 66). And this Sartre calls bad faith, or self-deception. Certainly it seems to be true that, for the self-actualizing person, a role can only be something false. It is a game to be played, and one has given up playing games. The whole aim of the kinds of growth, counselling and therapy work which we have been considering here is to enable people to give up playing games. This is quite explicit in the title of Eric Berne's most famous book (1964), and in the encounter literature we find titles like *The Game of No Game* (Thomas 1970). Or one can continue to play games, but this time one does not need to play games, one can just go into them and out of them consciously, like a game of chess or a game of tennis. This is the approach of Romey. The game here is quite explicit and not mystified into a hidden norm. Again, in Brown's (1971) book he gives two chapters over to two teachers who have actually tried these methods, and they speak of their difficulties and struggles in doing justice to what they believe in.

Later Brown (1975) edited a volume of chapters by various people involved in the confluent education project, which gives far more of the feel of the day-to-day struggle. There are lots of good examples here of exactly how teachers actually cope with teaching in the new way.

One of the best books on confluent education is the one by Castillo (1978), which contains 211 exercises which have been used in the classroom, some of them general and some of them specific to language, science, reading or mathematics. There is a brief but very useful annotated bibliography on humanistic education.

However, the confluent education movement did come to an end, and the story of how it was closed down by administrators is contained in the excellent book by Stewart Shapiro (1998). This book reviews the status of similar humanistic education programmes, and tries to arrive at some conclusions as to what makes such programmes live or die. Basically we have to understand the paradox that humanistic education can be too good. It can demand more than ordinary everyday people can cope with. It seems that the students can cope well enough – though they often resist freedom and responsibility in the early stages of the introduction of such programmes – but it is the staff and the administration who have many more problems.

So we come back to the paradox that humanistic education is and is not hierarchical. We somehow have to hold together the two sides of that statement, rather than imagining that we can miraculously abolish one half of it.

EXPERIENTIAL LEARNING

We come on here to the whole question of experiential learning, which is close to the heart of the humanistic approach. Most humanistic educators do a lot of work in the experiential mode, rather than in the didactic mode. There was a special issue of *Self and Society* devoted to this subject (vol. 10, no. 4, Jul/Aug 1982), which gives a good deal of information as to what it is and how it works.

It has also been made clear in recent years that experiential work taken on its own is much less threatening than the full-blown humanistic approach. Many people other than humanistic exponents are now using experiential methods. I have come across psychoanalytic courses which use experiential exercises, and also Jungian ones. Many management courses with highly conventional setups use experiential methods as important features of their work. But of course here we are concerned with the specifically humanistic use of these methods.

One of the best books in this area is by Terry Borton (1970), which not only gives an honest story of what he did himself, but also links up this whole approach to cognitive psychology. From this he derives a basic message that education is about the 'What', the 'So What' and the 'Now What':

> If, for example, a student is overly suspicious, then he must first discover What he is doing, perhaps by becoming immersed in a role-playing exercise so that he can see the pattern of his behaviour emerge there. He will then need to begin asking, 'So What?' What difference does his behaviour make? What meaning does it have for him, and what are its consequences? Finally he will need to ask, 'Now What?' Now that he sees that he is suspicious, what does he want to do? How can his new understanding be translated into new patterns of behaviour? Does he want to experiment with a new attitude, assess its consequences, and reapply what he has learned?
>
> (Borton 1970, p. 102)

Borton goes through example after example, showing how this simple structure can be applied to specific situations. He makes one important addition to the model: a curriculum based on it, he says, works best if the 'So What' part is carried out in two complementary ways:

The first is the analytic mode with which most of us are familiar – hard-driving, pointed, sharp, logical, tough and rigorous. But it is difficult for people to change if they are put under much pressure, so we also employ a contemplative mode, a more relaxed approach which avoids picking at one's self and allows alternatives to suggest themselves through free association and metaphor.

(Borton 1970, p. 96)

Here we are moving close to the points made in the large research project of Mary Belenky and her collaborators (Belenky et al. 1986), who say that the analytic mode is actually very masculine and does not do justice to the way in which women normally think. It seems clear that humanistic education does do justice to feminine as well as masculine ways of processing information.

This is the whole thing about the humanistic approach to education – it puts things together, rather than leaving things out. It also implies much more collaboration in the classroom. Johnson and Johnson (1975) speak of cooperative learning: in this approach children are encouraged to develop skills in collaborative relationships while working on academic learning tasks and other activities. Such collaborative skills include communicating in group settings, individual and group goal-setting and problem-solving skills, etc.

One thing which comes out very easily in this approach is that the personal experience of the student really matters. Somebody once said that there were four Rs in even the most basic education, and that the fourth R was Respect. The experiential approach makes it easy to respect the student, because the teacher/facilitator really has to listen to the experience which comes out of the exercise, game, simulation or whatever if any real benefit is going to be obtained from it. In this way we come close to the idea of enhancing the self-concept in the classroom (Canfield and Wells 1976) – a revolutionary idea for those of us who had their self-concept severely damaged in their own classrooms.

Some of the people working in transpersonal psychology have made important contributions to experiential education, particularly in books such as Hendricks and Wills (1975), Hendricks and Fadiman (1976) and Hendricks and Roberts (1977). The Religious Experience and Education Project at Nottingham University has done a good deal of work in this area (Hammond et al. 1990).

Another important contribution to the field of experiential education came from Sidney Simon and his co-workers, which is called 'values clarification'. Again this is not a sort of philosophical blue-sky approach, but a question of practical strategies for teachers and students.

What it says (Simon et al. 1972) is that valuing is a seven-stage process based on prizing, choosing and acting. It goes like this:

1 Prizing and cherishing
2 Publicly affirming, when appropriate
3 Choosing from alternatives
4 Choosing after consideration of consequences
5 Choosing freely
6 Acting
7 Acting with a pattern, consistency and repetition.

In the teaching based on this approach, the children are encouraged to follow this schema when talking about controversial subjects. And this results in far more self-respect among the students, because they now know why they think what they think, and can justify what they think in terms which will be convincing to others. Self-respect is also built up because the approach involves taking responsibility for what one thinks and does.

The authors emphasize that all school subjects on the curriculum can be treated in this way. We not only teach about rich and poor countries in geography, we ask the children what they feel and what they think about some countries being rich and others poor. The emphasis on action always makes it clear that any academic discussion of issues has practical consequences. Kirschenbaum (1978) has taken this further and shown that the general approach is applicable to organizations other than schools, too.

THE SCHOOL OR COLLEGE

So far, we have been seeing just what humanistic education is, but at the level of the individual classroom. What happens when we look at the educational institution as a whole? We find in most cases a hostile environment. There are very few places devoted to education, in this country or anywhere else, where the entire staff are committed to humanistic education.

And so one is faced with a number of difficult choices. Does one act as a teacher in an isolated way, doing what one can where one can? Or does one try to join up with other teachers who want to work in the same way, running all the risks of a subversive group? Or does one try to get the head of the organization turned on in some way? And what about the parents? And what about the students themselves? Bill Bridges says:

> Of course, I can bring them together on a purely interpersonal level (except for the 'I Ching' girl who doesn't relate well and the black nationalist who thinks that self-exploration is white, middle-class bullshit). And I can give them some growth-oriented experiences that fill up the class periods. But I can't really give them what they need, because the institution insists that we convert needs into three-

unit, semester-long classes that don't conflict with one another. Until we can restructure institutions to become educational resource places, we will mistakenly, but understandably, be trying to do the impossible – make each individual classroom what the institution ought to be.

(Bridges 1973, p. 11)

What wise words! One can only do so much on an individual classroom level. It is well worth doing, but it is not enough.

Carl Rogers has insisted that this wider context is always important. In his own work, he was driven more and more to consider the school system and the whole administrative set-up. And his view in his last years was that the right place to start is at the top of the hierarchy, with an intensive group meeting (basic encounter group) with members of the administration – whoever actually makes the decisions which affect the whole school or group of schools. This would last for about a week, and be residential. Negative feelings which had sometimes spoiled planning and work for years could now be safely brought out into the open, understood and dissolved. Rogers found that the intense sense of community which developed in such groups made it possible for the participants to risk new actions, new directions, new purposes.

After this stage had been completed and digested, the next step would be to hold similar intensive groups for teachers, again on a voluntary basis. The next step would be to run encounter groups for whole classes. At the same time, groups for parents should be organized, possibly just for a weekend.

However, Rogers (Rogers and Freiberg 1994) make it clear that the political climate can make it almost impossible to carry through and make permanent the gains which are made through such methods. This seems to be because the humanistic approach is much more radical than at first it seems; as the realization of this begins to come through, panic sets in amongst the more conservative elements in parents, teachers and administrators. Rogers deals in a sensitive way with some of the failures in the history of humanistic education, and much can be learned from these examples. One of the big differences between this book and the earlier editions is that we are more prepared now to admit that there are failures, and to assess in a much more rigorous way the advantages and disadvantages of the humanistic approach.

We have to recognize, with Godfrey Barrett-Lennard, that 'Dramatic or revolutionary change tends to bring strongly countervailing forces into play' (Barrett-Lennard 1998, p. 340). This is part of the dialectic of humanistic psychology, which we had cause to notice earlier. Humanistic psychology is critical of the status quo, and has to endure the fate of all such critiques – first opposition, then limited adoption in a system with different values.

Other approaches used in Britain are outlined in the book edited by Gray (1985), which specifically concentrates on working at the level of the whole organization, and shows a variety of ways of doing this.

There is a sort of enthusiasm which comes from the humanistic approach which is quite electrifying for the person who gets it, but quite scary for others who only see the thing from the outside. This enthusiasm almost always results in some attempt at action.

And if anyone says that it is employers who need to have some evidence of education, George Leonard (1968) has given us the answer to that one. As he points out very succinctly, the job dispensing agencies are not really interested in what you as a job seeker have learned in the school, but merely that, for whatever reason, you have survived it.

It is difficult to band together as teachers. Alix Pirani (1975) gave some of the reasons why this is so in Britain, at least:

> There is little cohesion or coordination, in spite of the frequently expressed desire for contact between at least somewhat enlightened workers, many of whom feel that they are waging a lone battle against reactionary forces . . . Everybody ultimately seems to want to do his or her own thing, in isolation and defiance.
>
> (Pirani 1975)

So why should we bother? Why is it important? One of the clearest statements of why it is important is provided by the work of Elizabeth Simpson (1971). The question she investigated was – What is the influence of the school on basic political attitudes?

THE WIDER SOCIETY

In Chapter 1 we talked of the psychosocial levels of development, and said that social action could either have the effect of allowing or encouraging natural development up the levels, or have the effect of driving people down. And we saw that any form of coercion tends to drive people down, as does any form of external evaluation. This links very naturally to the view of Maslow that there is a ladder of human needs, such that satisfaction of one need level enables movement upwards to the next (see Table 2.1 in Chapter 2).

What Simpson did was to develop a scale which could be given to children between 15 and 17, to measure which of these needs were being satisfied, and to what degree. What Simpson took as her dependent variable was a set of five fundamental democratic values:

1   Faith in human nature – the belief that human beings are basically good and trustworthy.
2   Belief that people have some power over their own lives, rather than being controlled by the environment or luck.
3   Desire to think for oneself, rather than accepting the opinions of others as to what is right.
4   Belief in the validity of the experiences and opinions of others – they have a right to be different. High tolerance and low dogmatism.
5   Belief that the rights of other people are to be respected, just because they are human beings.

Simpson argues – convincingly to me – that these five attitudes are necessary and sufficient to define a democratic outlook. Anyone who held these five views would always want a democratic system of organization; anyone who held the opposite set of views would prefer a strong leader to take all the decisions.

So how did the research come out? On her sample of 412 children from three different schools, Simpson found a highly significant positive relationship between need satisfaction and democratic values. In other words, the more psychologically deprived the children were, the less did they tend to hold a democratic attitude or outlook.

What this means in practical terms is that humanistic education, because it is continually trying to fulfil psychological needs in such a way as to bring children up the ladder in line with their own natural development processes, makes a genuinely democratic political system possible. This would be a system where people participated fully at each level in the state, and insisted on not being excluded from decisions which affected them.

Any form of education which adopted an authoritarian approach, laying great stress on hierarchy and formal roles, would actually make genuine political democracy in adult life either impossible or very difficult. So the educational system we adopt has enormous political implications, either way.

What seems to be happening too often these days is that teachers are giving up – or being forced willy-nilly to give up – the old authoritarian methods, structures and assumptions, but are not moving over into humanistic education either. Consequently they are simply trying to survive in a very uncomfortable situation where they feel out of control and subject to many anxieties. It may even be the case that many of them are going back to more authoritarian ways of working.

Humanistic education is uncomfortable too, but it is immensely hopeful, and that little spark can give comfort to a teacher in today's world. And it doesn't take much to start. The books already mentioned give some ideas for new ways of approaching the classroom and the curriculum. Jeffrey Schrank (1972) gives 101 suggestions for things to actually do. They open up lines of communication, enable students and teachers to see each other as human beings, and demand that adults in schools stop teaching-to and start learning-with.

Real freedom involves the students' ability to choose the alternatives they want rather than accept the one they are driven to. That is the concept of freedom which should be the goal of educators, yet a teacher cannot give it to students. They must win it for themselves. The best a teacher can do is to teach them the processes which will increase their ability to step aside from their own way of experiencing: to wonder at it, to question it and to modify it.

Yes. And ultimately it is impossible to separate change in the schools from change in society. One of the lines from self to society runs through schools, colleges and other educational institutions where real learning does or does not take place. Real learning affects the way people act in their own lives. And it is always self-discovered, self-appropriated learning, learning which makes a difference to who I am. That's what education is all about.

If we have perforce to work in other ways, we can still keep pushing and agitating, overtly or covertly, for the kind of reforms we require.

9

ORGANIZATIONAL

Most of what is valuable in management theory today comes from humanistic psychology. It is a field in which this school has been particularly active. In the comprehensive list of management development methods compiled by Huczynski (1983) over 40 per cent of them come out of humanistic psychology. In Carol Kennedy's later book on management theories (1991) and in the popular book by Stuart Crainer (1998) about the same proportion holds – higher than any other single outlook.

ORGANIZATION DEVELOPMENT

It started with the work of Kurt Lewin. In the 1950s the group of people inspired by him at the National Training Laboratories (NTL) moved over from calling their work 'training in democratic leadership' (partly, perhaps, because the word 'democracy' became a bit suspect during the McCarthy era) and began calling it 'the planning of change'. And instead of talking about 'trainers', they started talking about 'change agents'.

The early books were all about T-groups (Bradford et al. 1964, Golembiewski and Blumberg 1970) as the best way of inculcating democratic values, but during the 1960s they tended to be more about whole organizations (Bennis et al. 1970). In the 1970s a further change took place – people talked about Organization Development (often shortened to OD) instead of planned change. And in the 1980s the more frequently used terms have been human resources and normative systems, as in Allen (1980). In the 1990s there started to be more interest in transformational systems (Beck and Cowan 1996), which we shall meet in a later section.

The reasons for these changes in names and titles are important. The early humanistic practitioners became so impressed by the change that they saw in people who had been through T-groups – more open, more flexible, more creative, better at communication, altogether more nourishing – that they concentrated on doing that better and better. That led to the development of the encounter group (Schutz 1973). But what often happened was that you as a trained person went back to the home organization and were quite unable to be what you now wanted to be, because of the restrictions coming from the nature of the organization itself. So either you conformed, which meant giving up everything you had learned; or you resisted, which meant a long and often painful struggle, sometimes won and sometimes lost; or you left.

So the view gradually took root that it was not enough to work at the level of the individual person, or even the social atom (Bischof 1970). One had to start at the top of the organization, and work on changing the whole culture of the hospital, or industrial plant, or school, or whatever the organization happened to be. And in the 1960s a tremendous amount of work was done – the NTL produced an offshoot, the Institute for Applied Behavioural Science, which produced a new *Journal of Applied Behavioural Science*, in which started to appear a flood of humanistic research studies describing the new kind of work which was now being done in many different kinds of organizations.

At the beginning of this phase there was a great emphasis on the trained expert in applied behavioural science going into an organization and being able to see the problems very clearly, making a diagnosis, and then getting the management to make the necessary changes. And consequently there was a great deal of soul-searching about values. The consultant must have the highest possible ethical commitment, because of holding all this power.

But as the 1960s went on, the emphasis changed more and more away from this view. Organization development (OD) came more and more into line with the other fields we have been looking at already. The consultant, instead of being seen as an expert to diagnose and prescribe, now becomes a facilitator, whose job is to encourage the organization to work through its conflicts, in the knowledge that all the answers are there already.

Now one of the things which humanistic psychology has understood very well is conflict. It has a particular view of conflict which is unlike most of the received wisdom on the subject. It sets a very high value on conflict, and regards the serious pursuit of conflict as an important road to wisdom. This is clearest in some of the industrial applications, where people like Beckhard (1969), Blake et al. (1970) and Lawrence and Lorsch (1969) have spelt out in some detail how they actually encourage conflict to be developed and fully expressed, between departments of the same firm, between management and trade unions, and between functional groups in the same organization. All these people take it for granted that groups have different and perhaps opposed interests, and are not all of one mind. Mary Parker Follett's chapter on constructive conflict (Follett 1995) is a classic.

What do we do, then, faced with two parties who want apparently incompatible things? There are really only three possibilities:

Domination: one side wins and the other loses. This often leads to the losing side trying to build up its forces so that it can win next time round. It perpetuates or even sets in motion a win–lose relationship of low synergy.

Compromise: each side gives up a part of what it wants for the sake of peace. This is always unsatisfying to some degree, and each side may try to get its missing bit in some overt or covert way. This approach always tends to diminish integrity.

Integration: both sides get what they really wanted. This may need quite a bit of work to see what it is that each side did really want. Another way of putting this is to say that we look for the needs behind the wants. This way, when it can be found, is the most satisfying.

The great pioneer in this area is Mary Parker Follett (a humanistic psychologist before humanistic psychology was ever named or noticed), who takes it for granted that the thing to aim at is the interweaving of differences, because that is what one actually has got to work with. Conflicts are then carefully brought out and worked with, rather than being over-ridden, smoothed over or ignored. And the outcome of this is that creative solutions may emerge, which nobody had in mind at the beginning of the process. All growth is a process of differentiation and integration, and the differentiation is just as important as the integration. The first rule for obtaining integration is to put your cards on the table, face the real issue, uncover the conflict, bring the whole thing out into the open (Metcalf and Urwick 1941). Mary Parker Follett disappeared from view for a few years, but the magnificent work of Pauline Graham (1995) has restored her to her rightful place. Graham's appreciation, which includes contributions from a number of recent writers, shows how important her message is for today.

If we follow Follett's path, and attempt to bring out differences so that they can be worked on, it is possible to meet other people whom one knows to be opposed in interest and to confront them as a whole person, unafraid and ready to use whatever power one has. It is possible to be flexible and human and at the same time to stand no shit. And it seems that this is possible for groups as well as for individuals. It also seems that if we want creative solutions, this is the only way to get them. Rogers and Ryback (1985) show how this approach works at the level of international diplomacy, another field in which Mary Parker Follett was interested.

So the OD consultant becomes less like a doctor, and more like a therapist or group facilitator. If I am a facilitator, I cannot offer a blueprint of what the ultimate state of affairs will be. What I aim at is the production of an organization which can be flexible, engage in creative problem-solving, be proactive rather than reactive and so on, at every level. This means moving away from a 'power over people' orientation towards a 'power with people' orientation (Fordyce and Weil 1971). It means moving toward mutual empowerment (Culbert and McDonough 1990). It means moving from first-tier thinking in rigid categories and toward second-tier thinking (Beck and Cowan 1996), which is more dialectical. And because the organization itself is moving in this direction, the problems about the expert having power over people seem to dissolve too. In other words, if at every level people who know what they are doing can feel confident enough to talk back to someone who tries to push them around or manipulate them, people will also be willing to talk back to any consultant who tries to push them around or manipulate them (Rowan 1976b).

HIERARCHY AND BUREAUCRACY

So much for a thumbnail sketch of the way things have moved over the past 30 years or so. But what has been said may be very confusing to anyone who actually works in an organization. 'Surely,' such a person might say, 'all organizations are hierarchical, and depend for their very existence on some people giving orders, and others obeying them?' This is the voice of common sense.

But two things have happened over the years. One is that more and more research findings have piled up to show that hierarchy does harm to people, and the other is that various modifications of hierarchy have been tried, and found to work better, even in the strict terms of economic survival. This is not the place to deal with the whole tortuous business of the destructive nature of hierarchy – I have done that at length elsewhere (Rowan 1976a) – but here is a brief summary of the results.

Researchers such as Aiken and Hage, Grusky and also Lawrence and Lorsch (1969) have found these general effects of hierarchical organization.

- Feelings of inadequacy.
- Inability to express oneself.
- Inability to influence anyone.
- Feelings of being shut out.
- Increase in cynicism.
- Increase in destructive feelings.
- Feeling that one has to dominate or be dominated.
- Feeling that to conform is the best thing.
- Feeling that intolerance is all right.
- Feeling that prejudice is all right.
- Feeling that new ideas must come from the top.
- Feeling that there is no way of communicating with those at the top.

Studies by Inkson, Porter and Lawler and others, also show that there is a big difference between the way the organization feels at the bottom and the way it feels at the top. Those at the top see their jobs as interesting, challenging, not too predictable, satisfying and engaging a lot of their personality and skills. Those at the bottom feel bored and fatalistic, hemmed in and frustrated, and that very little of them is involved in the work. A study by Kornhauser in the US car industry found that nine out of ten of the assembly line workers felt trapped in a job which they wanted to change but did not feel able to; and eight out of ten said they were boiling with frustration inside. It seems, then, that hierarchy diminishes people, makes them less than they usually are, and much less than they could be. In terms of the psychospiritual ladder which we met earlier, hierarchical organization drives people down, rather than helping them up it.

In case anyone thinks that these findings are now out of date or reveal the prejudices of the early 1970s, the work of Kanter (1985) is saying the same thing, only with much greater sophistication and authority. More recently still, Beck and Cowan (1996) are saying that the hierarchical model belongs to first-tier thinking, and holds us back from moving into the much more rewarding territory of second-tier thinking, which is the humanistic way and the coming way.

ALTERNATIVES

If for all these reasons we want to have an organization which does not have an oppressive hierarchy, and does not reduce people to roles, how do we actually go about it?

Again, as with the school example we saw earlier (for after all, a school is an organization too), we can either work from the top or from the bottom. Most of the literature deals with working from the top, but there is some of the other, too.

An OD consultant is often called in by a company or hospital or other organization when something is going wrong. And it is a rough rule of thumb to say that the more that is going wrong, the more ready will the organization be to make real changes that are more than superficial. If, however, there is too much going wrong, the resulting panic will make any real work on the part of the consultant almost impossible. (This is very similar to the individual case!)

The first thing I as an OD consultant will do is to listen, not only to the person who has called me in, but also to other people involved in the problem which appears to present itself. One never takes one person's version as the final truth of the matter. On the basis of this preliminary listening phase, the consultant will draw up a proposal as to what programme of stages seems to be necessary to tackle the problem, and what kind of costs will be involved. There may also be some discussion of the values which the consultant holds, so as to make sure that there is no misunderstanding about that.

The programme itself will very often start with a research phase. This is sometimes called a diagnostic phase, but this is not really accurate, because what is done with the data obtained (usually unstructured interview plus questionnaires) is to feed it back to the people who have been questioned. This is often done at what Beckhard (1969) calls a confrontation and action planning meeting, where the consultant presents the results and they are discussed there and then, using whatever techniques may be useful to facilitate the constructive resolution of conflict.

Now I have shown elsewhere (see my chapter in Reason and Bradbury 2000) that research itself is best seen as a cycle, and Allen (1980) shows that OD can be seen as a cycle. He has four phases of intervention within an organization, which correspond rather well with the six phases of research as I have outlined them.

Phase 1. Have you found out just what your problem really is and decided what you want to happen? This is the diagnostic or research phase.

Phase 2. Have you helped others concerned with the problem understand the cultural impact of what is occurring and involved them in planning steps toward change? This is the consultation and action planning phase.

Phase 3. Have you put the agreed-upon objectives into daily practice, keeping track of results as you go along and rewarding everyone for his or her progress? This is the implementation phase.

Phase 4. Have you rechecked what you have done and kept your mind open to new factors that affect it? This is the monitoring phase, which may lead to a further cycle.

So a whole programme may be involved here, of further meetings, further research, encounter groups, team building (Woodcock 1979), creativity training and so on, depending on what action seems to be high on the list of priorities. Specialist consultants may be called in to help reorganize accounting procedures, or shopfloor layout, lighting fixtures, etc., if these things seem appropriate to all those concerned.

The consultant in OD works like a therapist or facilitator, bringing out conflicts and helping to get them properly worked through and dealt with, at the pace which the organization finds possible. Allen (1980) makes the important point that the programme must be owned by the people affected by it; this ownership must be genuine, and it must be felt. Kanter (1985) makes the point that it is not enough for creativity to be imposed from above, as if it were this year's fashion – it has to emerge from genuine participation.

There is an important distinction in all this work between 'process' and 'task content': in any meeting some of what is going on is to do with the task which the group has on the open agenda; but some of what is going on has to do with the hidden agendas which people have brought with them into the room, and which they are also trying to work through at the same time (which may have to do with power struggles, or personal relationships, or old feuds, or private aims, etc.) – these things are collectively known as the group process. Now if you are the consultant here, you contribute very little at the level of the task content – you do not have the detailed knowledge necessary to make much of a contribution there – but concentrate most of your attention on to the group process. This is where your skills lie. You as a consultant know how to make what is hidden open, and what was implicit explicit; and you also know how to deal with the emotions which are revealed when this happens.

What we have here is a process of: (1) generation of valid and useful information, which enables (2) free and informed choice to be made, and leads to (3) internal commitment to a course of action. Chris Argyris (1970) has done more work in this field than possibly anyone else, and these are the three points which he emphasizes.

The humanistic point of view, then, is that choice and decision are most effective when taken closest to the event – that it is harmful to full functioning if decisions which could be taken at a lower level are taken instead at a higher level. Some of the implications of this are drawn out well in the series of books which came out of the Norwegian experience (Bolweg 1976).

But how does this affect management? Does it take away from them all their work, and leave them with nothing to do? Some people argue for precisely this, as Martin (1983) has urged quite eloquently, saying that self-managing work groups are all that is necessary. Herbst (1976) has described several ways in which hierarchies can be avoided, and Emery and Thorsrud (1976) have given many examples of how this has worked out in practice. Most people, however, feel that managers are still necessary, but have to change their function. The new concerns are with aims such as these:

1 To help set up an open, problem-solving climate throughout.
2 To make sure that knowledge and competence goes with the work.
3 To find ways of locating decision-making and problem-solving responsibilities as close to the information sources as possible.
4 To help build trust among persons and groups throughout.
5 To see that competition is made more relevant to work goals, and to increase cooperative efforts.
6 To get a reward system which recognizes both the achievement of the organization's goals and the development of people.
7 To increase the sense of ownership of organizational objectives throughout the organization.
8 To increase self-control and self-direction for people within the organization.

All these things are quite specific and possible, and each of them has methods suitable for it. But they will only be satisfying to you as a manager to the extent that you come to appreciate those aspects of your work which have to do with the growth of people and your own capacity to facilitate the growth of people. And as Tichy (1977) has pointed out, this means great skill in coping with the political dynamics of organizational life. It means, as Beck and Cowan (1996) have argued, moving from the relatively static thinking of the first tier to the much more flexible and dynamic thinking of the second tier.

LEADERSHIP

A great deal of research, going back to the 1940s, shows that there are two main dimensions which any leader has to consider. One of the main studies which showed this was the factor-analytic study of Halpin and Winer (1952). This was confirmed by the quite different work of Bales (1958), Blake and Mouton (1964), Fiedler (1967) and others. The two dimensions are concern for people and concern for the task. The former is about social-emotional relations – paying attention to people as individuals with particular needs and feelings; a good social-emotional leader will make jokes to relieve tension, remember birthdays, show care about illness or other crises, be sociable and so on. The latter is about the task – getting the job done, being efficient, not making mistakes or wasting time – a good task leader will initiate, organize and direct in a firm and clear way, so that everyone knows what to do and when and how to do it. In the terms of Randall and Southgate (1980), who describe the healthy working cycle as Nurturing → Energizing → Relaxing, the social-emotional leader is good at the nurturing and relaxing stages of the cycle, while the task leader is good at the energizing stage.

Blake and Mouton had the idea of putting these two dimensions at right angles to each other to make a grid, and numbered each dimension from 1 (present in a low degree) to 9 (present in a high degree). They then devised tests for measuring where on each dimension a leader fell, so that each position could be described by two coordinates. They did this for managers in the first instance (Blake and Mouton 1978), and later for secretaries, salesmen (Blake and Mouton 1980), marriage partners and so on.

But Reddin (1977) suggested an interesting variation of this (see Figure 9.1). He said that if we look at the four quadrants offered by this grid, and say that a leader can fall into any one of the four, we get four different kinds of leader, rather than just the two mentioned so far. In the top left-hand quadrant we get the leader who is high on concern for people and low on concern for task; this Reddin calls the RELATED leader, who is seen as supportive or permissive. So far, so good. But it is here that Reddin pulls

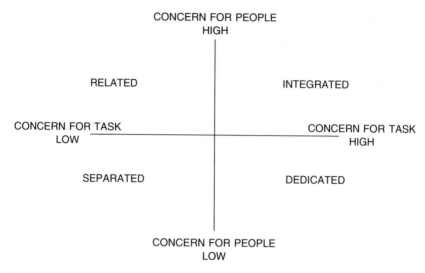

CONCERN FOR PEOPLE
HIGH

RELATED

INTEGRATED

CONCERN FOR TASK
LOW

CONCERN FOR TASK
HIGH

SEPARATED

DEDICATED

CONCERN FOR PEOPLE
LOW

Figure 9.1 Reddin version of Blake and Mouton grid

his masterstroke: he says that the RELATED leader can either be effective
or ineffective. So at each position we get two types, not one. At this
position on the grid the RELATED leader can either be effective – a
developer who nurtures followers at all levels and sets an example to them
of how to treat people – or can be ineffective, becoming a mere do-gooder
– someone who wants to be liked, and who confuses smiling with real
support, and talks about nurturing rather than being able to do it.

In the lower left-hand quadrant we get the SEPARATED leader, who is
not concerned too much with either the people or the task, and who is seen
as laisser-faire, leaving people to get on with their work. In the effective
version, this becomes the bureaucrat who holds the ring and sets up
conditions within which people can do what they need to do without
coming up against the rules of the organization; in the ineffective version,
the leader becomes a deserter who is simply not there, either physically or
mentally.

In the lower right-hand quadrant we find the DEDICATED leader, the
person who tells and sells, and is quite dominant in concentrating on the
task in hand. In the effective version (benevolent autocrat), this is the kind
of autocrat who inspires by dedication, and who energizes through a real
knowledge of and feeling for the job. In the ineffective version (autocrat),
this kind of leader can become narrowly and punishingly self-defensive,
dogmatically dealing out blame with both hands.

And in the upper right-hand quadrant we get the INTEGRATED leader,
the facilitating, encouraging type of leader who is interested both in the
people and in the task. The effective type is the good executive – a good

team worker, much concerned with motivation, adapting well to new situations; the ineffective type, on the other hand, is just a compromiser – unpredictable, indecisive and inconsistent.

The great advantage of putting things this way is that Reddin can now go to all the older theories of leader type and show that so often what happens is that the effective leader of one type (the type the author favours) is contrasted with the ineffective leader of another type (the type the author is against). This is what McGregor (1960) did – his Theory X and Theory Y contrasted the autocrat with the executive. This is what Lewin et al. (1939) did – they contrasted the deserter and the autocrat with the developer. And this, he says, is what Blake and Mouton (1964) have done – they have contrasted the ineffective forms of all the other quadrants with the effective form of the INTEGRATED quadrant, and this is not fair.

Hersey and Blanchard (1977) also adopt the four quadrant version of the model. But they bring in another consideration – maturity. They say that maturity is the ability and willingness of individuals to take responsibility for directing their own behaviour in a particular area. And they say that Reddin's DEDICATED quadrant is the one for the least mature groups, which need strong leadership. Groups which are a little more mature need the kind of treatment given by the INTEGRATED leader. More mature again, and they come into the realm of the RELATED leader. And the most mature groups need the attention of a SEPARATED leader. Like Reddin, they also say that all these leaders can be more or less effective. Hersey et al. (1979) add a discussion of different kinds of power to this analysis, showing that the more direct and coercive kinds of power are appropriate to the most immature groups, and so on up the scale of maturity.

But Blake and Mouton have not taken all this lying down. As humanistic psychologists, they have come back very strongly to argue that this is all wrong. There is one best style of leadership – the integrative style which is high both on concern for people and on concern for the task in hand – and different kinds of situation or group do not need different styles or types of leaders. What Reddin and the others have done, they say, is to confuse *adding* concern for people to concern for the task with the *integration* of these two concerns. If you take separate statements of concern for people and concern for the task, and simply add them together, what you get is some form of paternalism. Paternalism is an issue which is not dealt with either by Reddin or by Hersey and Blanchard – it is the view that the management, from a great height, will look after the people and get them to do the task, will take care of the people while the task is done. This is first-tier thinking. But what Blake and Mouton are interested in is genuine participation by all the people involved. This is second-tier thinking. It brings with it the kind of involvement which Allen (1980) and the others we have been looking at have all been talking about.

Blake and Mouton (1982) have pointed out that the questioning procedures which Reddin and Hersey and Blanchard have used in their research have actually made it impossible for them to come up with the idea that one style of leadership might be the best in all situations. There is just no room for what they call 9,9 leadership, and it could not emerge. So the humanistic view is that it is not true that in certain situations autocratic leadership is best – even if it is benevolent.

THE WIDER SCENE

Much of the older work seemed to ignore trade unions, but some important studies (Golembiewski et al. 1982, Nicholas 1982) show that unions can be involved with great advantage. OD can actually strengthen the effectiveness of unions, if used in the right way.

But it has to be recognized that there are three quite distinct fields within a unionized organization (see Figure 9.2). The first of these is the CONTROL field, which I call level C. This is usually some kind of oligarchy, where various interests are balanced, and this is where the high-level decisions about the organization are taken. It may be called a board, or given some other name, and there may be various ambiguities about exactly where it begins and ends.

The second main field is the HUMAN region, where conflicts emerge at all levels within the organization. Many low-level decisions are taken here, and many grades and types of consultation or participation may be involved in such decisions. This I call level H.

The third main field is the REGULATORY area where conflicts and other problems or moves are formalized through union channels. In Britain this usually takes the form of collective bargaining; other countries may have law, custom or compulsory arbitration. The outcome of the processes which take place here is a set of RULES jointly produced. This I call level R.

There is now a feedback loop whereby the rules produced at level R have to be implemented at level H. Such implementation has to be done in accordance with the norms of the workers involved, and therefore many small decisions may have to be made at this level to make the rules work.

This in turn gives us another feedback loop whereby the balance of the organization is disturbed by this change in rules, and this change is reflected at level C, where balance will have to be restored in some way, or moved to another viable state.

Now the main area for consultancy is level H, which forms a barrier between level C (where the management initiates action) and level R, where it is often the union which initiates action (though usually of a reactive kind). If level H is performing well, it acts as a damper or buffer which

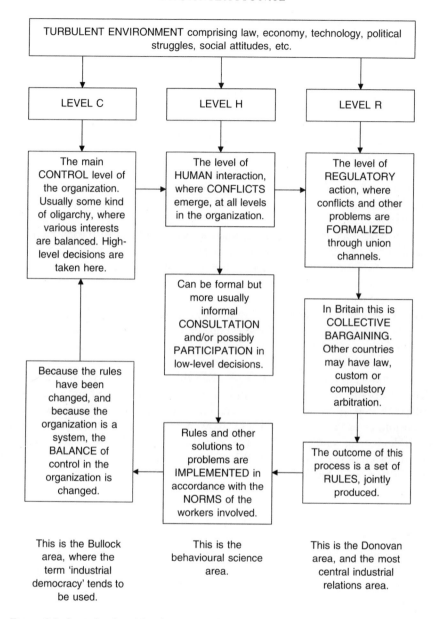

Figure 9.2 Organizational levels

stops the system going into positive feedback and going out of control altogether. If too much stress is laid on level H, however, level R gets starved and may not function properly when required. Level R is necessary because the conflicts sometimes run much too deep, in terms of opposing interests, for them to be handled in an integrative way – and this is where level R comes in with a whole system of handling disputes which is adapted to an adversarial mode.

Humanistic consultancy does of course have something to contribute at level C (e.g. top management team-building) and level R (e.g. theories of negotiation, bargaining and conflict resolution) but its home territory and most usable set of techniques are all in level H. Rather than adopt the imperialism of total systems theory, which only serves to remind us of the imperialism of extended collective bargaining or the imperialism of managerial prerogative, we humanistic consultants would do well, in my opinion, to settle for level H, but to make good connections with the other two levels, so that we do not act in ways which deny their existence or necessity.

This would mean, for example, making personal links with each member of the ruling oligarchy, and with each of the key people involved in industrial relations negotiations on the union side. It is my impression that the former happens more often than the latter. In terms of the model, we link better with level C than with level R. And if this does happen, it is not too surprising that both the union representatives and the company's industrial relations people look on us with suspicion, and are only too pleased to say 'I told you so' when our interventions run into trouble – trouble which they might have predicted.

Perhaps enough has now been said to make it clear that quite a bit is known about how to change organizations from oppressive hierarchies into places which allow for growth, personal development and genuine parti-cipation. (I have written elsewhere (Rowan 1976a) about the various levels and degrees of so-called participation.) But so far we have talked only in terms of change from the top. What about change which is initiated from the bottom of a hierarchy?

TAKING POWER

It is a quite common situation for a single individual to be turned-on and excited by the ideas and methods of humanistic psychology, and want to know how to pursue this new interest in an environment in which such ideas and methods are unfamiliar. You as such a person may try to do something on your own, which is rejected or misunderstood. You are almost certain to be asked to step back into your old role, as soon as what you are doing begins to be noticed. What do you do now?

I suggest that the first thing to get clear is the notion of synergy. Synergy is the kind of power which mutually enhances both giver and receiver – it is power through people, or with people. It is sometimes called the $2 + 2 = 5$ principle – a joining of two things or two people or two groups so that the outcome is more than the sum of the two parts. Abraham Maslow quotes Ruth Benedict's definition of social synergy:

> Social-institutional conditions which fuse selfishness and unselfishness, by arranging it so that when I pursue 'selfish' gratifications, I automatically help others, and when I try to be altruistic, I automatically reward and gratify myself also; i.e., when the dichotomy or polar opposition between selfishness and altruism is resolved and transcended.
>
> (Maslow 1973, p. 146)

Benedict used this analysis to show that some of the cultures she had studied were high-synergy cultures (the Zuni, the Arapesh, one of the Eskimo groups and the Northern Blackfoot), while others were low-synergy cultures: the Chuckchee, the Ojibwa, the Dobu and the Kwakiutl.

The high-synergy cultures tended to be secure, welcoming and high in morale: while the low-synergy cultures tended to be insecure, anxious, surly and low in morale. The high-synergy cultures were low in aggression; the low-synergy cultures had a win/lose attitude to most things, where the advantage of one individual became a victory over another.

Now I suggest that you as a person in an organization stand the greatest chance of success by keeping clearly before your mind the aim of turning the place into a high-synergy organization, where the more power you give away, the more you have. This is a tough aim, and may at first seem quite impossible; but it acts as a check at each point on whether one is moving in the right direction or not. Having accepted that, then, there are seven steps which may be necessary, as Ruth Leeds (1970) first stated. Obviously they need to be adapted to the nature of the specific organization which is in question.

The first step in taking power is finding allies. The isolated individual can do little except as a rare Titan. If one can make the person at the top of the hierarchy into an ally – and this is sometimes possible – the further steps may not be necessary; it just turns into a special case of working from the top. We are not in favour of opposition for the sake of opposition; only if it proves to be necessary.

It is better to look for allies than to wait for chance to create them. They should have something in common which can be used as an initial focus of activity – usually some form of dissatisfaction with an aspect of the power structure, or the way power is used in the organization. One of them at least should be a popular person, preferably with powerful outside contacts. And one of them should have access to the top levels of the organization. A group with these characteristics stands the best chance of taking power.

The second step is to find some form of activity, some definite project, which is likely to achieve success. This need not be directly concerned with the overarching aim of the group – it is important mainly as a sign that the group can work together to achieve something concrete. At this stage the group may acquire a name.

The third step is to settle the leadership issue. This may need some very honest and open talking, and some real working through of emotional issues. It is all too easy for a group to be named after one person who is seen as the leader, and if this happens it makes it much easier for the organization to prevent the group from achieving anything, by removing this person in some way. So if possible, avoid having a leader, and avoid using a person's name as a label, even informally.

The fourth step is to make some realistic demand upon the next higher echelon – let us call this middle management, on the understanding that it will have different names in different organizations. This demand must now be related to the main theme of higher synergy – the present structure is holding back necessary changes, and needs to be modified. New rules and procedures are needed which will permit increased effectiveness to the work of the group, by giving it greater control over decisions which affect it. It is essential at this point to maintain a group identity as nonconformist but not deviant. Leeds (1970) explains this distinction by saying that, unlike deviants, nonconformists do not hide their dissent from the prevailing norms.

Much depends on how middle management reacts to being asked to give up some of the decisions it has had in its hands up to now. It may agree, or may use one of four ways of fighting back: condemnation (threatening each member of the group and using pressures of various kinds, or trying to disperse the group); avoidance (memos are sidetracked, meetings postponed or cancelled, secretaries stonewall, supplies may be forgotten, delays seem to multiply, etc.); expulsion (direct coercive power used against one or more of the group); or co-optation (for example, promoting the most powerful person in the group). None of these methods will work if the group has taken the steps outlined so far.

The fifth step is to produce a lot of good work. The work at this stage may now form one of the distinguishing marks of the group, and there will be a great deal of informal pressure on members to live up to the group norms. The number of meetings will increase. There is a great danger here of going away from other groups at the same level, who may start to see the dissident group as big-headed, standoffish, superior and generally unsympathetic. But if the earlier stages have been carried out properly, then the group will find it easy to communicate with collateral groups, and explain the issues to them in a convincing way. The outside contacts also become important. This stage may be quite prolonged, and every means of maintaining high morale will be needed.

The sixth step is where top management steps in. And the tactic it is most likely to try is protest absorption. That is, embracing the group and treating it as a special exception, to be treated differently from anyone else. In return, they ask for certain assurances which will stabilize the position and make it acceptable to middle management. The unit's activity is limited to a particular sphere of operation, usually that for which the leader and his or her followers advocated their innovation.

This is quite clearly incompatible with the main overall aim of the group – it actively prevents the whole organization developing high synergy, and virtually restores the status quo. So this kind of approach must be seen through and resisted. The group insists that it wants power to control all those decisions, and those phases of decision-making, which it has by now decided upon. And the object is, at this stage, to get top management either to approve and institute such changes, or to bring in a suitable consultant who would be asked to report on the situation and take it from there. The group should, of course, insist on interviewing the consultant and having the right of veto.

The seventh step is to make friends again with middle management, and work out a new way of living together. For this reason it is best not to go too far in turning any one of them into some kind of symbol of evil at any of the earlier stages. In a high-synergy organization conflicts are brought out and worked through, not made an excuse for denying someone's reality (Graham 1995).

The final outcome will be an organization which is visibly different from the way it was at the start. Some of the blocks to self-direction will have been removed. The idea of taking power will be in the air, and to that extent the feeling of being a cog in a machine will have been reduced. The organization has been started on a whole new career as a basically innovative organization.

You have to make your own choice as to what to do in your own organization. It is more difficult to fight from the bottom than to make changes from the top – but maybe that is what we shall have to do, and support others when they do it. Something can be done.

Humanistic psychology is about not leaving it to experts, but taking responsibility for our own lives and our own actions. It is about human change and growth, about the realization of human potential, and about being an origin rather than a pawn. This means that you, the reader, are being at every point challenged to change and grow, to realize your potential, to become more of an origin and less of a pawn. What are you doing in your own organization?

TRANSFORMATIONAL MANAGEMENT

Since the second edition of this book appeared, a new school has taken the stage. Instead of Organization Development, this approach is concerned with Organizational Transformation. This change from OD to OT began in the 1980s, and is becoming more well-known and widely practised.

This approach says that we are essentially spiritual beings in a spiritual universe, that humans ultimately seek meaning within work, and that creative work is necessary for both psychological and spiritual growth. It represents an ecological approach to radical, second-order change in the entire organization. This involves transformative changes in the funda-mental nature of the organization: it is about giving the organization a new kind of vision and mission. This clearly pushes at the limits of the human-istic frame, and some people have thought it belongs to the transpersonal rather than the humanistic (Fletcher 1990). But my own view is that although it does touch on the transpersonal (what Wilber calls the Psychic level of development) it is for the most part within the humanistic outlook (see Harman and Hormann 1990, Evans and Russell 1989, Beck and Cowan 1996).

This approach means balancing the active with the receptive, the intel-lectual with the emotional, the body with the soul, the tough with the tender, and doing justice both to the male and the female.

One of the typical concepts is 'alignment'. A clear and timely vision catalyses alignment. Alignment is a condition in which people operate as if they were part of an integrated whole. It is exemplified in that level of teamwork which characterizes exceptional sports teams, theatre ensembles and chamber orchestras. When a high degree of it develops among members of a team committed to a shared vision, the individuals' sense of relationship and even their concept of self may shift. It channels high energy and creates excitement and drive (Harrison 1984).

Another idea is 'attunement', defined as a resonance or harmony among the parts of the system, and between the parts and the whole. As the concept of alignment speaks to us of will, so that of attunement calls up the mysterious operations of love in organizations: the sense of empathy, understanding, caring, nurturance and mutual support. Attunement is quiet and soft, receptive to the subtle energies which bind us to one another and to nature (Adams 1986).

Another concept is 'empowerment'. This word had been used before, mainly by humanistic people in the sense of self-actualization – that is, self-empowerment. But the new twist here is the emphasis on mutual empower-ment. This has particular implications for women in eroding the invisible barriers that tend to keep them in mundane organizational roles. With mutual empowerment people suppport each other rather than trying to put each other down (Culbert and McDonough 1990).

We say 'intuitive leadership' and encourage the development of intuition quite consciously and deliberately (Bourget 1988). Such leaders give inspira-tion and not just good ideas. They are often able to sum up the organ-izational vision in a memorable phrase (Tichy and Devanna 1986). The structure of the organization shifts in order to enable all these changes to take place, and to give them full scope. When this happens, excellence appears.

A final thought is summed up in the phrase 'planetary consciousness'. Everything done in the organization is related to this higher (or deeper) purpose. If we find on reflection that there is no longer joy in the struggle, that we are burning ourselves out in the effort, that we are no longer energized by what we do, then that may be a signal that it is time to move on to a new vision of what we are doing. Perhaps we have lost touch with our purpose on this planet. And perhaps the organization needs to change to reflect what is happening.

SPIRAL DYNAMICS

The latest thinking says that no one approach is going to be the best in all circumstances. If we want to do better than that – 'one size fits all' – we have to take note of where people are actually located.

Easier said than done. What is the actual method by which we do this, and what categories do we use in carrying it out? Again Ken Wilber is helpful, suggesting that the dialectical thinking used at the Centaur stage is what we need. If we think in terms of levels of consciousness, we can say that each person, each group, each organization functions at a particular level of consciousness.

This has been worked out in some detail by the authors of *Spiral Dynamics* (Beck and Cowan 1996), which takes developmental categories of consciousness and applies them to working within organizations. Their categories are parallel to those of Wilber (and other writers like Jenny Wade 1996), though out of tact when working with managers in the field they use the names of colours as labels instead of categories like Mythic-Membership or Mental Ego.

Beck and Cowan say that we are moving as an international culture towards a new form of consciousness which they call the Second Tier. All the previous forms of consciousness belong to the First Tier. And Wilber (1999a) makes the point that if we divide Centaur consciousness into three phases, the first phase is within the First Tier, while the next two phases are within the Second Tier. Thus again we find Centaur consciousness, and humanistic psychology, straddling the divide, just as we did with the personal and the transpersonal. And again this is an uncomfortable and tricky place to be, because we cannot settle into just one neat slot. As before, we have to use dialectical thinking and the language of paradox in order to handle the contradictions involved.

It is useful to look at the three phases which Don Beck and Christopher Cowan describe, because if Ken Wilber is right, they are highly relevant both to individual and to social development, as well as to organizations. They are called the Green, the Yellow and the Turquoise v-memes. This is unfamiliar language, and needs to be explained. A v-meme is a pattern of values (hence the v), which goes with a level of consciousness, and accounts for the way in which such levels of consciousness spread within a population. The Green v-meme (which follows on from the earlier and more basic Beige, Purple, Red, Blue and Orange v-memes and is still within the first tier of development) has to do with holistic thinking. It emphasizes building trust and openness. It is friendly to expanded awareness and the understanding of one's inner self. Wilber (1999a) points out that there is a positive and a negative version of this. In the positive version 'all perspectives and all stances deserve to be given a fair hearing and a fully equal opportunity; no perspective is to be unduly privileged'. In the negative version 'no stance is better than another'; Wilber calls this 'aperspectival madness', meaning that it denies the whole idea of having a stance or perspective.

The Yellow v-meme represents the first level within the second tier. It leads to an interest in the big picture, total systems, integration. No important distinction is made between the value of hard evidence and intuition; both are valued. At this stage we believe in the naturalness of chaos and the inevitability of change. We revel in paradox and do not fear technology. We are self-directed and expect others to become so, but not in any rigid way – flex–flow is the motto. We become aware that every step within the first tier was exclusive to some degree – the difference now is that we are truly inclusive. New times require new minds. We become able to recognize all the first-tier levels as being necessary; this is a quantum leap in thinking. Instead of, as previously, thinking that our approach is better than others and that others should join us as soon as possible, we now understand that every level is necessary. The terrible paradox that every step forward later becomes a ball-and-chain holding us back has to be accepted. The flexibility of this kind of thinking makes us much more able to solve problems.

The Turquoise v-meme pushes further into the second tier. And here the idea of spirituality comes into the picture, not so much as a concern with devotion, more a sense that there is more to life than systems, no matter how complex. Self is part of a larger, conscious, spiritual whole that also serves self. Global networking is seen as routine, and the idea of the spiral succession of v-memes as a sequence that has to be respected comes into its own. We can now move about within earlier v-memes in a fluid manner, and see the unity in their diversity. From the Turquoise perspective, there is nothing so very mystical about mystics. Business has a soul again, and the gaps between science and religion can now be bridged, as Wilber (1998) has laid out so well. Seeing-everything-at-once becomes the first aim in problem-solving, before doing anything specific. The idea of interdependence, already important at the Yellow stage, now takes centre stage. And dialectical thinking, already broached at the Yellow stage, now becomes the main way of thinking. 'Paradox construction and resolution is a good tool for tracking down the elegant, underlying order . . .' (Beck and Cowan 1996, p. 290).

This is of course a brief and inadequate account of a very well-worked-out model, but perhaps it will suffice to indicate how the humanistic way of thinking has to be brought in if we are to utilize the kind of thinking which is needed so much in today's world. Certainly it fits with Wilber's account and adds important elements to it. As Wilber says: 'The extensive research of Graves, Beck and Cowan indicates that there are two major waves to this second-tier consciousness (corresponding to what my system recognizes as middle and late vision-logic)' (Wilber 1999a, p. 115). As we saw earlier, vision-logic and dialectical thinking are one and the same.

But let us come back again to the wider world. Just as with the individual, where we found that it is not enough to develop the self, but have to go beyond that, here again we find that it is not enough to develop the organization, but we have to go beyond that. If the world we live in is run by crass multinationals and unfeeling governments, and oppressive systems, then we have to take that into account too (Capra 1983). We shall return to this point in Chapter 14.

10

TRANSPERSONAL

It must have been obvious all the way through this book so far that humanistic psychology is very interested in the experience of ecstasy. Maslow with his peak experiences, Perls with his satori, Moreno with his spontaneity – the list could be extended. If humanistic psychology is concerned with human potential, it must include all that we have it in us to be – and therefore must include ecstasy, creativity, unitive consciousness and so on. This means that it must touch on transpersonal psychology. One of the most characteristic things which the transpersonal approach says is that just as there can be repression of what is low and nasty about us, so also there can be repression of what is spiritual and beautiful about ourselves. As Maslow puts it:

> We fear our highest possibilities (as well as our lowest ones). We are generally afraid to become that which we can glimpse in our most perfect moments, under the most perfect conditions, under conditions of greatest courage. We enjoy and even thrill to the god-like possibilities we see in ourselves in such peak moments. And yet we simultaneously shiver with weakness, awe and fear before these same possibilities.
>
> (Maslow 1973, p. 37)

THE TRANSPERSONAL SELF

Why should we be afraid of our higher selves? Why should we be afraid of our most ecstatic insights? What could be so bad about them? Frank Haronian offers one explanation:

> . One possible reason why we do this is because the more one is conscious of one's positive impulses, of one's urges towards the sublime, the more shame one feels for one's failure to give expression to these impulses. There ensues a painful burning of the

162

conscience, a sense of guilt at not being what one could be, of not doing what one could do. This is not superego guilt, but rather the cry of the Self for its actualization.

(Haronian 1974, p. 61)

This mention of the Self may remind us of the Eastern approaches we noticed before, in Chapter 1. There has always been a great deal of interest in Eastern philosophy and practice, and in fact, as we saw earlier, this is one of the influences going into humanistic psychology as it is today. Alan Watts in particular did a great deal to make a bridge between the two. We have seen that Maslow wanted science to be more Taoistic, Barry Stevens learned T'ai Chi, Will Schutz practised Kundalini Yoga and used its thinking in his encounter groups, and so on. And a lot of the talk about the 'here and now' is explicitly Eastern in its inspiration.

So this interest in what we may call the higher self (though in some ways it seems better to call it the greater self or the inner self or the deeper self) has always been a part of humanistic psychology, and in the movements associated with it. The word 'transpersonal' was apparently used by Dane Rudhyar in the field of psychological astrology in the 1920s, and by Gardner Murphy in the field of parapsychology in 1949 (Murphy 1950). It was used by Erich Neumann in 1954 and by Ira Progoff in 1955, but it really only got popular after Maslow launched it: Stanislav Grof used it in 1967 and it then became the title of a journal in 1968. Assagioli thought it was a better term than spirituality. There is a good discussion of this in Boorstein (1996).

But today it is becoming more important than before. Partly this is because of the increased interest in the work of Jung (1959). He is being looked at a great deal more now that all his work has been translated and made easily available. The psychosynthesis people, in particular, have done a great deal to show the relevance of his thinking. And of course Jung was very much interested in transpersonal psychology, and in such Eastern ideas as the mandala, which is a very powerful symbol of what transpersonal psychology is all about.

Partly, too, it is because there are more and more new varieties of access to transpersonal states of consciousness of one kind and another, and the growth movement has been very hospitable to these. For example, T'ai Chi showed that there could be such a thing as moving meditation. Then Michael Murphy (1978) showed that golf could also be a moving meditation; from there it was only a short step to see that virtually any sport, any activity could be a form of meditation, leading to ecstatic states. It all depends on one's readiness to allow the experience to occur. (See Leonard (1977), Gallwey (1974) and Spino (1976).)

There are also new kinds of meditation, such as the active meditation of Osho (1992), which have become more easily available in Britain today.

The intense breathing and violent bodily activity of these methods are far removed from the traditional picture of the sage with his legs crossed contemplating his own navel. And they seem in some ways better suited to the Western way of life.

LSD

Another method of access to altered states of consciousness is to use psychedelic drugs such as mescalin, psilocybin, Ecstasy (MDMA) or LSD. Some of the recent drugs are interesting, too, but I would like here to mention only LSD, because that is within my own personal experience. It is unwise in some ways to discuss LSD, because it is illegal, but so much that is valuable has been found out by means of LSD that it seems out of the question not to deal with it.

By 1971 there were 2000 published reports referring to treatment outcomes for between 30,000 and 40,000 patients undergoing psychotherapy with LSD. Most of these reports were favourable or highly favourable (Wells 1973). They dealt with three main types of use – psycholytic, psychedelic and hypnodelic.

1. Psycholytic. Merely as an aid to other forms of therapy – a low-dose softening-up procedure.
2. Psychedelic. A powerful transcendental experience, aiming at significant change in personality organization. An unfreezing process, allowing access to hidden or buried possibilities within the person.
3. Hypnodelic. Patient is hypnotized before the session, and can therefore be guided into relevant areas by the therapist.

Also the therapists might use the drug themselves, on the principle that a guide to a territory should have been into that territory. In Czechoslovakia there was a rule that doctors must have observed 30 sessions and taken LSD at least five times themselves, before being allowed to administer the drug. A more recent account of some of this work is given by Grof (1980).

The approach of Timothy Leary (1970), on the other hand, was along the lines that LSD could get you into the same regions which had been described by the Eastern and Western mystics down the ages. But his account seems curiously eccentric and shallow.

John Lilly (1973) had a similar approach, and also charted various distinctions and differences between different states. This chart has now become part of the Arica training, which does not use drugs in any way. It seems to be a general truth that anywhere one can get with drugs, one can also get without.

Some of the early investigations found mystical effects from LSD – for example Pahnke (1972). A 25-year follow-up report (Doblin 1991) confirmed that an experience with psilocybin did in fact produce mystical experiences. It now seems clear that what you get with LSD is what is called in the mystical literature (Horne 1978) casual extraverted mysticism, which is one of the lower levels of mystical experience. It is very similar to the peak experience as described by Cohen and Phipps (1979) and by Hay (1982) based on the work of the Religious Experience Research Unit in Oxford (some of whose members have now set up their own project at Nottingham University). Such experiences are very common, about 30 per cent or more of the population having had them.

This approach to the psychedelics also produced one of the great ethical insights of recent years – the statement that 'You can't lay your trip on someone else'. This seems to me an enormously valuable insight, and it applies in so many areas – for example in education, in industrial consultancy and so on. What is true for you is true for you, and there is no need, apart from insecurity, for you to try to lay it on me, and say that it should be true for me, too. As Eric Hoffer (1952) has told us with a wealth of detail, the True Believer is the most dangerous person in the world.

And it seems clear that LSD and its associated substances has had a great influence on a whole generation and its way of thinking. As John Heider says (and I agree with his story):

> In my experience and thinking, the single major event forcing this development [of interest in transpersonal psychology] has been the widespread use and abuse of psychedelic or mind-manifesting substances such as marijuana, LSD and mescalin . . . The psychedelic drugs gave incontrovertible proof that altered states of consciousness had reality and that paths toward transcendent experience existed. Huxley's (1963) *The Doors of Perception*, originally published in 1954, provided the seminal bridge between rational and ecstatic experience. By 1960, drug experimentation was widespread within the Cambridge/Berkeley intellectual underground and no longer in the province solely of New York musicians and ghetto blacks . . . we were hunting for ways to stay high forever and bring home the New Jerusalem, the Whole Earth.
>
> (Heider 1974, pp. 29–30)

The curious thing about this is that mystical experience had always in the past been associated with passivity and quietism (in the minds of most Westerners, at least) and here it was now leading to political activity and commitment. So perhaps this mysticism was not so 'traditional' after all – perhaps it was something quite new.

LEVELS OF CONSCIOUSNESS

One of the most common concepts of the Eastern and the Western writers about transpersonal experiences, whether drug or non-drug induced, is that there is a finite set of regions which one can get into, each of which has its own describable nature. The fullest and best account of this which has yet appeared, and which threw a flood of light on the whole subject, is that of Ken Wilber (1983), who distinguishes these nine positions in a developmental sequence:

1. *Pleroma* – or material fusion, the lowest stage of structural organization, recapitulated in humans via the primary matrix. Pre-personal (PP).
2. *Body* – simple sensorimotor intelligence and emotional-sexual drives. Sense of being identified with the body. (PP)
3. *Magic* – the first symbolic cognitive mode, primary process: confuses inside and outside, whole and part, subject and predicate, image and reality. (PP)
4. *Mythic* – higher representational thought, but still incapable of formal-operational insight; still anthropomorphic; mixture of logic with previous magic. (PP)
5. *Mental ego* – egoic rationality and formal-operational logic. This is the 'normal' consensus consciousness of Western society. Personal.
6. *Centaur* – integration of vision-logic mind with emotional body; the unified bodymind. The existential self: autonomous, integrated, authentic. Transpersonal (TP).
7. *Psychic* – actual psychic capacity, or the beginning of transpersonal modes. Always some sense of the divine being involved. (TP)
8. *Subtle* – home of high archetypes, or exemplary and transindividual patterns of manifestation. Symbols and images cultivated to represent divinity. (TP)
9. *Causal* – ultimate unity in only Spirit. No symbols or images at this stage. (TP)

The Nondual is said to be a further stage of development beyond this, but could only be represented by the paper on which the whole diagram is drawn.

This list is so condensed as to be almost meaningless, but there is no space here to expand it. The interested person will have to go to the original. But perhaps there is sufficient to show that this is a process of psychospiritual development which we are all involved in, whether we want it or not and whether we know it or not.

Other useful maps are to be found in von Eckartsberg (1981) and in my own essay in this area (Rowan 1983a). The point I make there is that even the best maps seem to have bits missing and areas insufficiently well explored. But Wilber has achieved a magnificent task in reducing a huge mass of seemingly disparate material into some sort of order. In particular, I think he has done a marvellous job of showing exactly how humanistic psychology fits in to the whole picture. In his terms, humanistic psychology is almost all about the Centaur stage – how to take people there, how to explain what it is like, how to handle the phenomena which arise at that stage. If this is true, as I believe it is, then the function of humanistic psychology is immensely clarified and easier to carry out. It is also immensely important.

It is important because civilization, as Wilber (1979) has spelt out in detail, has now reached a stage of development which is all to do with the Mental Ego. The next stage has to do with a new spiritual step forward. But unless the Centaur stage is reached first, the Subtle stages can be quite disastrous because it is at the Centaur stage that we integrate all the previous stages. We go back and pick up all the pieces we discarded, as it were, at the previous stages; we fill up the holes in our personalities, we heal the splits in our personalities, and ultimately we transcend our personalities. We come out as a fully functioning person, in the terms we have learned from Rogers (1961). Wilber has the clearest possible description of exactly how this transition is made in his 1983 essay 'Where it was, there I shall become' now reprinted in Volume 1 of his collected works (Wilber 1999a).

In other words, it is safer and better to do our personal growth work before our spirituality, rather than leave it till later or try to avoid it altogether. It turns out that personal growth work is not an optional extra – it is an essential step on the spiritual path. In the past, people often embarked upon the spiritual path without having done this work, and promptly fell prey to demons, devils, elementals and so forth – most of which were projections of their own shadow, their own nastiness. By going the way of counselling, therapy, group work or whatever, we dispose of all these mistakes and confusions before we start; and hence, when we meet a demon, we know exactly how to handle it and how to speak to it, without giving it a status it does not deserve.

Similarly, in therapy we deal very thoroughly with all the big questions about oughts and shoulds and have-tos, throwing out all those compulsive guilts which plague us, and taking on instead a live conscience which lives by direct contact rather than rules. This is an immense help in dealing with the spiritual path at the subtle stage, where there are many, many rules, none of which has to be taken at face value. Unless we are sophisticated about rules in the way which doing this deep work on ourselves enables us to be, we are going to be caught up in years of misery sorting all that out afresh.

So for the first time we can have a clean spirituality, not cluttered up with womb stuff, birth stuff, oral stuff, anal stuff, oedipal stuff, shadow stuff, anima stuff, parent-adult-child stuff, character armour and all the rest of it. For the first time we can relate to Deity without wondering and worrying whether what we are relating to is just a projection of our own parents. So this argument of Wilber about levels of consciousness is very important for the understanding not only of the transpersonal, but also of humanistic psychology and its function in the whole process of development.

One practical thing about this process may be of interest. Some work by Elmer and Alyce Green (1971) suggests that on the way from the Mental Ego level to the Centaur level there is a particular feature which is quite often experienced – a narrow tube, tunnel or path. This is referred to independently by several Eastern traditions, and has been discovered by therapists such as Ira Progoff in the West. It seems that often in fantasy work, when the person is approaching the level of the real self (the Centaur), he or she will visualize a tunnel or well, and seem to be traversing it, until at the end a light appears, a golden sun or other object with which the person ultimately identifies. The Greens quote this clinical example:

> The power of meditation to bring transpersonal awareness is beautifully illustrated by the case of a 30-year-old physicist with whom we discussed occult metaphysics. During meditation he became aware of being in a long grey tunnel at the end of which was a bright light. With great joy he realized that this light was his life's goal and began running toward it. As he neared the light, however, its brilliance began to hurt him and he saw that the light came from an intensely illuminated figure of himself which was upside down, balanced head-to-head on top of another figure of himself . . .

The symbol of the illuminated man balanced upside down on the head of his normal self is particularly meaningful because it is generally maintained by teachers that the upper levels of man's nature have a correspondence in lower levels, highest to lowest, etc., and that man's personal and trans-personal natures meet at the fourth level, the point of balance. Merging with the illumined being consists of folding him down so that his feet come to the ground and the resultant figure is a completely integrated man. This is, in essence, Aurobindo's idea of the necessity in modern times of bringing down the transforming power of the overmind and supermind so that the man and his environment both benefit.

This is certainly something to watch out for when helping people to come to terms with the Centaur level.

PERSONAL AND SOCIAL IMPLICATIONS

Some of our hangups come from repressing those things about ourselves which we do not like (and this we can deal with very well in our personal growth work), but some come from repressing those things about ourselves which we do like. As we saw in the earlier part of this chapter, there is also such a thing as the repression of the sublime. But we do not need to suppress these aspects of ourselves any more than the others. They can all be explored, understood, transformed and made parts of our being (Tart 1990).

But what if we do? There is a persistent fear, which we mentioned before, that concentrating on one's spiritual path may make one passive in social matters. This may be true of some of the Eastern doctrines in their original homes, but it does not seem to be true of the versions we have been looking at which are integrated with humanistic psychology.

Many people have been through a lot of phases and come back to the community – there is now a great deal more work being done outside the growth centres, by people who learned what they know inside those centres.

My own way of looking at it is that there is a pulsation or cyclic movement in my life, so that at times I go inwards, and at other times I go outwards. This rhythm may have different periods in different people's lives, but I believe life is quite often like this. There is no need to fear that if one goes into a trance one will never come out of it, any more than there is a need to fear that if one once starts crying, one will never stop.

As we go up the spiral, more possibilities open up, and these are possibilities both for more intense personal experience and more intense social involvement and commitment. There are possibilities for more effortless personal experience and more effortless social involvement and commitment. How can it be intense and effortless at the same time? It is.

PAGANISM

Many people in the human potential movement have moved out in recent years into the sphere of the guru. Some of the best therapists I know joined up with Osho or Sai Baba or Da Avabhasa. Many others more informally adhere to Buddhism in some shape or other. There is a natural tendency, once one gets interested in the transpersonal, to specialize in it more and more, and to take up some kind of religious devotion. But I believe that there is an important political question to raise here. What is the type of religious devotion that is more helpful to the earth at the present time?

It seems to me that paganism has some claim to be considered, because of its close relation to the earth and its care for it. This connection has been well drawn out by Sjöö and Mor (1987). The group called Pagans Against Nukes (PAN) has issued a very good brief summary of the pagan faith, which among other things says the following:

> We consider as fundamentally Pagan all folk who hold the Earth
> sacred, who try to live in such a way that no living creature need

suffer that they might live, regarding the plants and creatures as kinfolk, whose needs are to be treated with respect; who seek to prevent the exploitation and poisoning of our Mother Earth; who seek to reestablish a culture that will live lightly on the Earth, taking only enough for its needs, and living in peace and harmony towards the Earth, fellow creatures and other human beings.

One of the big advantages of paganism as compared to the monotheistic religions is that it is pluralistic. There are many names for the Goddess and many ways of approaching her. There are many names for her son and consort the Horned God. As the PAN statement again makes plain:

> Paganism is not a dogmatic faith. We have no holy books, prophets or saviours. There is no One True Way with Paganism – rather a great diversity of approach to the faith, and a great variety of creative ways in which it finds expression, naturally arising from the infinite diversity of life.

This is perhaps the reason why paganism is becoming more popular today, as Margot Adler (1986) has described it with a wealth of detail. Excellent authors like Starhawk (1979) and Barbara Walker (1983) have opened up a broad path on which we can now walk in our examination of these questions.

Furthermore, it is paganism which has become the most political expression of the women's movement. Not only the Greenham Common women, but also many of the strongest protest groups in the United States, have used the pagan symbols of the spider's web, the snake, the ritual circle, the bird, the maze and so on. And so we get the feminist witch Starhawk telling us: 'If we are to survive the question becomes: how do we overthrow, not those presently in power, but the principle of power-over? How do we shape a society based on the principle of power-from-within?' (Starhawk 1982, p. 4). This political concern is found in many places today where women's spirituality is being developed, as we find in Spretnak (1982) and in McAllister (1982). I have argued strongly elsewhere (Rowan 1997) that men's spirituality also needs this kind of connection with politics if men are to come to terms with patriarchal consciousness – the biggest social problem of our time.

These are relatively new thoughts for me, and much has still to be done in working out how best to present them in print. The word 'paganism' has rather unserious connotations for many people, and it is hard for such people to take anything like this at all in the right spirit. But it seems so important that we just have to take the risk of being misunderstood.

In the last few years, there has been quite an explosion in the transpersonal field. The books have become more numerous, the international conferences have become bigger, the journals have grown, and the British

Psychological Society, normally a bastion of conservative respectability, sponsored two new sections, one labelled as Consciousness and Experience, and the other one labelled as Transpersonal Psychology. One of the best books was by Brant Cortright (1997), one of the most encyclopaedic writers in the field. He outlines and critiques virtually every aspect of transpersonal work, and clearly has read more or less everything which has been published on the subject. He teaches at the California Institute of Integral Studies, which is obviously a good place to be if you want to expound on this sort of thing. His book has to be read by anyone who wants to understand the full ramifications of transpersonal psychotherapy. It has little to say about the actual practice, but more than makes up for that by its excellent treatment of the theory. It does not take account of the Firman and Gila (1997) book mentioned earlier, which is a pity, because he is a bit dismissive of psychosynthesis.

Even more recent is the striking book by William West (2000) which not only discusses the relationship between psychotherapy and spirituality, but gives a number of case studies showing how the author actually deals with these issues in his own practice.

CROSSCULTURAL WORK

It has been pointed out that there is a particular role for the transpersonal therapist in the field of crosscultural work, because of the increased respect for all religious experiences which comes with transpersonal development. The research paper by Cinnirella and Loewenthal (1999) for example, shows that members of communities such as White Christian, Pakistani Muslim, Indian Hindu, Orthodox Jewish and Afro-Caribbean Christian have many different attitudes to counselling and psychotherapy. Some of these make them particularly suspicious of Western types of therapy. It is the transpersonal approach (not mentioned in that paper) which would be the most likely bridge for such people to use, in order to get the benefit of adequate therapy. The supervisor's role in this can be to encourage the transpersonal therapist to look for such experience and to make his or her presence known to the relevant people. Not quite in the same category, but offering the same kind of disconcerting experiences, is the crosscultural work involving discarnate entities of one kind and another, ranging from gods and goddesses to demons and devils, and from loas, orishas and zar to ghosts and witches. A good example is the extract from an interview with a patient in a mental hospital detailed by Eugenie Georgaca, which goes like this:

INTERVIEWER: So did, did something specific happen yesterday that made you feel so bad?
PATIENT: Yeah.

INTERVIEWER: What was it?

PATIENT: Those spirits. Spirits have been following me, spirits that, you know, they are coming up, they are coming out.

INTERVIEWER: Yeah. So what type, I mean, what type of spirit is it?

PATIENT: I would say a mind spirit.

INTERVIEWER: Yeah, yeah, I mean, obviously that's, I mean, you haven't seen it or heard it or anything, you just . . .

PATIENT: I feel it.

INTERVIEWER: Yeah, you're just feeling it. So how do you know it's a spirit then?

PATIENT: The world made up of, the world made up of body I just think it's spirit.

INTERVIEWER: Hmm mm, but it doesn't do anything else to you, does it?

PATIENT: That it makes me sick, it makes me sick.

(Georgaca 2000, p. 233)

The interviewer goes on to avoid all the issues raised by this extract, and to retreat to a rational form of dismissal of the experience as delusional. The first questions a transpersonal therapist might ask could be: 'Does this spirit have a name?' 'Does it have a personality?' 'What does it want?' Because the interviewer had no understanding of the mind-set of the patient, such a question could not be asked. But it is a well-known fact amongst people who believe in spirits that once you know the name of a spirit it gives you much more control of them. It makes it much easier to talk to the spirit and have a dialogue with it.

A great deal of fear may be aroused by such material for the client, and may be picked up by a therapist who is not well versed in this area. The transpersonal therapist is of course much better able to handle this material than other therapists, because their experience of the Psychic and the Subtle realms, and the transformations of consciousness, will stand them in good stead (see Wilber et al. 1986b). Also the whole idea of the pre/trans fallacy may be important, in placing the phenomenon into the right place. Again the work of the supervisor may be much needed here. Indeed, the supervisor may get out of their depth too, and have to refer to a specialist. But the simple fact of having been opened up to that level of spiritual reality may well be enough to deal with most problems.

KEN WILBER

Of course the greatest name in this field is that of Ken Wilber. He has continued to push the boundaries of what can be said and thought in the field of the transpersonal. In the last few years he has been bringing out book after book clarifying and developing his ideas. One of the best books to start on now is *The Eye of Spirit* (1997), because it begins by summarizing his work so far, and then takes off further from there. There are six chapters in which Wilber answers his critics. This is the most fascinating part of the book for someone who knows Wilber already. It goes deeply into all the most difficult areas of Wilber's theory and clarifies, explains more fully, extends even here and there, and does a magnificent job of throwing light into dark places. In doing so, he makes a useful distinction between phases I, II, III and IV of his own progress, and allows that there are significant differences between what he said earlier and what he is saying now. For the keen student of Wilber, this is the heart of the book. And in the final chapter, Wilber gives his account of the Nondual, the 'brilliant clarity of ever-present awareness', in the clearest way I have seen so far.

I have tried to go into much more detail about all this in my book on the transpersonal in psychotherapy and counselling (Rowan 1993), but anyone seriously interested in this area will have to read Wilber himself.

In 1998 a fascinating book entitled *Ken Wilber in Dialogue* (Rothberg and Kelly 1998) appeared which contains 16 chapters by critics, a reply by Wilber, further responses by 13 of them, and two final chapters summing up the results. He is clearly someone who has achieved an eminent place in the field, and has to be listened to very carefully.

11

FEMALE/MALE/GAY

In the late 1930s, Maslow began to study the relationship between sexuality and what he called 'dominance feeling' or 'self-esteem' or 'ego level' in women. He found that the more dominant the woman, in these terms, the greater her enjoyment of sex and her orgasmic potency. It was not that these women were more 'highly sexed', but that they were, above all, more completely themselves, more free to be themselves. They could give themselves more freely, because they had more of themselves to give.

Today we would tie this in to Maslow's self-esteem level, which we met in Chapter 2. Once a woman gets to this level, she ceases to underestimate herself in relation to men, and is able to gauge her own abilities accurately and realistically. As Maslow (in Friedan 1965) says:

> Such women prefer to be treated 'Like a person, not like a woman' . . . Rules per se generally mean nothing to these women. It is only when they approve of the rules and can see and approve of the purpose behind them that they will obey them . . . They are strong, purposeful and do live by rules, but these rules are autonomous and personally arrived at.

Now we have seen over and over again that it is difficult for anyone to get to this level. Our culture does not make it easy, and all of us need special help if we are to do it at all. It is as if our society puts a slope in the ground, so that psychosocial development after level 4 always takes place against resistance – always an uphill struggle. What has been found, however, over and over again in many independent pieces of research, is that the gradients are not equal for men and for women. If the gradient is 1 in 20 for men, it is more like 1 in 2 for women. The number of men who get to the genuine self-esteem level is small – the number of women seems to be even smaller. Most of us get stuck at the level of role-playing.

174

SEXUALITY

Even sexuality becomes a matter of role-playing. There have been two sexual revolutions in our time. The first was about getting rid of restricting and hypocritical Victorian morality. This reached its peak in 1962, with the invention of the Pill. The Pill was going to liberate sex once and for all from its old shackles. Now we could all be sexually free. With the fear of pregnancy gone, the road would be clear for us all to do exactly what we had always wanted to.

But pretty soon it became obvious to some women that what had happened was in fact that the way had really been made clear for women to do what men had always done – enjoy sex without responsibility. But was this what they had actually been wanting to do? It seemed highly dubious to them. Let Ellen Willis (1981) tell it:

> The libertarians did not concern themselves with the quality of sexual relationships or the larger social and emotional causes of sexual frustration. They were less influenced by feminism than their counterparts in the twenties; in theory they advocated the sexual liberation of women, but in practice their outlook was male-centred and often downright misogynist. They took for granted that prostitution and pornography were liberating. They carried on about the hypocrisy of the sexual game – by which they meant men's impatience with having to court women and pay lip service to their demands for love, respect and commitment. No one suggested that men's isolation of sex from feeling might actually be part of the problem, rather than the solution.

So the second sexual revolution was about women discovering that the first one was not in their interest, and trying to find out what sexuality might mean in their own terms.

This process of discovery has been long and difficult. It was made even more difficult by the fact that the family did not go away in the 1960s, as some of the liberators had hoped. It remained as unfinished business to be settled. As Willis (1981) has pointed out so sharply: 'There is a neat irony in the fact that leftists are now romanticising the family and blaming capitalism for its collapse, while ten years ago they were trashing the family and blaming capitalism for its persistence.' It is only the feminists, she says, who have consistently analysed the family and shown how sexuality is distorted and confused for both men and women in a patriarchal society. Her remark 'Women in a patriarchy have every reason to distrust male sexuality and fear their own', is a poignant cry about an impossible situation.

And the more recent writings on male sexuality (Rowan 1997) show all too clearly that the situation does not become any less impossible with the passage of time. The kind of authenticity which the humanistic approach makes possible still seems a minority affair. Most people rest content with roles.

SEX ROLES

But there is something particularly insidious about sex roles. They seem to be tied in with our identity in a way that most of our roles are not. We are sometimes told that the differences are biological, but humanistic psychologists do not believe this. We believe that women are just as capable of moving up the developmental spiral as men, and that if they are not doing it, this must be due to some internal or external barrier.

What has happened in recent years is that women themselves have become more and more aware of the arbitrary and hurtful nature of these barriers, and in increasing numbers have tried to dismantle them. In doing so, they have found it necessary to separate to some degree from men, because when men are present the old patterns reassert themselves all too easily. Or to put it another way, men are actually the reason why many of the barriers are there – it is actually in the interests of men's comfort and peace that women are pushed into service roles. No wonder it is hard to dismantle the barriers in the presence of those who put them there, or who at any rate maintain them.

At first, men reacted with antagonism or guilt (or a mixture of the two) to being accused of these things, but gradually they began to see that the culture, while narrowing women in one way, narrowed men in another. In 1970, a 'women's caucus' was formed within the AHP, and issued the following statement:

> Men are discouraged from developing certain traits such as tenderness and sensitivity just as surely as women are discouraged from being assertive and 'too bright'. Young boys are encouraged to be incompetent at cooking and child care just as surely as young girls are urged to be incompetent at mathematics and science . . . If sensitivity, emotionality and warmth are desirable human characteristics, then they are desirable for men as well as women. If independence, assertiveness and serious intellectual commitment are desirable human characteristics then they are desirable for women as well as men.

Both sexes have lost touch with their inner selves, replacing them with roles. To achieve a society of whole people, it is essential that these lost selves be found and realized. Potentially we are all whole human beings, but both men and women have been diminished and distorted.

The difference between this kind of distortion and the ones we normally come across in personal growth work is that it is a kind of distortion which is socially created, socially maintained and socially approved. And so it is what the Freudians call 'ego-syntonic' – that is, if in the process of working on ourselves we come across it, we ignore it, because both the therapist and the client take it for granted. As Judd Marmor (1974) has said:

> One of the clinical facts that has forced itself strongly upon my awareness has been the repeated observation of people who have undergone prolonged and painstaking analysis and yet have been left with clear-cut residual patterns of narcissism, exploitativeness, social aggression, rigidity, compulsiveness and other similar characterological attitudes.

In other words, if the culture tells us that such and such behaviour is normal, we will not try to work on it as a problem, even if it is causing suffering to others.

This is what we called earlier the result of living in an alienated society. It seems that we must take it as a basic premise that unless I as a person have worked consciously and often painfully at exploring and discovering my real self, I will automatically be alienated and shut off from my innermost core of being. In other words, to be alienated is to have developed normally. To be non-alienated means a conscious interference with normal development, in our male-dominated society, as Robert Seidenberg urges:

> Although it is a vast oversimplification to attribute mental illness to one cause, we are becoming aware of social forces that filter down to the family and mother–child unit. The effects of a male-dominant society on 'mothering' cannot be overlooked as potentially and actually disintegrative . . . In the unconscious of men as found in psychoanalysis, there is a deep-seated fear and loathing of women. All the songs of love do not displace this underlying contempt for those 'unfortunates' with gaping wounds where a penis ought to be. It is the loathing of differences that encourages and maintains the male homosexual culture from which females are regularly excluded . . . Women are different, but most of their purported differences are cultivated in the minds of men in order to justify oppressing them.
> (Seidenberg 1973, pp. 322–327)

The difference between an enlightened Freudian like this and a humanistic psychologist is that we don't see any of this as inevitable. It is because the 'fear and loathing' is permitted and encouraged by a million social forms that it becomes powerful. If it were denied by the culture it would become an individual quirk with few consequences.

One small instance, which feminists have drawn attention to, is the use of personal pronouns in books. A person of indefinite or general sexual reference, when referred to again, is called 'he' and the words 'him' and 'his' are also used. This produces a cumulative impression that the active subjects of sentences are male. In other words, most of the active and interesting things which are talked about in books are done by the male of the species. And this reinforces any cultural prejudices which are floating around which says that men are interesting and women are boring; that the things which men do are noteworthy, while the things which women do are not worthy of record. There are good discussions of this whole area in Miller and Swift (1979) and in Spender (1980), but this is a point which has now been widely accepted. Many publishers now have rules to eliminate such linguistic bias.

This is a minor one. There are also major ones, and medium heavy ones, and everything intermediate between these. And their cumulative effects are extraordinarily powerful – they actually affect our own consciousness of who we are. As Angela Hamblin (1972) says in a superb essay:

> When we accept our role and lose touch with the vital core of ourselves we are sick . . . It is a sickness that doesn't show, it doesn't noticeably affect our bodies, it doesn't impair our capacity to function. It doesn't prevent us from acting out our role. We are just dead inside . . . And most of the time it seems like normality. It is the striving for health, the groping towards self-realization that seems unnatural, unreal somehow . . . This is because in our sick role-playing society this inner core of self is never accorded recognition or legitimized. It is never acknowledged that such a thing exists, so how can it be lost?

Of all the roles which we can try to escape from, our sex roles are the hardest. Women have found that consciousness-raising groups help a lot in some ways, but are also very painful, which is perhaps why few of them have survived. To permit oneself the knowledge that one is oppressed, to open up one's awareness of the way that one's life has been fucked-up, is a recipe for pain. In such a group one may also find much laughter and new feelings of power, but in the end there is so much to fight against that it makes one mixed-up and angry and resentful. Su Negrin has written about this very well. It is almost as if in order to be a woman, one had to give up being 'a woman'. As if being a woman in relation to women was different from and incompatible with being a woman in relation to men. One simple way to resolve these contradictions is to become gay, or at least to open up to the possibilities of relating to other women on a body level, as well as on a mental and emotional level.

And something also happened with men. Men started meeting separately, and consciously experiencing their own feelings about relating to each other (Farrell 1974). They discovered how competitive they were, how devoted to power they were – often seeing couple relationships in terms of power rather than in terms of sex. (Key question 'Which gives you more pleasure, making love to a woman or getting her knickers off?') And again, after a while, this led to a real feeling of despair – there just seemed too much of it, there was no end to the ways of dominating women and putting them down. So maybe a simple answer was not to relate to women – at least one couldn't be accused of oppressing them then. And the gay men drove the point home:

> You claim to want to struggle against your own sexism and yet you refuse to make central and primary and before everything else, the task of breaking with gender roles. You want to stop being men, but without stopping being men. You want to postpone it until you've stopped being men . . . There are a thousand ways to deceive yourself. But in the end the only way forward is to really open yourself up to the mirror image of yourself and experience through another, yourself as a man (you are a male, remember) – and build something from the ruins of your male ego that will result.
>
> (Anonymous contribution to Brothers Against Sexism, 1974)

This was a strong challenge, and really got under the skin of those who were most sincere about trying to do something about their false socialized male selves. But it was very rare to be able to find a situation where anything could be done about this. I ran a workshop with a woman once, where we tried to get into these areas, and in it one of the men was confronted by the women over a period of about two hours. This led, with the help of Gestalt therapy, into his being able to have a kind of amazing vision of what it would be like to be a non-sexist person – and actually behaving like a real person. But it needed all that period of breaking down before he was ready to make that leap. Most of the time women are unable or unwilling to get together and spend that amount of time on one man, and it just doesn't seem to work very well to get men to confront each other. All these issues have been examined well in the magazine *Achilles Heel* in England over a period of twenty years or more.

CONSTRUCTIVISM AND SOME WAYS AHEAD

If this bit of potted history is anywhere near right, it seems that what has been happening is that some women have become aware that society is run in a patriarchal way, for the benefit of men. They have discovered that their alienation can be pinpointed very accurately as due to the separation of roles in a male-dominated society. Angela Hamblin (1972):

> The political class of men oppress and exploit the political class of women. Within the political class of men a few dominate and oppress the rest. It is for the benefit of these few that the patriarchal role-system is maintained, although all men derive direct or indirect political benefit from it. At no time is this system of benefit to women. This is why it is women who will bring it down . . . We have to dismantle the hierarchical power structure built up and maintained through social role-playing. And we have to start with ourselves. We have to put ourselves together again. We must become real. When we are real, then we are a real threat.

But we have also seen that men find it incredibly difficult to change, partly no doubt because we do derive direct or indirect benefit from the existing state of affairs, but also because the social conditioning works at an unconscious level as well as at a conscious level. I have written about this at much greater length elsewhere (Rowan 1997).

Now this seems very much like the situation between blacks and whites, in the relationship we call racism. Racism is the pattern where whites feel it is 'all right' to oppress blacks in various ways, because it is socially sanctioned. It is a mixture of prejudice and discrimination. And in recent years, of course, blacks have begun to resist this pattern, and to undo the ways in which their own selves have been made to feel inferior. Now the corresponding pattern between men and women is called sexism, and it seems to me that the analogy is very close, as Hacker (1951) has suggested.

If this is at all true, perhaps some of the same approaches which have been used in tackling racism might be useful here too. Jones and Harris (1971) tried using small groups to produce real change. They used six to eight weekly sessions of an hour and a half, followed by a six-hour session, with groups of 10 to 15 people, some white and some black. One leader is white, and one black. Their project showed that certain phases seem to be constant, and regularly arise to be worked through as the sessions progress:

1 Introductory phase. The main theme is of white people claiming to be free from prejudice.
2 Information phase. Black members come back with details of how they have suffered.
3 Competitive phase. The whites come back with stories of how they, too, have experienced discrimination or persecution, because of being Jewish, Catholic, longhaired, revolutionary, etc.

4 Competitive response. The blacks then emphasize how much worse their problem is, and it becomes clearer that it is white society which is responsible in their eyes.

5 Dissociation. The whites then try to dissociate themselves from white society generally, and also accuse the blacks of exaggerating. One way or another, they avoid accepting the black statements as applying to them.

6 Impasse. It becomes clear that the blacks and the whites are on two different wavelengths. There is a feeling of being stuck. Evasions of different kinds are tried. It seems that nothing is going to change or happen.

7 Moment of truth. Eventually one of the blacks will express unequivocal anger, strongly and honestly. The group now knows him or her well, and cannot fail to be impressed.

8 Follow through. The other blacks in the group sooner or later support the member who has spoken out. The emotional reality of what it is to be a black and not a white comes through clearly.

9 Realization. The whites gradually and painfully see the contrast between sympathetic understanding, warm-hearted liberalism, and the real awareness of the black experience. They see that they have been living in a different world, and systematically deceiving themselves about it.

10 Digestion. The whites start to go over their past experiences with blacks, in the light of the new consciousness they have now of what it means to be black. The blacks feel relief and surprised delight that the whites are really listening and struggling to understand.

11 Consensual validation. Both whites and blacks are able to work on their, and each other's, individual problems in an atmosphere which at last is relatively clear.

The main purpose of making this comparison is to show that deep-rooted ways of thinking and feeling need a great deal of effort to work through. Even in these groups, there were some people who never got the message, and seemed unreachable. It seems to me that there is no reason to believe that sexism is any easier to deal with than racism. And therefore something corresponding to these stages may need to be worked through between men and women too. There may even be more to it than that; I have suggested elsewhere (Rowan 1997) that the prejudices of men are so deeply ingrained that work at the unconscious and at the spiritual levels may be quite necessary, in addition to this kind of work at the conscious level of daily conduct.

One thing about it needs pointing up, perhaps, and that is that the blacks in these groups had an experience of expressing deep anger, and seeing it work. Daniel Casriel distinguishes four types of expression of anger, and says that it is only the fourth which is really effective in changing people. The first type is intellectual anger, quietly thought and expressed; the second is riddance anger, screaming but mixed with anxiety, coming from the throat; the third is more in the chest, a murderous rage:

> Individuals have to feel that third level before they can get to the fourth level. They have to feel secure enough for that third type of anger in order to feel the fourth level, which I call 'identity anger'. People feel it in their belly, and it comes out as a feeling that 'I'm angry because I've been hurt; it wasn't fair what happened to me, Goddammit, and I'm angry; I'm angry and nobody is going to do that to me again; no more. I'm not going to let anybody do that to me. No more; no more!' You feel it in your total body, and you feel aware of a total you, a total whole identity.
>
> (Casriel 1971, pp. 189–190)

This means that these groups not only reduced prejudice in the whites, but also gave an important therapeutic experience to the blacks. Similarly, if this work were done with men and women, it would not only be of benefit to the men (by confronting them and helping them to change) but would also be of benefit to the women, by enabling them to get into their identity anger, in the presence of the actual object of that anger, and with the support of the whole group structure.

It is important to be clear that we are not asking for people to take off one set of social clothes and put on another set. It is not a question of learning how to be 'Mr Nice Guy' so that one can get on better with feminists. For both men and women, it is a question of learning how to take off the clothes of social conditioning and walk naked. Or to put it more accurately, it is a question of getting in touch with the real self, and reintegrating the personality around it. This is the same process we have been looking at all the way through this book, only now it seems to have a more scary feel to it, as Angela Hamblin (1972) suggests:

> It will be a difficult journey back. It means peeling off layer after layer of social role learning. It is frightening. As more and more is discarded there is the fear that when the final layer is removed it will reveal nothing. This is existential terror, and it is this that makes us scurry back to the safety of roles, to the safety of what is known, and to deny our selves. It takes courage to go on – the 'courage to be'.

This is all true, and yet, as we have been seeing all through this book, there is no need to worry. In that scary void beyond catastrophe lives the real self

– who we really are. The way to wholeness and union is through the gateless gate.

This is where constructivism comes in. Constructivism questions the whole idea of roles and role-playing and indeed patriarchy, and indeed the real self. But it is a challenge which we welcome here, because it throws important and valuable light on the questions we are discussing.

A chapter by Sara Davis and Mary Gergen opens a key book (Gergen and Davis 1997), and here are one or two quotes to give the flavour: 'Sometimes one may emphasize sex differences, and sometimes one may minimize them. For example, in cases of job equity, arguing gender differences may (or may not) be essential to the effort of ensuring the rights of women' (p. 6). 'We are reminded that there are multiple ways of giving words to create worlds, and no one way is the only way' (p. 6). 'From this position it is possible to acknowledge the multiplicity of worldviews, and to work toward creating conditions wherein the separate parties can find opportunities for mutuality, tolerance, and compromise' (p. 7). 'One can ask questions about the world, but cannot claim to have discovered the truth' (p. 7). They suggest that there are five qualities which the chapters in this book have in common:

1 Reflexivity in their approach to their subject matters . . .
2 Knowledge claims are seen as continually developing, never reaching a permanent endstate . . .
3 The authors continually affirm that they and those with whom they are working are identified with particular groups that influence their own formations . . .
4 The search for new forms of cultural life is a central focus . . .
5 Research endeavours should be contextualized so as to enhance their usefulness to people . . .

(Gergen and Davis 1997, pp. 9–11)

It is immediately obvious that this is not like the old liberal feminism, it is not like the old militant feminism, it is not like the old spiritual feminism: it is something quite different and new. And it can be quite critical of earlier formulations. For example, one of the contributions of Gilligan and others was the idea that relationality was a part of the outlook of women as such: that women paid more attention to personal relationships and that this was part of their nature. But Janis Bohan says:

To illustrate the difference such a perspective makes, consider the case for relationality as a worthy human quality. Excising it from individual psyches and locating it firmly in context transforms our change strategies. Our task becomes the enhancement of contexts that elicit doing relationality, a far different undertaking from encouraging women to lay satisfied claim to relationality as a trait of their sex.

(Gergen and Davis 1997, p. 41)

This an important point to make, and it chimes in with the humanistic emphasis on dialectics and taking nothing for granted.

Later on, bell hooks is even bold enough to take up the slogan 'The personal is political' and take it apart for closer examination. She finds that it does not really say enough. It somehow seems to say that the personal can take the place of the political, and she wants more attention paid to the political as such. We shall see in Chapter 14 of this book that the humanistic case has to say the same thing.

The chapter by Leonore Tiefer makes some good points about the word 'natural' and how it is used in discussions of male and female psychology. By the time she is finished, we can only use the word with a painful awareness of its limitations. Humanistic writers have sometimes been guilty of using words like 'natural' in an unaware way, as if they represented something fundamental, instead of being a matter of agreement.

Celia Kitzinger and Sue Wilkinson tackle the newish ideas of 'virgin heterosexuality' (Marilyn Frye) and 'queer heterosexuality' (Judith Butler) and show that they won't work as justifying feminist heterosexuality, because they both retain a notion of essential and natural sexuality. They say that 'We are still a long way from having a politically and theoretically adequate solution to the problem of heterosexuality' (Gergen and Davis 1997, p. 418). This is close to the humanistic view that we co-create our sexuality in engagements with others, rather than just finding it automatically.

There are some instances here of a kind of language imperialism, where it seems as though language is taking over completely, as if there were no other kinds of reality. Mary Gergen's chapter on 'life stories' contains a few instances of this, such as where she quotes Michael Sprinker (1980) as saying

Every text is an articulation of the relations between texts, a product of intertextuality, a weaving together of what has already been produced elsewhere in discontinuous form; every subject, every author, every self is the articulation of an intersubjectivity structured within and around the discourses available to it at any moment in time.

(Gergen and Davis 1997, pp. 204–205)

This goes much too far, it seems to me, as it does when she says herself: 'Language seems almost magical. Only through its powers to name can we identify our experiences and our persons. There are no social structures that bear upon us beyond this linguistic order. All that exists is within it' (Gergen and Davis 1997, p. 217). Of course language is important, but other things are important too. If language were everything, there could be no experience before language, and as recent books confirm (e.g. Wade 1996) there is a great deal of experience before language, which can be very important for later life. If existing language were everything, it would be impossible to create new words, yet writers and others are inventing new words all the time: don't let's make poetry impossible.

One of the best chapters is by Susan Bordo, on anorexia and bulimia. This paper has quite a history, because it first came out in 1985, and has been commented on a great deal since. Bordo's own ideas have changed somewhat in the meantime, and anorexia is much more clearly distinguished from bulimia than it was at that date. But the essay stands as a deep and fundamental examination of all the issues raised by these 'eating disorders'.

A chapter which appealed to me particularly was one by Jeanne Marecek on abnormal psychology. She says things like this: 'Their discussion of categories of disorders portray them as if they were forged in the scientific laboratory, not in the fray of human relations and cultural contestation' (Gergen and Davis 1997, p. 547). There is so much of this in psychology, and this book continually comes up with such discoveries. This is of course in line with recent books such as the one by Kutchins and Kirk (1997) on DSM-IV and the psychiatric classification of disorders, where they show quite conclusively that there is nothing very scientific about it.

Another key chapter is by Susan Oyama, on essentialism, women and war. She has a quite brilliant examination of the feminist arguments here, arguing against the view that women are naturally more peaceable. She says 'What I am saying is that analysis should be conducted in the interests of the eventual synthesis of a complex, multilevelled reality . . .' (Gergen and Davis 1997, p. 527). Humanistic psychology has long urged that there is nothing about women that makes them fit only for roles defined culturally as 'feminine'.

One of the most exciting chapters for me was the one on love and violence, a study of relationships by Virginia Goldner, Peggy Penn, Marcia Sheinberg and Gillian Walker. Why do men appear loving and then descend to violence? Why do women go back to violent men? 'We decided to maintain a position of "both-and", arguing that one level of description or explanation does not exclude another' (Gergen and Davis 1997, p. 578). For example, are men sinners or victims? 'We believe that both are true: that male violence is both wilful and impulse ridden, that it represents a conscious strategy of control, and a frightening, disorienting loss of control' (Gergen and Davis 1997, p. 578).

In discussing what makes a woman codependent, they are forced to discuss what makes a woman a woman in our culture.

> The central insight in all the new work about women is the idea that women form a sense of self, of self-worth and of feminine identity through their ability to build and maintain relationships with others . . . The daughter, like her mother, eventually comes to measure her self-esteem by the success or failure of her attempts to connect, form relationships, provide care, 'reach' the other person.
> (Gergen and Davis 1997, p. 592)

Understanding this makes it easier to understand that going back to a violent man can be experienced not as a failure, or as a submission, but as gender pride and self-respect.

It is hard to stop writing about a book as good as this one is. Everyone interested in these issues would, I believe, find it valuable. It casts a lot of light in a lot of murky areas and for me, at any rate, makes feminism seem once again vital and unique in its contribution to all our thinking about social and political matters.

But there is another area which we need to look at. So far, we have been assuming that the whole world is heterosexual. But it is quite clear, from the little bit of history which we looked at, that the various movements within sexual politics have now become very much aware that an important alternative is to be gay or lesbian.

And once we start to look at this, we find that just as men in quite real and important ways oppress women, so the straight world in quite real and important ways oppresses the gay world.

Now humanistic psychology does not have a particularly good record in relation to gay people, and some therapists who otherwise have a right to be included in this book have been excluded from it mainly because of their strong prejudices against gays.

Most people in humanistic psychology seem to be quite open to homosexual expression, and quite accepting of gay people, but somehow they don't talk about, don't write about, don't research about anything to do with the gay experience. They just leave it alone, quietly and politely. I'd like this to change. But gay people are going to have to do the real work of confronting and raising the issues, just as women and blacks had to do the real work before straight men and whites would take them seriously.

In February 1975, I helped to organize the first 'four-way workshop' to be held in Britain (Rowan 1975). This had two gay and two straight leaders, and enrolled both gay and straight men and women. We all learned a great deal from this, but it was very hard to arrange, and a planned follow-up workshop never happened.

186

There are two good papers on the difficulties involved here in the book on radical psychology edited by Phil Brown (1973), and Su Negrin's book helped me a lot in getting some understanding. She says:

> To me, lesbianism is not so much a sex issue as it is a life-style issue and a political commitment. The life-style aspect involves putting my energy into relationships with women, finding my pleasure in the company of women, developing my sexuality among women, struggling with my oppression in solidarity with women, satisfying my daily needs in community with women. My habits always oriented me to relate in these ways only with men, as straight women do . . . Being a lesbian helped me to become a whole person. As a straight feminist I got in touch with anger; but I experienced myself as a rhetoric reciting, vengeful, conflict-ridden ghost. As a lesbian, I got in touch with love; and I experience myself as a more confident, joyful, powerful person.
>
> (Negrin 1972, pp. 122–123)

It would seem quite wrong to me to say that Su Negrin was sick, or needed treatment. The ability to love somebody of the same sex seems to me a valuable quality, which should be wider spread than it is. (I feel uneasy about that 'should' but let it stand.) I don't do it myself. I have very few close relationships with men, and those that I do have are not on a physical level. (See also Clark 1972.)

And the implications of this include a complete change in the way we might think about sex education. I have never seen a book by a humanistic educator which included suggestions about sex education to include an understanding of same-sex relationships. Yet every book I have ever seen on counselling adolescents says that worries about homosexuality are high on the list of concerns which come up in their sessions. There is a contradiction here.

There is a lot of work being done now on breaking down sex roles in children's books and so on. But whenever an anxious parent raises the question 'But won't playing with dolls make little Johnny into a homosexual?' the answer is always given 'Certainly not'. Which is fair enough, in factual terms, but leaves all the prejudices intact. Maybe we could think of some alternative answers now:

- We believe that each child has the right to be gay in his or her own way, and we wouldn't try to force it.
- We try not to indoctrinate them with any particular sexual orientation.
- We try to help children to be as adaptable as possible in a fast-changing world.
- This is not a single-sex school.
- Are you prejudiced against homosexuals?

Perhaps heterosexuality is like Anglicanism – something we used to teach in schools, but now you have to go to a special school if you want to get it; the ordinary schools are interdenominational. Then sex education would be sex education, not heterosex education.

It is interesting that recently there has been some attempt to put these thoughts into action, and that the backlash has been very strong, assisted by the current anxieties about AIDS. Acknowledging homosexuality becomes encouraging homosexuality, and encouraging homosexuality becomes abetting buggery, and abetting buggery becomes the spread of AIDS. It seems obvious that each of these links is very shaky and can be challenged very easily.

In general, it seems that humanistic psychology needs to be a lot more consistent in its approach. If it is in favour of the full development of human potential, this must mean the full development of sexual potential too. In the present historical situation, where there is such considerable inequality as between men and women, straights and gays, this may have to include periods of separate development and separate exploration. But it also needs to include new kinds of coming-together.

It seems to me that humanistic psychology has a lot to offer in helping to understand these phases, and work them through. It is not afraid of sex any more than it is afraid of any other of the basic motives of human beings, and it has a lot to say about human relationships. The basic principles outlined by Bach and Wyden (1969) in their book on couple relationships apply not only to heterosexual couples but also to homosexual ones, and even to larger intimate groups than the couple.

And this may mean shattering our self-image. Specifically, it may mean shattering our image of ourselves as a woman, or a man. This is what we have been saying all through this book, though. Fritz Perls puts the point with his customary bluntness:

> Many people dedicate their lives to actualize a concept of what they should be like, rather than to actualize themselves . . . This difference between self-actualizing and self-image actualizing is very important. Most people only live for their image. Where some people have a self, most people have a void, because they are so busy projecting themselves as this or that.
>
> (Perls 1969, p. 19)

And what we have seen over and over again is that this void is all right; it is only by going into that void that we can have any inkling of what it might be like to be a real person, who is free to play games or not to play games, and never has to play games.

This process is never easy, and in a historical situation where the straight white male has to do very little to win, and the others have to work like hell to avoid losing, it is harder still. The problems and burdens of men are real enough, as Pleck and Sawyer's book (1974) makes clear, but they are the burdens of privilege; the game is not even. There is a long way to go. And if we want to hold all these complex ideas together, we have to be able to think dialectically, and meet the constructivist challenge.

Part 3

THE FUTURE OF HUMANISTIC
PSYCHOLOGY

12

THE SPREAD OF HUMANISTIC PSYCHOLOGY

As we have seen, the Association for Humanistic Psychology (AHP) was formed in 1962. All through the 1960s it was growing in the United States, but outside there was little overt sign of the ideas or methods catching on. Probably most of what activity there was tended to be in the established fields of counselling (the Rogerian influence) and in organizational psychology (the influence of Maslow, largely channelled through the National Training Laboratories and other management professionals).

It was not until 1969 that the AHP started in Britain, through some people happening to come together at a conference of the British Association for Social Psychiatry. It was out of that meeting that Ruth Lassoff, John Wren-Lewis and Leslie Elliott started the British organization off. And in 1969 the first British growth centre was started up by Paul and Patricia Lowe, and called itself 'Quaesitor', which means seeker.

The AHP in Britain began by running a number of open experiential events, attended by some 50 to 60 people each time, and quickly built up a mailing list of about 500 names and addresses. It began to issue a Newsletter early in 1970, and set up a task group to decide how best to organize. The group consisted of Mel Berger, Eve Godfrey, Roger Harrison, Caron Kent, Ruth Lassoff, Paul and Patricia Lowe, Hans Lobstein and Bill Schlackman. Anne Elphick, Nina Quinn and John Adams (whom we shall meet again later) were also involved at the start of 1970.

By May 1970 the AHP had 41 members in Britain, and the committee included Ann Faraday, Val Peacock, Peter Spink and Colin Sheppard, in addition to those mentioned before. Already there was pressure to start a British journal, and make specific contacts with industry, education, social work and academia.

In 1970 a big boost came through the visit to London of several leaders from the Esalen Institute, who put on two big events at the Inn on the Park, and also two for students in Paddington (organized by the radical psychology magazine *Red Rat*). Michael Murphy, Stuart and Suki Miller, Alan Watts, Jackie Doyle, Will Schutz, George Leonard, Betty Fuller and others were here, and aroused a great deal of interest in the whole area. By August 1970 the membership list had gone up to 76.

In 1971 it was decided to make a definite attempt to become better known in the field of academic psychology, and to get more members from that area. So the AHP set up two evening events on the campus of Exeter University, at the same time as the annual conference of the British Psychological Society (the big orthodox equivalent of the Americal Psychological Association in the US). The first event was a talk by John Heron on the different ways of attending to behaviour, followed by an experiential event led by Paul Lowe and Jackie Doyle; and the second was a talk by Jacob Stattman on the concretization of affect in groups, followed by an experiential event led by Carmi Harari and Stanley Graham. These two events were extremely successful, about a third of the entire conference attending one or other of the events, and most of these attending both. To explain and supplement the experience, a booklet was put on everyone's breakfast place, containing a general introduction by Charlotte Buhler, information about the AHP, a book list and a sprinkling of quotations. This was also available later in the main conference office.

This event gave a lot of confidence that the British AHP knew how to do things, and knew where it was going. And it reflected some things which were going on elsewhere. In August 1970 the first international conference of the AHP had been held in Amsterdam, and participants came from the USA, the Netherlands, Britain, Denmark, Sweden, Norway, Belgium, France, Germany, Switzerland and South Africa. Also in 1970 the first groups were started in Israel under the AHP banner.

In Japan in 1970 there were something like 400 people leading groups ranging from person-centred groups to T-groups to open encounter and psychodrama. This again started in the organizational field but became more oriented towards personal growth. Some became quite political, wanting 'to popularize the movement for the masses to liberate individuals from all that keeps them from being themselves'. There was an Institute of Group Dynamics at the University of Fukuoka and a professional association of T-group trainers with a membership of 150. A great deal of work was being done by the Japan Institute for Christian Education, with 40 trainers doing a wide variety of workshops, many of which had no connection with the church as such. Some indication of the level of interest at that time was shown by the fact that the complete works of Carl Rogers had been translated into Japanese (18 volumes).

At the same time in the Philippines there was a great deal of activity and a Philippine Institute of Applied Behavioural Science, with a growing network of trainers doing groups for industry, the church, the university and a variety of community development projects. There was also a good deal of interest in the Department of Psychology at the University of the Philippines in developing a research programme on humanistic psychology.

All this was reported in the second number of the Bulletin which the British AHP started to bring out in 1971. Also reported in the same Bulletin was the very successful conference held by the Group Relations Training Association (GRTA) that September. This was organized in a much more flexible way than the average conference, and included a much wider variety of activities – talks, demonstrations of leadership style, board games, encounter tapes, intergroup exercises, large group experiences, a marathon, a couples group, creativity training, achievement motivation training, Gestalt awareness exercises, 'The Marriage Grid', management simulation, and so on. It was arranged like a fair, with plenty of choices and repeats of some sessions, and it was very cheap. Before it happened some of the session leaders were worried about the disjointedness of the thing, and worried about how their work would be separated off. But:

> What happened in practice was that feelings generated in one session were often carried over into other later sessions. In effect, what was created was not a tightly bound series of self-contained learning groups, but a much more flexible and open learning community.
>
> (AHP Bulletin 1971)

The GRTA was not committed to humanistic psychology, but this particular conference probably went further in the direction of that orientation than anything they have done before or since, both in form and in content. Sadly, this organization no longer exists.

In April 1972 the first Scandinavian Conference on Humanistic Psychology took place at the University of Stockholm, with about 140 people. And in the same month the British AHP participated in the annual conference of the British Psychological Society (BPS), this time on an official basis, with a half-day symposium on humanistic psychology. This started off calmly enough with papers by John Heron and Peter Smith – but the third paper was by Sidney Jourard, who had come over from Stockholm specially for this session. It was called 'Psychology for control, and for liberation of humans':

> The agencies that believe it worthwhile financing research into human behaviour typically believe that their interests will be furthered if man's behaviour becomes less unpredictable. They want men to be transparent to them (while they remain opaque to the others), and they want to learn how to make men's actions more amenable to control . . . My hypothesis is, that unless the behavioural scientist explores the broader social, political and economic implications of his work, then he is a functionary indeed; worse, if he does not realize it, then he is being mystified by those who employ him.

195

This was hard-hitting political stuff, and it fitted in very precisely with the concerns of the *Red Rat* collective, who had in fact organized an informal meeting on ethics the previous day. They had been saying much the same thing – only here it was being said more fully and more eloquently, and by a distinguished professor, and in the name of humanistic psychology, to a packed audience in a large lecture theatre. (Two years later Sidney Jourard died in an accident, which was a sad loss to us and to the world.)

The rest of that conference was dominated by these events, which formed a major topic for the open meetings which followed. And out of this conference it was decided that the time had come to start a British journal. The time was ripe.

The International Conference was held in Tokyo in 1972, and aroused a great deal more interest in Japan, though it was rather far to travel for anyone from this country.

In September 1972 the AHP (by this time I had been the Chairperson since the departure of John Wren-Lewis and Ann Faraday to America) together with the GRTA and Leslie Elliot's 'Ananda' organization, put on its most adventurous event yet, a four-day workshop under the title 'Creative Change in Higher Education'. This again was arranged in 'fair' style, with many choices, but this time the afternoons were devoted to small group sessions where people could find ways of taking back what they had learned in the mornings to their own home environments.

About 150 people attended this event, and it showed how much interest could be aroused in the whole humanistic approach to education. Those giving presentations included: Roger Harrison, Gurth Higgin, Angela Steer (later Summerfield), Brian Thorne, G.W.H. Leytham, Jacob Stattman, Bill Tibbett and Laurie Cureton, Emily Coleman, David Warren Piper, Eve Godfrey, Peter Spink, Anthony Blake, Nick Georgiades, John Heron, Alan Dale and John Shotter. This was an encouraging event, which should have led to a spurt in activity; but around the end of the year (1972) Leslie Elliott left to live in America and Bill Schlackman withdrew from active participation. Both of these two men had contributed substantial resources of premises and secretarial facilities. We realized how much we had depended on these generous subsidies. From then on, everything we wanted we had to pay for, in time or money or both.

Not to be too parochial, however, it was also in 1972 that the AHP had a very successful meeting in Moscow on psycho-energetics and parapsychology, with 70–80 people, half from the USSR and the rest from France, Belgium, Austria, Switzerland, West Germany and the United States. Stanley Krippner and Carmi Harari, as well as several others, brought back information about important experimentation going on, essentially relating to tapping fields of psychic energy, which corresponded to the work of a number of US scientists closely associated with the AHP.

In 1973 the second AHP Scandinavian conference was held at Roskilde University; 250 people attended, and about 100 had to be turned away because of lack of facilities.

And in March 1973 the first issue appeared of *Self and Society*. This was the culmination of a year's thought and struggle, often difficult and trying. It was an independent venture by Vivian Milroy, but had a close relationship with the AHP, printing two pages of AHP notes every month. As soon as it could be formally arranged, it was made part of the AHP subscription package, thus ensuring a basic circulation. This made a great difference to the whole identity of the AHP in Britain; for the first time it had a living demonstration that humanistic psychology was active in a wide variety of fields. Contributions started to come in from many countries, and clearly it was of more than narrow interest.

At the same time the University Circus was operating. This was a small group of people within the AHP who were willing, for expenses only, to go to any organization which could provide 20 people at least and suitable premises, and put on a five-hour presentation of the theory and practice of humanistic psychology. This proved to be a successful enterprise, and the Circus went to over 20 different universities and colleges.

In July a big seminar was held in India, and a number of visits made, which aroused such interest in Indian universities that a conference was mooted for the following year. The main centres were Dehradun and Aligarh, and many important connections were made between humanistic psychology and Indian philosophy.

In September the International Conference was held in Paris, and several British members went to it. It was poorly organized, and a great deal of dissatisfaction was expressed that it seemed to be an American event held in France, rather than a European event. This was really the turning point in setting off the idea of a genuinely European conference.

In October 1973 in Britain the AHP attempted to get together all the organizations working in the field of humanistic psychology, so that they could actually meet and see each other. This turned out to be very exciting, and there was a lot of enthusiasm to take things forward and see whether some form of cooperation might not be possible. Two more meetings were held in November and December, but it became clear that if anything concrete was to come out of this, a great deal of time and energy would be needed. It seemed that a professional organization, separate from the AHP, was one possibility, but nobody wanted to found it. It was not until 1980 that this idea was brought to fruition with the formation of the AHP Practitioners group (AHPP).

The winter of 1973–4 was very active for the AHP in Britain, with six monthly workshops, including an important one on therapeutic communities, which was attended by 17 different organizations, most of them outside the National Health Service. It was quite apparent that humanistic psychology and therapeutic communities fitted together, and that much could be gained by making those working in such places much more aware of how much they were using our approach, and how they could gain by doing it in a more self-conscious way.

In April 1974 we again put on a symposium at the BPS annual conference, with papers by John Raphael Staude, Peter Spink and myself, followed by an experiential event. About 300 people came to the papers, and 100 to the event. Also films of Fritz Perls were put on by Ken Holme of the Churchill Centre. By this time we were also able to distribute the AHP booklist, which we had got together the previous autumn, and which had been printed with the great help of George Brosan of the North-East London Polytechnic. This gave an annotated rundown of the books in the area of humanistic psychology which were felt to be central, and it was updated twice over the next four years.

International conferences were again held in Scandinavia and in India, at Andhra University. Later in the year, there was an important AHP symposium put on at the InterAmerican Congress of Psychology at Bogota, in Colombia. As a result of it, an AHP chapter was set up in Venezuela. In the following year, the sixth International Conference was held, this time in Cuernavaca, Mexico. About 500 people came, and it was felt to be a big success.

The year 1977 was a very important one for Europe in a number of ways. In Britain the Association for Self-Help and Community Groups was founded by Hans Lobstein; the Antioch University MA in Humanistic Psychology was set up by John Andrew Miller; the first Primal Integration course was set up by William Swartley; and the first European Conference was held in London, organized by the AHP in Britain.

This conference, entitled 'Self Renewal', was very successful. About 200 people turned up, and seemed determined to make it a high-energy event. Five major presenters failed to turn up, and nobody seemed to mind too much. The schedule of lectures and workshops was in a continual state of flux. But some very important ideas were put forward. One presentation on 'A basic qualification in psychotherapy' sparked several efforts in the next year or so to start up training institutes with the humanistic approaches. And another on 'Research in the human sciences' started in motion the formation of the New Paradigm Research Group and its publication later of the book *Human Inquiry* (Reason and Rowan 1981).

In 1978 Michele Festa was inspired to put on the first Italian Congress of Humanistic Psychology in Rome, and to start publishing a magazine, *Psicoterapia Umanistica*. Carl Rogers went to Spain and put on a big international workshop and then came to England and did a week-long workshop for the Facilitator Development Institute. A second European Conference was held, this time in Geneva, thanks to the marvellous entrepreneurship of Sabine Kurjo and her centre, *Vision Humaniste*. As a result of the success of this enterprise – again about 200 participants came – the European Association for Humanistic Psychology (EAHP) was formed, with Arnold Keyserling as its first President, and Sabine Kurjo as Secretary-General. In September a French AHP was formed, with Jacqueline Barbin as the most active moving spirit.

Nor was this all. In Britain two very important educational enterprises were started. One was the Institute for the Development of Human Potential, initiated by David Blagden Marks together with John Heron, Tom Feldberg, David Boadella, Frank Lake and others. This ran a two-year diploma course, which was later extended to run at a number of different centres all over Britain. The other was the Institute of Psychotherapy and Social Studies (IPSS), which put on a three-year diploma course in psychotherapy, covering both the psychodynamic and humanistic approaches, together with a good deal of attention to the social context within which all psychotherapy takes place. This was initiated by Giora Doron, and in the first year the staff included Joan Meigh, Helen Davis, Alan Cartwright, Luise Eichenbaum, Susie Orbach and myself. Unfortunately this was too heady a mixture, and there were splits and problems, leading to Helen setting up her own somewhat similar course under the title of the Association for Psychotherapeutic Process (later changed to the Minster Centre). The IPSS still continues with a high-level course, but has now abandoned its humanistic orientation and turned over to a purely psychodynamic approach.

In America Jean Houston was elected President, and initiated a three-year programme of social involvement. This led in the following year to an event which is best described in Jean's own words:

In April there was an extraordinary conference in Easton, Maryland. The US Departments of Commerce, Energy and the Interior pooled resources and under the sponsorship of the National Institute of Public Affairs brought together over 120 leading government officials and change agents from virtually every department to consider with AHP leaders how the possible human could lead to the possible society. For three days of intense exchange, speeches, small group seminars, and, yes, physical and mental exercises, we explored together the implications of humanistic values and practice on social change. Linear-analytic thinkers were in abundance as were hardnosed bureaucrats whose pathos was one of hopelessness. In the opening small seminars there were ten negatives given for every suggestion, the conversation rife with current trappings of Catch-22. But as we all continued in the atmosphere that we tried to create of real caring, of shared and deep inquiry, of acknowledgement and empowerment as well as fun and fanciful disinhibiting exercises, many among them came to feel differently about themselves and their roles. They discarded despair and began to explore in depth and detail the practical policy alternatives that could help engender the possible society. Networks were formed there, transformational lunch bunches agreed to meet and share regularly to enable each other's vision and to help bring these perspectives into government policies. We in the AHP were asked by a number of key officials to continue to assist and consult with their departments. And several weeks ago *The Washington Post* featured a long editorial applauding the conference and its efforts to improve government by first extending the vision and mind-sets of bureaucrats.

This was an activity which some of us would like to see reproduced in many other countries and much more frequently. But to the best of my knowledge it has never been repeated.

However, on 28 August 1979 another aspect of the new attention to social action came to fruition, when at the Annual Meeting of the AHP at Princeton University entitled 'Evolutionary Ethics: Humanistic Psychology and Social Change' a resolution on nuclear power was passed. This was something quite new: the AHP had always set its face against political involvement. The resolution was so important that it seems worth while to give it here in full:

NUCLEAR POWER AND SOCIAL TRANSFORMATION

We the Executive Board of the Association for Humanistic Psychology wish to affirm our positive vision of the human potential and our conviction that a truly free, just and peaceful way of life can be achieved in our times. We believe, in fact, that our society may well be at the beginning of a new era of human progress.

But our reliance on nuclear power and nuclear weapons – the two are inseparable – endangers and could destroy this positive prospect. The immediate possibility of nuclear accidents and the difficulty of containing radioactive wastes for thousands of years threatens our children and their children with a legacy of birth defects, cancer, and an environment that will not support life. The excessive security requirements of safeguarding nuclear materials and vulnerable nuclear facilities threaten our political liberties. The institutional requirements for the concentration of wealth and power in huge, publicly unaccountable bureaucratic organizations, and the need for secrecy and public deception threaten to undermine democratic government. The safety requirements of infallible operation for thousands and tens of thousands of years put intolerable demands on fallible human beings and social systems.

The expansion of nuclear technology increases conflict, stress and anxiety throughout the world.

We believe that all these dangers can be avoided. A more humane, less extravagant way of living is easily possible through greater emphasis on conservation, appropriate technology, and renewable sources of energy. We believe, in fact, that the turn away from nuclear power can mark an historic turn toward a more human growth-oriented society.

Nuclear expansion depends upon a distorted image of the human being as a consumer whose well-being and sense of identity demand an ever-increasing use of energy and other resources. An evolution to higher levels of personal and social development requires the unfolding of a more holistic and positive vision of human nature. Beyond the failing nuclear dream is a new dream, a dream of deeper human relationships and more humane institutions, of lifelong learning and growth, of greater personal responsibility, more supportive human community, of lifestyles that are more efficient in the use of scarce resources, gentler on the earth, more ethical, more fulfilling.

We therefore resolve to take initiatives in support of research, education and social action dedicated to the emergence of a non-nuclear, human-growth-oriented society. We will seek helpful ways of dealing with the social and psychological transitions that must inevitably accompany a collective change of mind about nuclear power. And we will strive to articulate and realize new adventures of person and planet.

We of the Association for Humanistic Psychology publicly call for global nuclear disarmament, a moratorium on the construction of nuclear power plants, a phased decommissioning of existing plants, and a comprehensive program to conserve energy and implement the alternative, renewable energy technologies which already exist.

This was approved unanimously and confirmed in 1980. The AHP in Britain adopted it in 1980. Some members did not like us taking this stand, and one or two actually resigned over it, but it marked a turning point in the history of attitudes within humanistic psychology. No longer could anyone maintain that it was neutral or value-free.

In Europe we had, for the most part, not gone that far; we were still occupied with spreading the word more generally. The European Conference in 1979 was entitled 'Reaching Out', and a strong attempt was made to do exactly that. And it was very successful – again in Geneva organized by Sabine Kurjo, and this time under the aegis of the EAHP. There were 650 participants, and 100 presenters from 14 different countries – the biggest gathering in Europe we had had up to that time. *Self and Society* was inspired by this event into renaming itself the *European Journal of Humanistic Psychology*.

In the following year, the Association of Humanistic Psychology Practitioners (UKAHPP) was founded, with John Heron as its first Chairperson. This was another groundbreaking effort, because this had never been done in America, and still has not been done there or in any other country. What it does is to set up and maintain standards in all the fields where humanistic psychology is applied. There is a strict accreditation procedure whereby people first of all assess themselves, and then are assessed by their peers. Individuals are accredited in a specific area of practice for five years only, after which they come before the Membership Committee for reassessment.

Members of this group have to satisfy strict criteria of training and experience, and since education is seen as a lifelong process, they are required to continue their own professional and personal development while they are members. They must subscribe to a code of ethical conduct and professional practice which means that any dissatisfied client has recourse to a complaints procedure which has ultimate powers of expulsion.

This group in its first year developed a method of self and peer assessment which has spread to many other groups and other countries. It consists of a formal sequence of operations, where a person conducts a live counselling session (or other activity) in front of a group of peers for 20 minutes or so, and then gets feedback from the group. This is extremely valuable for purposes of professional development.

In 1981 came a new magazine – *Human Potential Resources* – from the enterprise of Maureen Yeomans. For a number of years this was a useful resource.

Later in the year came the fifth EAHP Congress, this time in Rome. This was an excellent conference, with Laing and Laborit (from France) as the two main protagonists. Five hundred people came to this one, mainly from Italy. The sixth Congress was in Paris, and even more people came to that one, breaking all records with about 800 participants.

It was interesting what was happening at this time. Two quite different movements were both progressing at the same time – one towards an increasing interest in the social aspects of humanistic psychology, and the other towards an increasing interest in spirituality. In 1982 there was a joint conference of the AHP in Britain with the Wrekin Trust – rather New Age type of people at the spiritual end of the spectrum – and a special issue of *Self and Society* around psychology and spirituality.

The two things came together in Joanna Macy (1983), who in 1982 and 1983 began to do far more work on what she calls 'pain for the world'. This is a particular kind of pain, which is not psychological in the sense of being due to early trauma or existential angst, but is both social and spiritual. She ran workshops where people could face and own up to their despair at the state of the world – nuclear threats, ecological devastation, political oppression and all the rest – and come out the other side feeling refreshed and empowered. She encouraged further networking.

And networking was the theme of the AHP Annual Meeting in Toronto in 1983. Out of it came a number of networks and an extraordinary initiative by Wendy Roberts. She had had advance notice that a film called *The Day After* was to be shown on TV in some months' time – a film about what happens after a nuclear attack. She had the idea of setting up at least 100 community forums where people who had seen the film and been affected by it could talk to each other and find common cause and common meaning through it. Not only did she succeed, with a lot of help from AHP members and members of Joanna Macy's Interhelp groups, but in the end over 500 community forums took place, involving some 25,000 people, not only in the USA and Canada, but also in Hawaii, Britain and Germany. That same year there was a special issue of *Self and Society* on peace, and the following year one in the *Journal of Humanistic Psychology*, which normally never had special issues on any political subject.

In 1983 came the first issue of the Japanese *Journal of Humanistic Psychology*, edited by Shoji Murayama. In September of that year 30 members of the International Association for Humanistic Psychology visited Moscow and other centres in Russia. This was to be the first of many yearly visits, usually for a fortnight, talking to Russian psychologists and other practitioners about matters of common interest.

In 1984 the European Association of Humanistic Psychology held its conference in Britain, at Surrey University. The weather was brilliant, and the preparations excellent, Wendy Freebourne doing most of the organization. About 400 people turned up from 21 different countries, and the closing ritual was very moving.

March 1985 saw a big celebration in San Francisco of a quarter century of humanistic psychologies. All the big names were there, and over 1000 people took part over the three-day event. In the same year there was something quite new – a conference which started in Baden and then went over the border into Budapest. This was the first time that a really strong effort had been made to have a joint conference with a country like Hungary, and it was mainly due to the initiative of Laszlo Honti that it happened.

In 1984 and again in 1986 there was an attempt made to set up a real international committee which would genuinely represent humanistic psychology worldwide. But it seems that it is very difficult to do this, and maybe it is not really necessary.

The EAHP conference was held in Zurich in 1986. This was a splendid event, again on a big university campus, and Stanislav Grof was one of the star performers.

The last EAHP conference was in 1988 at Barcelona. At first it looked like being a great success. Michele Festa in Rome had found a marvellous organizer, a woman with diplomatic experience and access, who had the ability and the money to travel round and do what was necessary. She got the three Gestalt organizations in Spain to cooperate on the ground, and a good hotel to host the conference, and all seemed to go well. Then she fell ill with cancer, and had to withdraw. Michele Festa tried to carry on without her, and might well have succeeded, except that the Gestalt organizations fell out and could not agree on anything, and handed it all back to him. Consequently the numbers were small, and it was hard to break even. To add to the problems, Ronnie Laing was up to his usual tricks and insisted on an expensive suite, where he ran up large drinks bills for all his many friends. The result was a disaster, which virtually bankrupted Festa and put the whole organization into a decline from which it never recovered.

Since then things have been much more quiet. In the US there has been a lot of devolution, with separate sections of the AHP being devoted to Somatics and Wellness, Women for Change, Student Communities, and a big International Programs effort, which mounts yearly conferences on Conflict Resolution in Russia and different workshops in other countries.

But of course the spread of humanistic psychology does not depend on the efforts of the AHP alone. Organization psychologists, counsellors, people in various fields of education and ordinary people who feel their consciousness to be changing are all affected. They read Carl Rogers, they learn group work and discover Moreno, they attend more to their peak experiences and find Maslow, they do management training and are exposed to the work of Argyris, Blake and Mouton and the rest, they go to self-help groups and learn about Fritz Perls and Gestalt awareness, they go to demonstrations of body work and hear about Lowen and Reich, and so on and so forth.

It seems that still there are many people – perhaps most of those affected – who have the ideas without the experience, or the experience without the ideas. Both of these are lacking – it is as if the former had the words without the music, and the latter had the music without the words. But humanistic psychology is the kind of song which needs both words and music to carry its full message and its full effect.

In 1989 something remarkable happened in England. Around 1980 there had been rumblings about the dangers of uncontrolled psychotherapy. In response to this there had arisen an organization called the Rugby Conference, which met once a year and tried to draw in all the existing training and accrediting centres in the United Kingdom. In 1989 this resulted in the formation of the UK Standing Conference on Psychotherapy. This was divided into sections, the two biggest of which were the Psychoanalytic and Psychodynamic Psychotherapy Section, generally known as PPP, and the

Humanistic and Integrative Psychotherapy Section, generally known as HIP. Other sections were devoted to Analytical Psychology (the Jungians), Behavioural and Cognitive Psychotherapy, Experiential and Constructivist Therapies, Family-Marital-Sexual Therapies, Hypnotherapy and the pompously named Psychoanalytically-Based Therapy with Children Section. Also included were Institutional Members: the Association of University Teachers of Psychiatry, the Tavistock Clinic, the Universities Psychotherapy Association, the British Psychological Society and the Royal College of Psychiatrists.

The UKAHPP (mentioned earlier) was one of the founding members, and when the time came for each section to draw up its defining statement, two of the three members who wrote this statement were members of the UKAHPP.

Later this became the UK Council for Psychotherapy (UKCP), and in 1993 it issued the first National Register of psychotherapists, comprising the membership of all the 70 or so organizations which belonged to it. It was thus the umbrella setup for the whole of British psychotherapy, and when the European Association for Psychotherapy was formed, the UKCP was one of its founding members. This was a remarkable achievement, and it was good to see humanistic psychology take such a prominent part in it. The first President was a psychoanalyst, but the second was Emmy van Deurzen, a leading existential analyst and member of the HIP Section, and one of the foremost people in making the European connection.

The AHP in the US went through a strange evolution during this period, losing a number of members and having much smaller conferences than it did in the days when I attended a meeting of 2000 people at Princeton. But in the year 2000 there was a striking new move: the Old Saybrook 2 conference was held at the State University of West Georgia, in the spirit of renewal and regeneration. Out of this came a number of initiatives which look like fostering a new spurt of growth. Also it was revealed that a major book was on the way, edited by Kirk Schneider, James Bugental and Fraser Pierson, including chapters by Amedeo Giorgi, Thomas Szasz, Donald Polkinghorne, David Feinstein, Clark Moustakas, Stanley Krippner, Maurice Friedman, Alvin Mahrer, Eleanor Criswell, Myrtle Heery, Maureen O'Hara, Art Bohart, Roger Walsh and others. The title is *The Handbook of Humanistic Psychology*, and it is expected to weigh in at about 1000 pages. This seems an encouraging portent for the future.

So in the spread of humanistic psychology there are a number of contradictions. On the one hand it is probably more universal and less culture-bound than any previous psychology, but on the other it is always seen as very American, and arouses a lot of resentment and anti-Americanism. On the one hand it deals with what is common between people and works more often than not in group settings, but on the other it is seen as very individualistic and does actually seem to lead to people working separately rather than together. On the one hand it is very well integrated and consistent, but on the other it is seen as very fragmented, and often leads in practice to people working in a fragmented way. On the one hand it is very open and receptive, opposed to laying trips on people; but on the other, it is seen as very intrusive and aggressive, and very heavily laden with values which it is busily pushing. On the one hand it is seen as too active, leading to panic and breakdowns; but on the other it is seen as too passive, leading to withdrawal from political involvement, and personal responsibility.

There have always been criticisms of humanistic psychology, and I suppose there always will be. We have touched on many of them in this chapter. But to me they are evidence that the whole of humanistic thinking is based on the dialectical thinking we looked at in the Introduction. Of course there are contradictions, because humanistic psychology is based on contradictions. In an outlook founded in dialectics, how could it be otherwise?

13

DIRECTIONS FOR THE SELF

Is there any way of drawing the threads together and seeing what is common to all the fields we have been studying? First of all, is there any consistent message about the self – any indication of where we might go from here? Let us start off with that which seems most obvious – the personality.

THE PERSONALITY

What now seems to be true, and to be coming through from the ever-increasing amount of research now available (Verny 1982, Blum 1993, Wade 1996), is that experience starts early, way back in the womb, if not before. The mass of respectable academic research now being done on infants shows that babies are perceiving the world and making decisions about how to interpret it right from the word 'go' (Bower 1977, Chamberlain 1998). As far back as we know how to make any kind of tests, we find that babies are making sense of the world, not just responding to it blindly or automatically.

And in doing this, they soon find that certain kinds of ways of relating seem to work for them; they may be about getting what they want, or they may be about how not to care when they don't get it, and so on (Mahler et al. 1975, Stern 1985, Gopnik et al. 1999). As time goes on, babies find that they have to relate differently in different circumstances; what works for one person does not work for another, and what works in one setting does not work in another. Also processes of identification are going on – 'This is me; this isn't me' – and people in the environment start to get internalized in this way, often under strong pressures. All this makes the personality, even in the first couple of years, become differentiated – one region, as it were, becomes specialized in one way, and others in other ways. I have called this (Rowan 1990) the formation of subpersonalities. And in all this there is a powerful element of fantasy – this specialization is not done in relation to the environment as it might appear to an impartial observer, but as it appears to a panicky person with a rich fantasy life, very willing to make up stories and paint pictures, and with very little sense of time before and time after (Segal 1985).

So by about four years old, the child has made some very important decisions about the world and relationship with it, and split off various regions within the personality to deal with the people and situations which have been noticed (Rowan 1999).

I have put this in rather general language, but the same kind of story is in fact common to most forms of psychology which have attempted to deal with the same ground. Kurt Lewin (1936) puts it like this:

> The degree of dynamical connectedness of the different parts of the person can be nearly equal within the whole region of the person, or certain regions can separate themselves to an especially high degree from the others and develop relatively independently. This can be observed in the normal person . . .

If we take this point seriously, it makes us wonder why there is no discussion of this sort of thing in any of the texts I have been able to discover so far on the study of personality, with the single exception of David Lester (1995). But if this is true, it makes a great difference to the way we do our research and conceptualize our results. Which subpersonality is answering our questionnaire? Which subpersonality is taking part in our experiment? Which subpersonality is attending our group? As Gurdjieff (Ouspensky 1949) put it dramatically:

> Man is divided into a multiplicity of small I's. And each separate small I is able to call itself by the name of the Whole, to act in the name of the Whole, to agree or disagree, to give promises, to make decisions, with which another I or the Whole will have to deal. This explains why people so often make decisions and so seldom carry them out. A man decides to get up early starting from the following day. One I, or a group of I's decide this. But getting up is the business of another I who entirely disagrees with the decision and may even know absolutely nothing about it. . . . It is the tragedy of the human being that any small I has the right to sign cheques and promissory notes and the man, that is, the Whole, has to meet them. People's whole lives often consist of paying off the promissory notes of small accidental I's.

Once we begin to think in these terms, many things become clearer – we can start to see how our subpersonalities torture each other, how they play games with each other, how they play into each other's hands, and often how little they know each other. And once we know our subpersonalities and give them names, and find out what their nature is, what their motives are, they become powerless to harm us. A shadow is only strong when it is dark; once some light is shed on the scene, it changes colour and may disappear altogether.

But not only does this way of looking at things do good in freeing up our own internal world, it also does good in our relationships with others. Elizabeth O'Connor explains this very well:

> If I say 'I am jealous', it describes the whole of me, and I am overwhelmed with its implications. The completeness of the statement makes me feel contemptuous of myself. It is little wonder that I fear letting another know when my identity with the feeling is such that it describes the totality of who I am . . . If I respect the plurality in myself, and no longer see my jealous self as the whole of me, then I have gained the distance I need to observe it, listen to it, and let it acquaint me with a piece of my own lost history. In this way I come into possession of more of myself and extend my own inner kingdom.
>
> (O'Connor 1971, p. 23)

If each of us understood ourselves in this way, we would be able to give up saying things like 'Well, if she is that way, I want nothing to do with her', as though the 'way' of a person could be known just because one of her selves was glimpsed for a moment. We are able to listen to one subpersonality, and do justice to that, because we are not forced into the judgement that that is all there is. We can wait for the dialectical movement which is going to bring the next subpersonality out into the picture – maybe a directly opposed one. And this makes the job of listening much easier, because we have given up the impossible task of understanding a person all at once. We can genuinely give ourselves up to following the energy to see where it leads today.

The theory of multiple selves seems to make a lot of sense, but it gives a lot of problems for the researcher. Kenneth Gergen (1972) has shown one approach, James Vargiu (1974) another, Hal Stone and Sidra Winkelman (1989) another, Stanley Krippner and Susan Powers (1997) another, and so forth – I have also done some work on this myself, which is written up fully in my books on the subject (Rowan 1990, 1993, 1999). It is obvious that if we have a number of subpersonalities and also a number of levels, then the possibilities for the number of combinations extend alarmingly.

Multiple selves also raise problems for the therapist. If we are busy trying to get people to take responsibility for themselves, is it not a cop-out to allow them to say – 'Well, you see, it was this subself that did it'? This is actually not as difficult in practice as it might seem in theory. Whatever form of therapy we go in for, we almost always come across subpersonalities in some form or other. It may be Freud's Ego, Id or Superego; or Jung's complexes or archetypes; or Berne's ego-states; or Peris's top dog or underdog; or Klein's internal objects; or Shapiro's (1976) sub-selves; the names change, but the reality is still there. It may be interesting to point out that even behaviourism, in the person of B. F. Skinner (1974), has its version – in this case 'repertoires of behaviour'.

Humanistic psychology prefers to talk in terms of subpersonalities rather than regions or repertoires because this makes them easier to deal with in practice, and also because it seems truer to the pictorial way in which they are laid down in the first place.

Now it often happens that one of these subpersonalities becomes a general functionary, and gets given more and more jobs to do. This is usually the most highly socialized of the subpersonalities, and is often closely tied in with the male or female role. This is the one which most of the people in the child's circle will call forth by their expectations, by rewards and punishments, by referring to cultural norms. It is the sub-personality which we know we are supposed to be, whatever we actually are. When people praise us, and try to raise our self-esteem, it is often this subpersonality that they are boosting. It is usually called the ego.

Now the tragic thing is that we can easily be taken in by this, to think that this subpersonality is our real self. It is so much us. It is what every-body knows and relates to – why wouldn't it be who we really are? But in fact it is just what Esterson (1972) calls an alterated identity – that is, it is something trumped up for someone else's benefit; it is something they wanted, and we survived because we produced it (see also Winnicott 1975 on the false self).

To the extent that we firmly feel identified with this false self, it will be dangerous for us to entertain notions of self-actualization, self-realization and so on. What it will mean for us is some form of ego-boosting, some kind of inflation of this subpersonality. And we know very well that this is just going to magnify our existing faults and impose them more fully on other people. So the whole enterprise becomes ridiculous. And if, in spite of this, we go along with the therapy group or therapist or guru or whatever, and come to believe that we have achieved satori or some other kind of enlightenment, we are likely to have incredible difficulties in reconciling our sainthood with our humanity, and have to resort to all the methods which pseudo-saints down the ages have used. McNamara (1975) has a very good discussion of some of these points.

As Perls said, it is the difference between self-actualization and self-image actualization. The latter leads to the desperate straits of the man who said to me once: 'I think I've got this spiritual thing pretty good now, but I still can't get on with my wife.'

The more we can work with the subpersonalities and really get to know them, the more easy it is to see that none of them is the real self. And when at last we allow ourselves to get in touch with the real self, we find that we don't have to take any special measures to deal with our subpersonalities – they take care of themselves and just become colourful facets with a lot of light, but no harm in them.

This may seem hard to believe, particularly because there is often one of our subpersonalities which seems evil, destructive, black and horrible. This may come to light during therapy, or in some other way, but it seems always to be a heavy experience to go through, when we discover it. Jung (1938) has described this as the archetype of the Shadow:

> Unfortunately there is no doubt about the fact that man is, as a whole, less good than he imagines himself or wants to be. Everyone carries a shadow, and the less it is embodied in the individual's conscious life, the blacker and denser it is. If an inferiority is conscious, one always has the chance to correct it. Furthermore, it is constantly in contact with other interests, so that it is steadily subjected to modifications. But if it is repressed and isolated from consciousness, it never gets corrected. It is, moreover, liable to burst forth in a moment of unawareness.

But this again is just another subpersonality, sometimes brought into being as a servant whose job it is to destroy the child's enemies, but who then starts to take over and get out of hand (the basis of the fascination with the Frankenstein story). But there is no need to destroy it; it contains a great deal of locked-up energy and excitement, which when released makes the person more alive and spontaneous. There is a lot of real love and real anger tied up in that congealed hate, and when it melts and starts to flow the results can be incredibly beautiful.

Although he uses different language, this is also the view of Mahrer (1989), who speaks of deeper potentials. These deeper potentials, he says, always have a good form, although they usually appear to us at first in a bad form. And again the answer is to own up to and enter into the deeper potential, so that we can reclaim the original good form it always really had.

So it seems that this way of looking at the self, and the personality, and the subpersonalities, is potentially very rich, and deserves much more research to discover how best to conceptualize and describe the phenomena. Some of this is reported from a number of different angles in a recent book (Rowan and Cooper 1999). Also perhaps there may be ways of handling children which are less likely to produce these very deceptive and over-inflated socialized subpersonalities, which as we saw in the chapter on gender can be very destructive both to men and more particularly to women.

Research in this area might also be productive because it may be that the way in which we treat people in our environment is closely connected with the way in which we treat our own subpersonalities. If one's first reaction to a subpersonality judged to be bad is to say 'Cut it out, destroy it', then this will perhaps be one's attitude to social, financial or political enemies. It might make sense to say that subpersonalities are to the whole person as social classes are to the whole society. There are many thoughts we could pursue along these lines, as I have suggested elsewhere (Rowan 1983b). If we can find out how to deal with the internal society, this may help us in our understanding of the larger society we live in.

The important thing is that in humanistic forms of therapy we do not try to get rid of the subpersonalities, but we do try to transform them (or allow them to transform themselves or each other). Ultimately we want all the subpersonalities to be merely seen as integrated filters to the real self.

THE REAL SELF

Using the term 'real self' in this way suggests that the subpersonalities are in some sense false. And insofar as they act independently they are false. They are not an adequate expression of who I am. They are partial versions of me, scraped up to meet a particular purpose, and resorted to in a kind of panic of choice.

But there are very difficult paradoxes involved in any notion of the real self. Let us see how they arise by taking it very slowly and watching our language very carefully. Do we simply mean the body? This is what Rogers (1961) calls the organism. From one point of view, it is identical with the self, and from another it is part of the environment of the self. It is this ambiguity which makes the body schema or body image such an important source of discontent for most of us, as Seymour Fisher (1973) demonstrates. Masters and Houston (1978) have shown with a wealth of detail how important the body is as a centre for our identity. And recently I have been trying to say that the body is much more complex than has been imagined in the past: there is the conventional body, there is the bodymind unity, and there is the subtle body too (Rowan, 2000).

Or do we mean some kind of original self? This can be thought of from the inside as the 'I' (first person use) and from the outside as the 'me' (third person use). Heron (1972) refers to the primal self, and says that it can be looked on as a set of hypothesized potential capacities. Duval and Wicklund (1972) call it the 'causal agent self', and they make the point very strongly that this self does not need any outside agent to bring it into being – it is there all the time. But it has no nameable characteristics – nothing specific can be said about it. When it relates to the internal or external world, it is the content of the relation, and itself the process of relating. It is empty and void of any content, and at the same time full of energy and life.

Or do we mean the embodied self? Will Schutz (1977) makes the important point that any really adequate approach to psychotherapy or to group experience must take the self and the body as being a unity, and he often speaks of the body/person/process where another writer might refer to the person. He makes the point, too, that the body contains the whole history (or histories) of the self in its encounters with the world. Perhaps the best discussion of this point of view is to be found in Dreyfuss and Feinstein (1977), where they say:

> Contemporary understanding of human functioning is tending to abandon the old notion that mind and body can be thought of as being separate entities and is adopting more holistic concepts, such as the soma: the total living, breathing, experiencing, indivisible being, whose parts cannot be meaningfully considered except in light of the whole person.

They go on to consider the body as a map of the past, as a map of our limitations, as a map of our potentials, and as a map of our universe. But it is also a gate to transcending the map. They talk about unhindering and unfolding, in the typical humanistic fashion, and this has been even more thoroughly brought out in Houston (1982).

Or do we mean the deep intention of the person? Sartre (1963) makes the point that in an important sense our projects are the most significant part of our self structure. What I want to do, what I want to be, what I want to happen – this is what defines my direction. It arises out of my values, my needs, my wants:

> The most rudimentary behaviour must be determined both in relation to the real and present factors which condition it and in relation to a certain object, still to come, which it is trying to bring into being. This is what we call the project. Starting with the project, we define a double simultaneous relationship. In relation to the given, the praxis is negativity; but what is always involved is the negation of a negation. In relation to the object aimed at, praxis is positivity, but this positivity opens onto the non-existent, to what has not yet been . . . Man defines himself by his project.

Again, this is not easy stuff to handle. But it is simply a part of the dialectic which we have to come to grips with if we are going to make any sense in this area. There is no particular reason why men and women should be as simple as noughts-and-crosses. It is intentionality which makes the

213

difference between behaviour and action (Torbert 1972). In humanistic psychology we are often reluctant to talk about behaviour, and are more interested in talking about action, for this very reason.

Or do we mean the realized self? Heron (1972) talks about this as the personality as re-created by systematic self-direction. We have seen a great deal about this in the course of these chapters. With Charles Hampden-Turner (1971) we can perhaps best see this as a spiral or helix where we have gone away from the original self into all the complexities of personality and role, and where we now come back again to the original self, only now on a higher level. Mahrer (1989) has an excellent discussion of integration and actualization as two distinct steps in the process of realization. This would also be the view of Jung, in his work on individuation (von Franz 1964).

Or do we mean the Subtle self? When we first come across this, it always seems to appear as an outside force. We picture it as something which in some sense has something particularly to do with us, but as something unchangeable, which is not moved by the wheel of fortune. It is 'above the battle'. It has 'stopped the world'. It is like a star to guide us, or an angel to watch over us, or like a wise person on a mountain peak who can see it all. And we can be this star, be this angel, be this wise person.

All these different versions seem to have some claim to be considered as the real self. But recently the work of Ken Wilber has given us a way of sorting out this business much more satisfactorily. By referring to his map, we can see that the primary self is not really relevant – it is too bare and too primitive to be much use to us, except as a conceptual starting point. At the other end, the Causal self (as found in mysticism) goes beyond the realm of humanistic psychology and therefore cannot be what we are looking for. The body is again too primitive, going back to the very earliest forms of experience. The realized self is perhaps a bit ambiguous, but as described by the people we have quoted, it seems close to what we mean by the real self. Similarly the embodied self, because it implies a process of realization, can be very relevant to us. And the deep intention of the person also seems relevant; it is crucial to what Wilber calls the Centaur stage, which is what we are mainly concerned with here. It is at the Centaur stage, so well described by Ken Wilber, and also (under the heading of the Authentic self) by Jenny Wade (1996), that we get the vision-logic, the dialectical thinking, which is central to the humanistic position.

We have avoided talking here about the soul, because up until recently there has been no treatment of the soul which seemed at all useful to the humanistic psychologist. But now in the work of Frances Vaughan (1986) we do have a version which seems to make sense, and to be quite usable. One of her main points is that 'How the soul is envisioned depends on the level of consciousness from which it is perceived.' I have tried to build on this in my own work (Rowan 1990, Chapter 12).

MULTIPLE LEVELS OF CONSCIOUSNESS

One final point we need to make here is that there is not just one condition or state to be studied under the heading of 'human consciousness'. People move into and out of a number of different states and stages in their development. And this is true not only in the trivial sense that we are sometimes awake and sometimes asleep; we are talking about a wide range of different 'spaces' that we can get into.

Now it is true that there is as yet no agreement on this variety of states, or even as to what kind of dimensions might be useful in describing them. Leary (1970) has seven levels. Lilly (1973) has nine levels. Stanley Krippner (1972) describes twenty states, but the waking state is just one of them. Maslow, Kohlberg, Loevinger and Piaget (see Maslow's chart, Table 2.1, this volume, pp. 25–26) describe six or seven states, but they are all waking states. Ring (1974) describes nine different states, most of which are contained in one of Krippner's. And so on. It seems that we have a great number of things here, few of which have been studied in any detail, by psychologists or anyone else.

But the main point to see about this is that if we are genuinely trying to explain human behaviour, or understand human actions, or interpret human conduct, it must be absurd to ignore these different conditions.

Tart (1975) has talked about state-specific science, and has suggested that a phenomenon can only be studied from a state of consciousness which is adequate to that phenomenon. Wilber (1983) has reinforced this view, and has criticized academic psychology for not paying more attention to this. We have already seen in Chapter 10 how he has his own list of such states.

So what we are talking about all the time is a set of levels or states which a person can move into and out of, though not necessarily merely by wishing to. It is here that a question arises which seems worth discussing thoroughly: should we talk about levels (which seems in some ways an elitist way of talking) or should we talk simply about states, or spaces, with no implication at all that some of these are more rarefied than others?

It seems as though those who have gone furthest into the whole business of altered states of consciousness are all of the same opinion about this. Whether we look at John Lilly or Abraham Maslow, at the Greens or at David Wright; whether we look at the Eastern tradition or Western science, the same answer comes out – it is a matter of levels, and some levels are higher than others.

And there is a precise sense in which this is held; the higher levels are higher in that they include the lower levels, in a way which is not true the other way round. From a lower level, one cannot understand a higher level; but from a higher level, one can understand a lower level. This is, of course, related to the fact that one progresses from one layer to the next, so that one cannot rise above a level, in any genuine sense, without having been through it. So the person at a higher level can understand the lower level not least because of having been through it. A fuller account of this argument may be found in Wilber (1997).

We are obviously talking about hierarchies here, and humanistic psychology on the whole does not like hierarchies. Is this another contradiction, another paradox? Actually not, because of the important distinction, spelt out very clearly by Riane Eisler, between two kinds of hierarchy.

> In connection with the dominator model, an important distinction should be made between domination and actualization hierarchies. The term *domination hierarchies* describes hierarchies based on force or the express or implied threat of force, which are characteristic of the human rank orderings in male-dominated societies. Such hierarchies are very different from the types of hierarchies found in progressions from lower to higher orderings of functioning – such as the progression from cells to organs in living organisms, for example, These types of hierarchies may be characterized by the term *actualization hierarchies* because their function is to maximize the organism's potentials. By contrast, as evidenced by both sociological and psychological studies, human hierarchies based on force or the threat of force not only inhibit personal creativity but also result in social systems in which the lowest (basest) human qualities are reinforced and humanity's higher aspirations (traits such as compassion and empathy as well as the striving for truth and justice) are systematically suppressed.
>
> (Eisler 1987, p. 205)

What we are now saying, therefore, is that the kind of levels we have been talking about form an actualization hierarchy.

Now is this elitist? It seems that it is only so if two conditions are satisfied: first there is an implication that only a few can reach the top levels; and second there is an implication that those at the top levels are generally superior to those at the lower levels.

As to the first of these points, humanistic psychology says that people can naturally reach the further levels, and that it is only if they are held back (by cultural pressures or their own choices) that they will fail to do so. There is an innate capacity for self-actualization, which only needs a real intention and a supportive environment to be realized. So it is not elitist in this respect.

On the second point, humanistic psychologists are not always fully in agreement. Rogers is quite clear that his 'fully functioning person' is just one possibility, and that some people would rather aim at a person who is tightly controlled and rigidly disciplined; and he certainly doesn't come across in his films or books or tape-recordings as someone who thinks of himself as superior. Maslow is quite clear that his 'self-actualizing person' has faults and defects, and is by no means free from guilt, anxiety, sadness, self-criticism and internal conflicts. Perls I am not so sure about, but if we take Barry Stevens as a living example of what Gestalt therapy is all about, certainly she doesn't see herself as superior to anyone. Here is where she is talking about Herbert Talehaftewa, a Hopi Indian who was at this time working on a construction job as a carpenter, while Barry was on the same job as office manager:

> Cab, the owner and boss, was a Boston snob who looked down on *everyone*, belittled them to the point where most people who were subjected to it went to pieces and had to pull themselves together again. One day I saw this man look and speak to the Hopi in this way. Cab was a small man, and the Hopi was quite tall and broad, but Cab still managed to look down on the Hopi. I saw the Hopi look at Cab so *equally* that he drew Cab down to his own level – precisely, and not one bit lower – so that they seemed to be two people eye-to-eye. I was so impressed by this that I looked up to the Hopi as though he were some sort of god. The Hopi turned to me with that same strong *equalness* in his gaze, and I felt myself being drawn *up* until we were on the same plane.
>
> (Stevens and Rogers 1967, p. 35)

Whatever we may feel about the language in which this is expressed, it seems to express an attitude pretty clearly, which is not an attitude of superiority. It is an attitude which, if anything, is critical of assumed superiority.

So it seems to me that, at least in its most central and substantial representatives, humanistic psychology is not elitist in this way either. It says that being a real person may be very rare at present, but it is just ordinary, not a cause for exaggerated respect, and not carrying with it any special privileges. I have been arguing in this book that Centaur consciousness is quite specific and limited, not a final aim or a great ideal. It is quite achievable if one is prepared to do the work.

Some of the Eastern approaches seem to be much worse in this respect. If someone calls himself a Perfect Master, and carries on as though he did have a general superiority, this seems to be indefensible. But no one within humanistic psychology has yet done this.

It seems, then, that although the concept of levels is a dangerous one, and we rightly look upon it with suspicion, it does not necessarily lead to an elitist view. And we can surely accept this conclusion when we look over the various fields dealt with in this book, and see how in every field there is a general opposition to hierarchical social relationships. However, there is yet one more challenge we have to meet.

HUMANISTIC PSYCHOLOGY AND THE SOCIAL CONSTRUCTION OF REALITY

There is a question which humanistic psychology has to answer. It has to do with the challenge of social constructivism, social constructionism, deconstruction and postmodernism. Its most acute point, it seems to me, is at the question of the self. All of these challenges say in their different ways that there is no 'real self' in the sense usually proposed by humanistic psychologists. Therefore there is no such thing as being authentic (true to oneself) or autonomous (taking charge of one's life) or self-actualization (being all that one has it in oneself to be). If this is true, then humanistic psychology is obsolete, overtaken by a postmodern wave which has passed it by. It is incumbent on those of us who call ourselves humanistic psychologists to answer this challenge.

The basic case of social constructionism, as described for example by Kenneth Gergen (1985), is that knowledge, scientific or otherwise, is not obtained by objective means but is constructed through social discourse. Hence the study of dialogue and discourse and text become extremely important. No single point of view is more universally valid than another, because all points of view are embedded in a social context which give them meaning. 'Such a view does not obliterate empirical science; it simply removes its privilege of claiming truth beyond community' (Gergen 1997, p. 729). However, within this general outlook there are a number of important differences.

The first step seems to be to outline the various approaches within this field, and to see what they are actually saying, and whether they are all saying the same thing. Scott Greer (1997) suggests that we should distinguish between constructionists and constructivists. The constructionists (like Kenneth Gergen and John Shotter) advocate a more anti-realist and anti-foundationalist position, while the constructivists (like Rom Harré, James Averill and Donald Polkinghorne) believe that while knowledge is to a large extent a social artefact, there is still a 'reality' beneath, behind and between our discourse about it. Greer makes the point that Nietzsche was one of the first people to take up a social constructionist point of view:

> That the value of the world lies in our interpretation; . . . that every elevation of man brings with it the overcoming of narrower interpretations; that every strengthening and increase of power opens up new perspectives and means believing in new horizons – this idea

218

permeates my writings. The world with which we are concerned is false, i.e., is not fact but fable and approximation on the basis of a meagre sum of observations; it is 'in flux', as something in a state of becoming, as a falsehood always changing but never getting near the truth: for – there is no 'truth'.

(Nietzsche 1967/1901, sec 616)

This is a radical and starkly stated position, which is strikingly similar to the current issues within the social constructionist critique.

Kurt Danziger (1997), on the other hand, makes a distinction between light constructionism and dark constructionism. Light constructionism says that 'among those points of view which do not claim a monopoly on the path to the truth, which do not prejudge the nature of reality, tolerance must be the order of the day. A thousand flowers may bloom, provided none of them is of a type that threatens to take over the entire field, if left unchecked' (Danziger 1997, p. 410). Dark constructionism (often referring to Foucault) says that discourse is embedded in relations of power. Talk and text are inseparable from manifestations of power. While light constructionists such as John Shotter emphasize the ongoing construction of meaning in present dialogue, dark constructionists emphasize the dependence of current patterns of interaction on rigid power structures established in the past and protected from change by countless institutionalized practices and textual conventions.

Art Warmoth (personal communication, 1997) says 'The fact that power relations are an aspect of communication (social discourse) should not surprise humanistic psychologists, especially those familiar with Gregory Bateson's work. But we should be alert to tendencies to stereotype or rigidify categories such as class and gender structures.' There is a delicate line to tread here, because the humanistic approach is like the constructionist approach in having a liberatory tendency: in this respect we are on the same side, so to speak, in relation to the forces of mechanistic thinking. And the feminist critique of gender certainties is part of this effort for both parties, as has recently been made very clear by Leslie Miller (2000) in her discussion of discourse analysis and feminism.

Cor Baerveldt and Paul Voestermans (1996) make a distinction betweeen weak social constructionism, which says that there can be such a thing as natural emotional responses (although they can become connected with a sense of self only within the context of a cultural system of beliefs and values), and strong social constructionism, which denies the relevance of physiological processes altogether. 'From this perspective, the states and functions of the body become a cluster of cultural instead of natural, that is, biological constructions' (Baerveldt and Voestermans 1996, p. 695). It must be remembered, however, that this is not positing physiology and culture as polar opposites: it is merely saying that physiology is not to be taken for granted as foundational. Alvin Mahrer (1989) makes exactly the same assertion from a humanistic point of view.

Perhaps the most radical form of social constructionism is that put forward by Paul Stenner and Christopher Eccleston, when they say that the more the distinction between the real and the discursive is examined, the more it becomes obvious that it is precisely the meaning something has for people and what it matters to anyone (both discursive questions) that constitute its reality. So their approach, which they call Textuality, sees the usual objects of psychological inquiry as so many texts which we read and discuss as opposed to fixed entities or essences which we strive to know.

> Another way of putting this is that Textuality serves to worry or trouble the commonly held dichotomy between subject and object or knower and known. For us, neither subject nor object is accorded the status of already existing fact or pre-given essence. Rather, both are viewed as socially constructed: as continually (re)produced in discursive (and other) practices in the course of social activities.
>
> (Stenner and Eccleston 1994, p. 89)

This enables them to question in a radical way the importance and even the existence of such things as attitudes, emotions, memory, personality, prejudice and thought. 'It is a deconstructive strategy which serves to dissolve the very "thingness" of the entity by drawing attention to the discursive work necessary to constitute and uphold the impression of "thinghood"' (Stenner and Eccleston 1994, p. 94). This vision of contexts within contexts within contexts is a difficult one to get hold of, and these authors are careful to distinguish themselves from various misdescriptions and misunderstandings which have been imputed to such a position.

It does seem clear, however, that they are strong and dark constructionists in the senses described earlier.

> We encourage a social constructionism whereby people are viewed as readers and writers (written upon and read) within the Textuality of culture. People (and this includes people who are psychologists or social scientists) actively construct (and are actively constructed by) versions of the 'way things are', versions which are always-already enmeshed with the moral, political and ideological concerns of Being.
>
> (Stenner and Ecclestone 1994, p. 96)

So in the end they settle not for a critical realism, but for a critical poly-textualism.

There is of course a danger in all this of paying insufficient attention to the ground on which the social constructionists themselves are standing.

And in recent times they have started to question this themselves. A rather long quote from Kenneth Gergen, one of the classic pioneers of this approach, makes the point very well:

> While constructionist critiques may often appear nihilistic, there is no means by which they themselves can be grounded or legitimated. They too fall victim to their own modes of critique; their accounts are inevitably freighted with ethical and ideological implications, forged within the conventions of writing, designed for rhetorical advantage, and their 'objects of criticism' constructed in and for a particular community. The objects of their criticism are no less constructed than the traditional objects of research, nor do their moral claims rest on transcendental foundations.
>
> (Gergen 1997, p. 739)

This seems an appropriately humble statement, and it shows us how the social constructionists are capable of taking their own medicine. This is the kind of reflexivity which humanistic writers have often championed.

This kind of critique, it seems to me, is very effective in undermining and even sometimes demolishing our taken-for-granted assumptions. But does it undermine or demolish any idea of a real self? At first it seems that it must. Is not the truth of the real self just the sort of truth which social constructionism is here to destroy?

But there seem to be at least four lines of thought which can lead in different ways to the reinstatement of the real self. The first of these, and the most obvious, is simply to put the real self into quotes. Then we could say that the 'real self' is simply the way the self appears in certain contexts, and that humanistic discourse favours this way of talking. This would enable us to continue to use the term 'real self' with the approval of social constructionists. However, this usage might not be acceptable to many of those within humanistic psychology, because it is difficult to think of oneself as something in quotes.

The second position we could take up is to say that the real self is real only in a particular context. If we participate in the humanistic psychology language community, we can very easily talk about the real self, because it makes sense in terms of other constructs like self-actualization, authenticity and autonomy, all of which form part of that field of discourse. We would not be claiming universal or exclusive validity for that field, but simply saying that it was as legitimate as any other. This would be taking very much the Wilber (1997) line that what we have is a series of nested truths, none of which can stand alone, each of which depends on others. We would be arguing that the real self was a text in a context, and in that sense valid and meaningful. We could also say that the Centaur self is precisely a situated self, well defined for its purpose and not applicable outside its own context.

A third line to take would be to say that the real self is not a theoretical construct. In fact, as we can see quite easily in issue after issue of the *Journal of Humanistic Psychology*, no one has ever come up with a good theoretical description or empirical investigation of the real self. I suggest that this is because the real self is not a concept but an experience. When we have a breakthrough into what Ken Wilber (1995) calls the Centaur stage of psychospiritual development, we have an experience which we in humanistic psychology have named as an experience of the real self. While we are having that experience, which is usually for only a brief period at first, though it may well extend over time, we are authentic. We relate to others in an authentic way; we own our bodies in a new way; other people experience us as clear and direct and truthful. It is basically an ecstatic experience, and I believe it is a mystical experience, although on the foot-hills of mysticism, rather than on the great heights. After it, we are more likely to say that we *own* our experience in a new way.

Like all mystical experiences, it is ineffable. That is, it goes beyond the categories of our ordinary discourse. It can only be described in paradox, or in poetry. If we try to bring it down into everyday discourse, the language of the Mental Ego (the previous and much more familiar psychospiritual stage of development), we can only distort and misrepresent it. From this third point of view, we would want to say that social constructionism in all its forms is firmly located at this Mental Ego level. It glories in reducing all forms of experience to some form of conversation. It relies totally on language (hence the emphasis on the text) and regards anything which cannot be put into language as not really existing at all. Just as the positivists (arch enemies of the constructionists) used to say that anything which could not be empirically tested was excluded from the field of science, and therefore beyond the pale, just so the constructionists say now that anything which cannot be part of a form of discourse is excluded from their consideration, and therefore beyond the pale. So if mystical experiences cannot be forms of discourse, and if contacting the real self is a mystical experience, the real self is beyond the pale so far as they are concerned.

Of these three positions, it is the third which puts us in the greatest difficulty with academia. Academia mistrusts and hates anything which cannot be put in a book. Whether positivist or constructionist, academics continually try to put beyond the pale anything which is experiential. That is why psychotherapy courses have such a hard time persuading academics that such things as experiential training groups, personal therapy or supervision belong at all in their field. They are hard to assess, hard to describe, hard to evaluate. They are potentially messy and hard to control. And so we have the spectacle of academic courses in psychotherapy and counselling which include no practice at all. There are some of these now and I predict that there will be more in the future. In a group, in one's own therapy and even in supervision one may have a breakthrough: one may have a mystical experience – even one which may change one's life. This is not controllable: and if there is one thing which academics are about it is control. It doesn't matter whether they are old nasty positivists or new shiny constructionists, they are all about control. Nietzsche would have laughed.

The fourth position we could take up is to say that behind and beneath the constructivist positions we have been looking at there is a more fundamental issue – that of dialectical thinking. We have been arguing all through these pages that the humanistic position is the Centaur position, and that Centaur thinking is vision-logic, dialectical logic. If we think dialectically, it is clear that we have all the time been saying something paradoxical. If we say that we believe in subpersonalities, and also believe in a real self, this is a huge contradiction. Where is the truth?

The truth, as Hegel used to say, is the whole. It is only when we can say everything at once that we can say 'This is the truth!' But since we cannot say everything at once, we must agree with the constructivists and the discourse analysts and the Lacanians and so forth that we have no basis, we have no foundation.

What we also do not have, and what the constructivists do unfortunately have, is a belief in the 'either-or'. They ignore the warning of Mary Parker Follett (a closet Hegelian): 'Never let yourself be bullied by an either-or'. They ignore the magnificent words of Hegel himself: 'It is the fashion of youth to dash about in abstractions: but the man who has learnt to know life steers clear of the abstract "either-or" and keeps to the concrete' (Hegel 1892, p. 146). Constructivists have a bad habit of making an excellent case for the primacy of discourse, and then letting themselves down by denying the importance of realism. It is an immensely valuable exercise to see through the pretensions of foundationalists, and to emphasize the importance of sheer human discourse; it is not a valuable exercise to then say that that is all there is. If there were nothing but discourse there could be no foetal experience, there could be no birth trauma, there could be no memories of anything before language, there could be no poets creating new words and new languages, there could be no out-of-body experience, no near-death experiences, no mystical experiences going beyond language. The mad effort to redefine all these things as forms of discourse is reminiscent of paranoid thinking, which sees the same conspiracy everywhere.

The either-or is a madness. It is closely connected to the idea of being right, which is one of the most dangerous positions in the world, and one which the constructivists explicitly reject. If we maintain our dialectical thinking, we do not have to slip into this dangerous mode. We can hold to the 'both-and'.

I am not sure that there is any great contradiction between the four positions I have outlined. I have some respect myself for all of them. And I have some respect for my real self.

223

14

DIRECTIONS FOR SOCIETY

And so we come to the social scene. What does humanistic psychology have to say about that? Again it seems important to be personal here. This is not just an abstract question. One of the main discoveries I made is that there are three approaches to politics: one is to develop the best possible intellectual case, so that you can be more correct than anyone else; one is to be so militant and so activist that you never cease from some kind of action or other; the third is to see politics as about feelings and the way you live. It is the third kind of politics which seems to be closest to what humanistic psychology has to say. And when I get in touch with my feelings, what do I find?

When I look at most of what goes on in psychotherapy I get frustrated. When I look at the relations between men and women I get frustrated. When I look at the relations between straight and gay people, I get frustrated. When I look at what goes on in our offices and factories I get angry. When I see what happens in our schools I get angry. I have tried in this book to be positive rather than negative; to say what can be done, and what has been achieved, rather than dwell on the worst aspects of what is. But really I agree with Michael Glenn (1971) where he says:

> Therapy is change, not adjustment. This means change social, personal and political. When people are fucked over, people should help them fight it, and then deal with their feelings. A 'struggle for mental health' is bullshit unless it involves changing this society which turns us into machines, alienates us from one another and our work, and binds us into racist, sexist and imperialist practices.

And it is in and through the growth movement that I have come to see the world this way. It is with a taste of liberation, a touch of some new sensibility, that what I see around me turns into something unsatisfactory.

I see a society which compels the vast majority of the population to get a living in boring and badly-organized jobs; which conducts its booming or failing business on the back of ghettos, slums and internal and external

224

colonialism; which is infested with violence and repression while demanding obedience and compliance from the victims of violence and repression; which uses its vast resources for waste, destruction and an ever more methodical creation of conformist needs and satisfactions; which systematically puts children down under the guise of educating them; which turns women into drudges and men into image defenders; which condemns marijuana and Ecstasy while swimming in a bath of alcohol and cigarettes; which does not care about the environment, does not care about pollution, does not care . . .

The courts are not all right, the police are not all right, the local councils are not all right, the mental hospitals are not all right, the nuclear family is not all right, the universities are not all right, the medical profession is not all right, the way handicapped children are treated is not all right, the newspapers are not all right, IQ tests are not all right, what happens to the homeless is not all right; nuclear power is not all right; international diplomacy is not all right.

Even language is not all right. Somehow those who want things to stay as they are have captured the language itself (Miller and Swift 1979, Spender 1980, Cameron 1985). We find ourselves using their categories, fighting on their ground, talking in their terms, copying their style. I have tried to write this book directly, without jargon and without hiding what I meant under a hail of words – and of course I have failed. The horror and the twisting and the distortion are not just out there – they are right here, in me. I have written about the pain of awareness – well, this is it, this is what it feels like.

If, in spite of all this, it is all going to come out all right, we need to be really strong, and not let it overcome us. Luckily we don't get the awareness without the strength, they come together, in the same package. As Joanna Macy (1983) tells us, the only worthwhile hope comes up out of despair. In her workshops I learned just how this works. And they enabled me to see that not only must we not give up, we mustn't get desperate about the pathways of change. The absurd situation is that the established democracy still provides the only legitimate framework for change and must therefore be defended against all attempts to restrict this framework – but at the same time, preservation of the established democracy preserves the status quo and the containment of change. There are no one-way, open-and-shut answers. All we know is that we have to struggle with love as well as opposition in our hearts. If we just have the love (as some of the New Age people suggest), the old ways continue their disgusting course, only touched with a certain glow, like phosphorescence; if we just have the struggle (as some of the political groups suggest), we soon become wooden soldiers fit for nothing but being pushed around by some leader. It is about love and struggle.

There is a very important misunderstanding here. New Age people often say that by paying attention to some evil we give it energy, we somehow

225

feed it. But it was the people who ignored the Nazis who allowed the death camps and the pogroms to continue. It is not enough not to give energy to some social evil – we sometimes have to question it, to raise awareness about it and if necessary to fight it.

Once we see the way we treat our bodies as political, the food we eat as political, the raising of children as political, the way we look at people sexually as political, we cannot rise above or turn away from the challenges which face us day by day and hour by hour.

The ideology of consumerism and globalization is so hostile to everything we stand for that we cannot just stand back and see it rise and rise without any comment and without any response. We have to care for our fellow human beings who are alienated and deprived: material deprivation is common enough, but emotional and imaginative deprivation is important too. When I notice these things, I find it hard to keep calm.

That is where I have to start from. But although anger is a good starting point, it is not much good as a guide to what to do. In trying to spell out the implications of this, I want to say that there have been three phases in the way humanistic writers have spoken about society. In the first phase humanistic writers talked mainly about humanity as a whole; while in the second phase there has been more awareness of the depth of the patriarchal split which has divided women from men. And in the third phase we are still learning how to take up a more integral attitude to politics.

PHASE ONE: THE UNIVERSAL APPROACH

One of the best writers in this area is Christian Bay, who has written a number of pieces, the best known of which is the book *The Structure of Freedom* (1968). He was a political scientist, and wrote:

> I am convinced that our profession will never help us advance from our wasteful, cruel pluralist pseudopolitics in the direction of justice and human politics until we replace political systems with concepts of human need and human development as the ultimate value framework for our political analysis.
>
> (Bay 1967)

He made an important distinction between politics, which is all about the power to satisfy real needs, and pseudopolitics, which is all about satisfying the vocal demands of pressure groups, no matter how narrow the interests being served. The crucial thing is not to obstruct human development: 'How can people construct a society so as to provide for maximum growth opportunities and satisfaction of their needs?' (Bay 1965). Bay argues that only a society in which people are positively encouraged to reach Maslow's self-actualization level (what we have been calling the Centaur level) can ever be truly free. People at this level actually have a capacity to cooperate voluntarily, and not to demand control. At this level social freedom is possible, because people can set up a structure which allows the necessary opportunities to act or refrain from acting as they desire. (See also Bay 1971.)

Another writer who has written along these lines is David Wright, a sociologist much influenced by the research of Jane Loevinger (1976) on ego development. Her well researched and empirically grounded work ties in, in a remarkably strong and apt way, with the more speculative work of Maslow. In particular, the final stage which she calls *Integrated* fits in very well with Maslow's (1987) self-actualization level. Wright says of people at this level that they are autonomous and genuinely individual:

> Yet 'autonomy' and 'individuality' should not be mistaken for 'individualism'. There is a social context to their independence that is implied by their principles. By taking everyone's perspective into account in any particular situation, they are explicitly 'other-oriented' (though not 'other-directed') and view their selves within a larger context of mutual interdependence. Moreover, these people have a deep feeling of identification, sympathy and affection for human beings in general and they view their selves and others as part of a common humanity.
>
> (Wright 1973)

Wright makes an important distinction between indoctrinated control and voluntary cooperation as a basis for social order, and argues that the former comes essentially from the middle levels of development, and holds people back at those levels.

> Thus, to emphasise the contrast, one basis views meaning and action as derivative from the social order; the other sees the order itself as derivative from the people's meaning and action. One postulates the society's creation and control of members; the other postulates the people's creation and control of their society.
>
> (Wright 1974)

In a major effort at theory-building, Wright uses Maslow's ideas to build a synthesis between the conflict perspective of people like Marx and Dahrendorf and the equilibrium perspective of people like Parsons and Smelser. He points to the necessity for social transformation involved in taking Maslow's ideas seriously:

In sum, we have presented support for the view that people located at stage 6 and the self-actualized need-level [or the Centaur] tend to actively respond to situations of perceived injustice. Thus, people at earlier need-levels will struggle to become self-actualizing and, once there, will tend to act on their universal moral principles. As a result, change is ubiquitous and continuous, no matter where people are located on the need-hierarchy.

(Wright 1973)

Wright therefore argues that it is worth contending for a society where this happens more readily – a society where the positive nature of human needs is better recognized. Charles Hampden-Turner (1971) is excellent on the whole process of psychosocial development and its problems, and what Wright is saying here chimes in well with the position taken up by Hampden-Turner.

A third writer who has spoken of these things is Walt Anderson. He again speaks of the higher levels of human development, and of what happens when the social scientist reaches those levels:

Scientists will no longer think of themselves as detached from nature, as disembodied intellects in the sense Hannah Arendt (1958) meant when she described the rise of modern science as the point, the place to stand outside the world. Rather, they will understand and feel that they are a part – the conscious, deciding and responsible part – of the very evolutionary process they study.

(Anderson 1973)

So he, too, comes out in favour of a society where more people are encouraged and allowed to reach the higher levels of development – Maslow's self-actualization, Loevinger's integrated state, Kohlberg's level of conscience and principle – and he sees this as definitely possible:

I believe that the drive toward self-actualization is, as Maslow insisted, species-wide and not peculiar to any race, culture or sex. The predominance of white males among the historical figures considered to be examples of self-actualized people is not so much a flaw in Maslow's research as evidence of the inadequacy of a society which offers such a narrow spectrum of its members the opportunity to reach their fullest development as 'human beings'. I would argue, therefore, that the middle-class bias is relatively superficial, and that humanistic psychology is in fact a compre-hensive set of ideas relevant to the needs of all people.

(Anderson 1973)

It is this sense of important possibilities being ignored which runs through all the arguments we have been looking at here. Society as organized at present has little notion of human development in the Maslow sense, and holds people back to the levels at which they can play fixed and predictable roles most efficiently.

> When we look at politics this way we naturally turn our attention to the things which obstruct human development. And I believe that the most important single limiting factor is the idea that any society has about what the possibilities of human development actually are. A stunted or narrow conception of the human potential, especially when deeply built into cultural norms and reinforced by a society's art and science and philosophy, is as narrow a form of tyranny as any political institution.
>
> (Anderson 1973)

Another implication of all this is that the person-centred society would be decentralized. We have seen that in organizations it has been found best to place the decisions as near as possible to the place where the knowledge to make those decisions first becomes available. The same applies in society generally. It is bad for a larger and higher organization to arrogate to itself functions which can be performed efficiently by smaller and lower bodies. There is work to be done at every level, and the responsibility for what can be done at lower levels must not be allowed to gravitate to the top. The general principle of autonomization applies all the way through.

In a later book, Anderson (1983) carried on the theme of decentralization, and many of the contributors to this book had much to say on how we have to go beyond liberalism. This means that each citizen can and should have the experience of genuine participation, which means having a direct say in the relevant political decisions. There is a spirited discussion of this whole area in Hampden-Turner (1983). The desire for this kind of participation comes both from greater opportunities, and also from the feeling of being competent. As Brewster Smith (1974) says:

> the motivational core of competence is a cluster of attitudes toward the self as potent, efficacious, and worthy of being taken seriously by self and others. Such a cluster of attitudes sets a kind of self-fulfilling prophecy in operation. In the favourable case, the individual has the confidence to seize upon opportunities as they present themselves. He tries. He therefore acquires the knowledge and skills that make success more probable – which in turn lend warrant to his sense of efficacy.

229

Such a society would be likely to be high in synergy, since there would be no need to see everyone else as competitive for limited goods. The power of imagination would be released to solve problems creatively. Don Beck and Christopher Cowan (1996) have been arguing similar points more recently.

Thus this scenario has a gradual movement towards a different state of society, along the lines outlined by Charles Reich (1972) in his popular book. Instead of Consciousness I (go-getting individualism) or Consciousness II (conformity, the organization man and the domination of technique) we have Consciousness III (person-centred). A similar view has been put in different terms by Capra (1983) and by Ferguson (1982). Or as Maslow (1973) puts it: 'The movement toward psychological health is also the movement towards spiritual peace and social harmony.' If only it were as simple as that.

PHASE TWO: QUESTIONING PATRIARCHY

All this sounds perfectly plausible, but there is something still missing from it. And what is missing is any real appreciation of the feminist critique. Feminism has raised the issue that in our present society women are put down and all that is female is downgraded. In a future humanistic society, they say, that could easily continue. Just because so many men in the field of humanistic psychology have developed their feminine characteristics to some extent, and have to that degree stopped downgrading the female inside themselves at least, that does not mean that they will stop oppressing women. It often means that they do it better, more efficiently. In a typical centre for training people in the caring professions, 80 per cent of the participants will be women, but 80 per cent of the leaders will probably be men.

So if we are to do better than this, if we are to enable some kind of non-oppressive society to dawn, we have to understand something about patriarchal consciousness and how it works to the detriment of both women and men – not to mention children, animals and nature.

The diagram in Figure 14.1, taken from Gray (1982), shows the basic structure of patriarchy. It exposes, with pitiless clarity, the simple nature of the oppressive structure. All other oppressive relations are based upon this model. This comes first. And once we see the world exposed in this way, it enables us to connect the political with the personal, it even applies to the conscious and the unconscious mind, it includes the material and the spiritual. 'Patriarchy is a society which worships the masculine identity, granting power and privilege to those who reflect and respect the socially-determined masculine sex role' (Warnock 1982, p. 23). But patriarchy is a historical structure, which came into being and can go out of being, and has internal dynamics which are changing it. It is nothing to do with biological determinism, as some critics suggest. It is about socially/historically defined gender, not about biological sex.

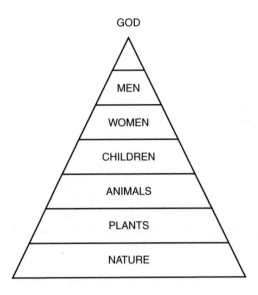

Figure 14.1 Patriarchy

It was feminism which allowed us to see that all the struggles against oppression are one struggle, the same struggle, the struggle with patriarchy. And this includes the struggles for children's rights, animal rights and the concern for ecology against the exploitation of nature. It is very important that the black struggle and the lesbian and gay struggle are one with the women's struggle. A member of the National Black Feminist Organization said:

> We are often asked the ugly question, 'Where are your loyalties? To the Black movement or the feminist movement?' Well, it would be nice if we were oppressed as women Monday through Thursday, then oppressed as Blacks the rest of the week. We could combat one or the other on those days – but we have to fight both every day of the week.
>
> (Quoted in Dunayevskaya 1982)

I have argued at length elsewhere (Rowan 1997) that questioning patriarchal consciousness is just as important for men as it is for women, blacks, lesbians or gay people. Men lose a great deal under patriarchy, and would gain a great deal from a non-patriarchal society. It is in the interest of men to work for change in this area (Connell 1987). But it is harder for men to change than it is for women, because at a conscious level they often seem to gain from patriarchal power (Reynaud 1983), at an unconscious level they are at the mercy of their conditioning (Metcalf and Humphries 1985), and at a spiritual level they have no notion of the Goddess (Starhawk 1989). So men often have to work at all three of these levels in order to change their internal responses to women and to power in the world. And unless they are willing to do some of this work, they are going to stand in the way of the oppressed groups who need change much more urgently.

Women have already seen a lot of this, and particularly, it seems, those women who have made links with ecological issues, peace issues and the issues around the development of a new spirituality. Hazel Henderson (1982) has made an acute economic analysis showing that we have to keep all the connections in mind if we are to think reasonably about society. It is not enough to talk about decentralization – some very dubious politicians can talk about decentralization too, in their own way – we have to keep in touch with all the relevant factors, and listen to the voices from below. And this means listening to nature. Henderson (1982) says about this, after discussing the basic economic realities:

> The planet, Gaia, and the universe are now teaching us humans directly, nudging us along in the direction we must change, reconnecting us with the most fundamental living force, the urge to become all we can be, to evolve and to love it. We have this optimal program encoded in the proteins of our DNA. We know how to be healthy, how to co-operate as well as compete. These are older, deeper programs than our cultural programming. We are learning to tune back into them and to Nature, our surest teacher.

This speaks of a kind of eco-feminism which goes beyond the male eco-philosophy which preceded it. It speaks of what Wright (1982) calls moon-power. See also many of the contributions in Spretnak (1982), and the special issue of *The Humanistic Psychologist* (1998, *26*, Nos 1–3) devoted to ecopsychology.

POWER AND CHANGE

All this, of course, makes us ask the question 'What do we do about it?' How are we to take power to change the patriarchal system? And how are we to use it? Zaltman (1973) has given us seven types of power; Hersey et al. (1979) give us seven bases of power; combining the two gives us these nine forms of power:

1   Physical force; coercive power. This is a form of power which can produce compliance. It is seldom any use for any length of time, unless accompanied by one of the other forms of power.

2 Connection power. Based on connections with influential or important people. Induces compliance from others because they try to gain favour or avoid disfavour of the powerful connection.

3 Rewards and punishments; reward power. Another form of coercion, where the stick and the carrot are used to ensure compliance. Not very effective unless accompanied by fear on the part of those on the receiving end.

4 Manipulative. Behaviour is influenced rather than ideas. Rewards and punishments may be used as in behaviour modification. All sorts of Machiavellian tactics, including cue control. Many examples in the book by Varela (1971).

5 Normative-legitimate; legitimate power. Norms, rules and values are referred to in using and maintaining power. The strength of this will of course be strongly related to the strength of the relevant norms, etc.

6 Expert power. Based on possession of expertise, skill and knowledge. The expertise to facilitate the work behaviour of others. This leads to compliance with the leader's wishes.

7 Charisma; referent power. A non-coercive form of power which relies on identification as the psychological mechanism for ensuring the correct behaviour. People will go along as long as they feel drawn to the leader.

8 Rational-persuasive; information power. Use of relevant information to persuade and influence, such data being related to the subject in hand rather than the person to be influenced.

9 Synergy. Growth-oriented power, obtained through facilitation of the needs and interests of others, as in organization development, individual therapy or experiential learning, or community development. This is the one which is often called power-with, as opposed to power-over, and it is compatible with what Starhawk (1982) talks about as power-from-within. Can be creative.

These categories can of course overlap, or be mixed. But they make quite a useful list of what is available. The question now is which of these can be used in dealing with the problem of patriarchy? And as soon as we ask the question it must be evident that many of these forms of power actually reinforce patriarchy, or take it for granted. If we want to question patriarchy, we must question some of the ways of attacking it. Types 1, 2, 3 and 4 seem very difficult to use without setting up the very social relations which we want them to overthrow. Types 5, 6, 7 and 8 are also rather dubious, though much will depend on the actual content of the norms, etc. If the norms or values are deficiency-motivated, they are likely to be helpful to patriarchy, while if they are abundance-motivated (see Chapter 15), they are likely to be incompatible with patriarchy.

But the type of power which is most useful for dealing with patriarchy is obviously synergy, since this is all about power with people, rather than power over people. And one of the most distinctive and characteristic features of patriarchy is that it is dedicated to, and depends upon, the notion that power is always over people.

However, synergy is by no means an infallible password, any more than is decentralization. For example, I find Peter Russell's (1982) discussion of synergy to be far too blue-sky and over-optimistic in the New Age manner. I think we have to keep our feet on the ground with synergy as with everything else.

With this in mind, let us look at the acute analysis of social action developed by Philip Kotler (1973) where he makes some very important distinctions. He suggests that there are five main elements:

1   Cause. A social objective or undertaking that change agents believe will provide some answer to a social problem.
2   Change agency. An organization whose primary mission is to advance a social cause.
3   Change targets. Individuals, groups or institutions designated as targets of change efforts.
4   Channels. Ways in which influence and response can be transmitted between change agents and change targets.
5   Change strategy. A basic mode of influence adopted by the change agent to affect the change target.

Now what is the cause here? It is tempting to see it as the overthrow of patriarchy, but it seems more modest and more appropriate to see it as the questioning of patriarchy, so that at least it is not taken for granted and hidden or mystified. Another point worth clarifying is that when we question patriarchy, it is not because we want to put matriarchy in its place – it is the whole system of domination of one set of people by another set that we are questioning, and not the substitution of one set of dominators by another. Riane Eisler (1987) has been very clear about this.

Kotler suggests that there are three basic types of cause; helping causes, which seek to help the victims of a social problem; protest causes, which seek to discipline the institutions contributing to it; and revolutionary causes, which seek to eliminate the institutions contributing to it. The cause of questioning patriarchy seems to contain elements of all three: there do need to be answers for individual victims; the contributing institutions do need to be disciplined; and ultimately we do want to eliminate patriarchy. This being so, it seems that more than one change agency might have to be involved. This is a problem which extends from the family to the whole industrial system.

And there is one extra difficulty which does not apply to most other social problems: in questioning patriarchy we are questioning something which is built into the nuclear family, and therefore built into the growing psyche of each child in our culture. Juliet Mitchell (1974) has spelt out the extraordinary way in which patriarchy has entered into our language and our thinking at deep unconscious levels. John Southgate (Southgate and Randall 1989) has suggested that it makes sense to talk in terms of a Patripsych – an internal structure which exists inside all of us and which is easily hooked by authority figures, producing exaggerated reactions of one kind and another. If anything like this is true, it means that we have not only to contend with the patriarchal structures in our society, of which social class is one of the most important; but also the Patripsych inside us. This thought has also been taken up by a group of radical psychiatrists in the United States, of whom the best known is Claude Steiner. One of them, Hogie Wyckoff, (1975) has written:

> In women's groups, women can become familiar with what insidiously keeps them down – not only the obvious, overt male supremacy . . . but also oppression which has been internalized, which turns women against themselves, causing them to be their own worst enemies rather than their own loving best friend. This internalized oppression I have called the Pig Parent. It is the incorporation of all the values which keep women subordinate . . .

This is not unlike the self-denigration of minority groups, which has often been investigated. But Wyckoff and her group have been working on ways of breaking down these patterns in individual people.

So we must be concerned with the dancers as well as the dance. A system as all-embracing as patriarchy has to be dealt with on many levels at the same time – no one approach is likely to be adequate on its own. This again suggests rather strongly that more than one change agency will be required to deal with the problem.

It is enough to think of a few of the contenders in various parts of this field to see at once that not only are the various efforts very uncoordinated (for some excellent comments on this problem see Rowbotham et al. 1979), but that also there are patriarchal elements still surviving within many of them. Probably the most consistent one, in avoiding all kinds of relapse into patriarchy, is the women's movement.

And within the women's movement we find the kind of eco-feminism which is very close to the vision of humanistic psychology, deeply concerned with the integration of all the forces in nature and society. As Kornegger (1975) says so well:

> Together we are working to expand our empathy and understanding of other living things and to identify with those entities outside of ourselves, rather than objectifying and manipulating them. At this point, a respect for all life is a prerequisite for our very survival.

Radical feminist theory also criticises male hierarchical thought patterns – in which rationality dominates sensuality, mind dominates intuition, and persistent splits and polarities (active/ passive, child/adult, sane/insane, work/play, spontaneity/organiza- tion) alienate us from the mind-body experience as a whole and from the continuum of human experience. Women are attempting to get rid of these splits, to live in harmony with the universe as whole, integrated humans dedicated to the collective healing of our individual wounds and schisms.

This is very much the voice with which we have been familiar all through this examination.

Coming back to our question, then, what kind of change agency would be suitable for carrying on the struggle to question patriarchy? It seems that it must probably be an organization dominated by women, or at least the kind of vision which women have particularly been responsible for developing, and that it must be organized in such a way as not to set up all over again the social relations of patriarchy. There is a very good discussion of all this, with many practical hints, in Coover et al. (1978). We saw earlier that organizations did not have to be hierarchies, so it is by no means impossible for such an organization to exist. But the men in such an organization would have to have been through the men's movement, or something like that, in order to be able to work in such a set-up.

The men's movement is something I have tried to describe elsewhere (Rowan 1987). A good summary of many of the issues involved is to be found in the book by Kenneth Clatterbaugh (1990). It arose mainly as a result of the women's movement making it clear to men that their behav- iour was not acceptable in certain ways. After a number of one-to-one struggles within couple relationships, men began talking and finding that they had things in common. Their eyes had been opened to things about themselves which they did not know before. And so they started meeting to try and work things out, and see how they really felt about themselves. These meetings were often very tense, because the men felt pressured into self-examination, and defensive about many things. The meetings were often unsatisfying because of this defensiveness, usually manifesting itself in a persistent tendency to go off into theoretical diatribes or compulsive activity rather than real attempts to get in touch with feelings and to critique daily actions. But imperfect as they were, and are, these meetings are seemingly the best way for men to find out at least something about how they are affected by the social relations of patriarchy, both internal and external. The magazine *Achilles Heel* deals with these matters, and so does the international IASOM Newsletter.

However, if these groups are to be effective, as I have argued at greater length elsewhere (Rowan 1997), they have to work on three levels. On the

236

first level, they have to enable the participants to examine their current consciousness and actions. This is the basic consciousness-raising function which can work very well in enabling men to change their assumptions as to what is proper masculine behaviour, and to enable them to relate much better to other men. A new psychology of men is developing (see Levant and Pollack 1995) and this may be a hopeful sign.

On the second level, they have to enable the participants to go into the unconscious determinants of their actions. This is more difficult, and requires a commitment to some form of personal growth work. Only in this way can men really get down to their mother stuff, their father stuff and all that material which unconsciously prejudices them against women and all that is female. (Many ways of doing this are outlined in the earlier part of this book.) At the same time this process enables them to come to terms with the feminine within themselves, and this is also a useful and perhaps necessary step. There is a poetic side to this, which has been movingly contributed to by Michael Meade (1993).

On the third level, they have to enable the participants to come to terms with female power. The only way I know for this to happen is that we find out about the Great Goddess and the Horned God, and to understand something about paganism. The reason why this is so necessary is because there are very few images of female power in our present society, and we need to go back and pick them up if we are to believe in them (Noble 1991). Unless men genuinely believe that there is such a thing as female power, and accept it as good, they will never hand over their male power.

It is for this reason that I do not really believe that there are any other ways for men to pick up this kind of thing. Those who have been through the 'hippie thing' often picked up something of it, though not at all reliably; those who have been through encounter groups or co-counselling, have often discovered some of the same things, though again not reliably; those who have mixed a good deal with feminists have often changed quite substantially as a result. But none of these things is on a mass scale.

It seems, therefore, that the change agency for questioning patriarchy on any large scale is going to be rare and hard to find. Perhaps the nearest thing to it is the Green movement. But as we have been seeing, work has to be done at many different levels, and it would not be right to leave everything to a political party, no matter how enlightened.

This means that we also have to consider change agencies which can challenge patriarchal attitudes and practices at the organizational level – what Kotler calls the 'protest' approach. This is obviously an easier, though never an easy, task. But it still entails having an organization which is not itself patriarchal, and aims at synergy. Coover et al. (1978) give many hints how this may be done.

237

Believing, then, in the importance of conflict and the possibility of integration, we can go out for what we want as individuals, as groups, as communities and even as members of social classes.

Out of this, then, what needs to be said is that the way of working through conflict and integration favoured by humanistic psychology works best with reasonably small units, which can be easily visualized and mentally grasped.

We have already seen that humanistic psychology can handle very well the conflicts between management and unions, black and white races, gender opponents, teachers and students and opposed interest groups in local communities. Why should it not be able to handle class conflicts too, so long as these are expressed in terms of genuine demands for real needs? In fact, this outlook should make class conflict more frequent and more productive, because of its emphasis on becoming aware of what is real for each person, instead of suppressing needs in favour of what is supposed to be felt.

So the humanistic view has been to say that there is only one way through: to become real, to learn to take a stand, to develop one's centre.

PHASE 3: AN INTEGRAL APPROACH

If we want to go beyond that, it seems that we have to adopt a more integral approach. What we mean by that is that it is not enough to have a vision of a better society (phase 1) or to have a real understanding of the prevalence of patriarchy (phase 2). We have to adopt an approach which does justice to the whole world we are living in, and use it to guide us into the most useful paths. The kind of thinking we need for this is the dialectical thinking we referred to earlier, the vision-logic which sees more widely and more finely.

If we adopt a planetary vision, and make sure that it is not a reductionist vision, we have to admit that we are still a long way short of doing it justice. But we can at least say something about it.

The first thing seems to be that we are envisaging a world movement into the Centaur phase of development. Just as the Industrial Revolution speeded up the adoption of the Mental Ego stage, so that it is very wide-spread today, in the same way new developments in all aspect of society are speeding up the next phase of development. Our sense of possibility has expanded enormously. And Ken Wilber (1996b) has argued that social evolution (chiming in with the ideas of Jean Gebser and Jürgen Habermas) is due to take another turn, this time from the Mental Ego into the Centaur. This book itself contains a multitude of hints as to what this might mean in practice.

It would mean moving into the dialectical thinking which comes so naturally to psychotherapists but not so easily to business people, academics or politicians. It would mean moving into the ways of thinking which Beck and Cowan (1996) describe as the Green, Yellow and Turquoise levels of action, moving into the second tier of social and political development. And with this would come a new attitude to morality, which has been spelt out very clearly and helpfully by John Kekes.

I have been struggling with postmodernism for some time now. Attracted by its opposition to the tyranny of the one big truth which is true for everybody at all times, and which therefore must become oppressive sooner or later. Repelled by its empty relativism, which has no point of purchase to say that anything is better than anything else, and therefore leaves us floundering. Now here comes a book (Kekes 1994) which gives me a way of avoiding the tyranny of the one big truth, and also the fragmentation of postmodernism.

It is a book of philosophy. It says that there are three basic attitudes to morality: monism (the one big truth or the one big ordering of truth); relativism (the proliferation of many little truths, each good in some area or other); and pluralism, where we allow for more than one truth, but want to know precisely how the various truths relate and make sense in relation to one another. I want to say that it is pluralism which comes most naturally to people within humanistic psychology.

Monism is so oppressive because it has just one answer to everything. My own position, on the other hand, is that questions are OK, answers are not. There is of course a paradox here – how can there be questions without answers? The way out of this is to see that there is nothing wrong with answers, plural – what is death is THE answer singular. When we have THE answer, we feel powerful. If knowledge is power, it comes most often in the form of answers. There is a twist which can make this even more dangerous. If we believe we have found the person or organization which has THE answer, we can devote ourselves to it. We can become a true believer. 'The less justified a man is in claiming excellence for his own self, the more ready is he to claim all excellence for his nation, his religion, his race or his holy cause' (Eric Hoffer 1952, p. 27). Hoffer's whole book is a warning against people who have found THE answer. When answers turn into certainties – then we all die. We have interposed a fact-proof screen between us and reality. As soon as you settle with a finality, you have ceased to live. This is exactly the position of pluralism, as outlined by Kekes, in relation to monism. But we also need to guard against relativism. How does Kekes pull this off?

He outlines six theses of pluralism. First there is the distinction between primary and secondary values. Primary values are universally human, and may be physiological, psychological or social. Secondary values vary with persons, societies, traditions and historical periods. Monists think that there must be one highest value, and that in cases of conflict this overriding value must settle the matter. Pluralists understand that all values are conditional.

The second thesis is that conflict between values is unavoidable. This is partly because some values are incompatible – that is, they cannot all be realized at the same time – and partly because values can be incommensurable. The basic idea of incommensurability is that there are some things so unlike as to exclude any reasonable comparison among them. 'Square roots and insults, smells and canasta, migrating birds and X-rays seem to exclude any common yardstick by which we could evaluate their respective merits or demerits' (Kekes 1994, p. 21). This is a good reason for rejecting monism, because monism has to assume that values may be incompatible, but can never be incommensurable.

The third thesis is that conflict-resolution is possible and desirable. Because we live in a shared culture, our conceptions of the good life or the importance of the traditional system of values to which we adhere will be wider and more general than the particular points in dispute. We can reflect on what would be best not only here and now but in the long run, given the values of our tradition or our conception of a good life. And Kekes points out that this not only refers to conflicts between people or groups of people, but also to conflicts within ourselves. We too can refer back to our more general conceptions of a good life or of our traditions. 'And this fact about us provides both a common ground on which we, who may be the factions of our divided selves, can agree to stand and a device for resolving our conflicts' (Kekes 1994, p. 25). I think it is a pity that Kekes has never read Mary Parker Follett (Graham 1995), who teaches us so much about the integration of different points of view in conflicts of all kinds. He never goes beyond balance and compromise, and appears not to see that integration – where both parties to a dispute get all that they really want – is a better possibility.

I wish Kekes had said more about the question of truth. With pluralism, we still want to know the difference between truth and falsehood. We still need to seek for more truth and deeper truths. But when we find them, we modestly say that we have found a truth, not THE truth, and that makes all the difference. Even when we utter a truth, it matters very much who utters it, and in what context, and what ground we are standing on when we utter it. I think Kekes would agree with this, but he doesn't actually say so.

The fourth thesis is that by the expansion of our possibilities and the imaginative exploration of them we can obtain a moral space which can be described as freedom. To lead a good life we need a rich supply of possibilities, a sufficiently developed imagination to enable us to explore them, and the enlargement of our freedom. 'For the more numerous are the available possibilities and the better we appreciate the nature of these possibilities as possibilities we may try to realise, the greater will be our freedom to make for ourselves what seem to us like good lives' (Kekes 1994, p. 28). This is the respect for human potential which seems to me very important.

The fifth thesis is the need for limits. Kekes here introduces the notion of deep conventions, as distinguished from variable conventions. 'Deep conventions protect the minimum requirements of all good lives, however they are conceived. Variable conventions also protect the requirements of good lives, but these requirements vary with traditions and conceptions of a good life' (Kekes 1994, p. 31). Deep conventions have a context-independent justification, and this is what relativists cannot admit.

The sixth thesis is that there can be such a thing as moral progress. This again distinguishes pluralism from relativism, as Kekes argues well. It also chimes in very well with the thought which runs right through the present text – that there can be such a thing as a developmental actualization hierarchy.

> For individuals, moral progress is toward recognizing richer possibilities, growing in their imaginative appreciation of them, and increasing their freedom. For traditions, moral progress is toward creating a context in which individuals are encouraged rather than hindered in their aspiration to make a good life for themselves.
>
> (Kekes 1994, p. 141)

We then get a discussion of the limits to morality: of how non-moral values are important too and need to be taken into consideration, sometimes even taking precedence over moral values.

The final chapter moves on to the political scene, and contrasts pluralism with liberalism, with which it may sometimes be confused. This again is very thorough.

So what emerges from all this? For me it is a very satisfying answer to the problems which postmodernism raises. It manages to reconcile my desire to be able to hold two ideas in my head at the same time with my desire to avoid the directionlessness of relativism. The secret is to take nothing absolutely for granted. If we do that, we can hold on to whatever we may feel we need to hold on to, but in a provisional and friendly way, not in a fierce and compulsive way.

It is the compulsion and the fierceness which make belief systems into killers. If we wear our belief systems lightly, we can be free to entertain possibilities for long enough to explore them properly. Kekes in this book gives us the philosophical foundation to make this possible.

If we can get the morality right, other things come right much more easily. The humanistic approach can help us to do this. Ken Wilber is apparently writing a political volume, and I look forward to seeing this: it should have many hints as to how to think about politics from a Centaur point of view.

15

SOME POINTS ON THEORY AND RESEARCH

This book is about what happened and what is going on, rather than about detailed theoretical argument. The main reason for this is that such finer details are only of real interest to a minority – those who have had psychological training of one kind or another. My other books were mainly written for them, and contain quite a lot of scholarly material which can be chewed over in the usual academic way. But in reading over this book, I have become aware that there are certain theoretical points which perhaps need to be clarified, because they are referred to every now and again without any real explanation being given, and this may be frustrating to the reader. So I'd like to try to mop up at least a few of these points here.

BASIC ORIENTATION

Humanistic psychology says that it is all right to look inside yourself. And it sets no limits on that. It is all right to look as deep and as long as you want to, on your own or in company, and whether you call it meditation, counselling, psychotherapy, confluent education or whatever.

Now there is a basic difference here between humanistic psychology and two other main dominant schools of psychology – behaviourism and psychoanalysis. Both of these other schools, in their various ways, say that it is not something to be encouraged. Let us look at psychoanalysis first.

Psychoanalysis says that if we look inside ourselves deep enough and long enough, and in the right way, what we will find, deep down underneath it all, is the Id. The Id is seen as the basic foundation for all motivation in the individual person. It is an extraordinarily dramatic concept. It seems to be impossible to describe it without excitement. It is a 'seething mass', 'primitive repository of primitive and unacceptable impulses', 'completely selfish and unconcerned with reality or moral considerations', or 'unorganized chaotic mentality', according to various commentators. Freud's own words are 'a cauldron of seething excitement'.

242

The Id works on the basis of the pleasure principle – that is, it seeks immediate gratification, regardless of circumstances, ignoring other people's rights or needs in an almost crazy way. For Freud, the unconscious system works according to the laws of the Id. There is no time in the Id – past, present and future mix without distinction. The laws of logic and reason do not exist for the Id, so that contrary wishes can exist side by side quite happily. One thing can stand for or symbolize other, incompatible things, and so on. If the Id were a person, it would be mad. There is a very sophisticated discussion of all this in Blanco (1975). This is what makes so striking the words of Groddeck, which Freud accepted: 'We are lived by our unconscious.'

There is a powerful picture here, of a primitive energy source frightening in its intensity, and actually guiding our actions. No wonder it is thought to be unwise to go anywhere near it without a highly trained and skilled therapist by our side, to see that we come to no harm! And it is not surprising that one of the main efforts of the therapist is to help the Ego to get some kind of control over the force of the libido which comes from the Id. Nor is it surprising that psychoanalysis takes very seriously the importance of social rules and norms, and believes that society is right to set limits on what we naturally want to do. The answer to the problems of the Id is good socialization, where we learn how to adapt in terms of the reality principle, and become acceptable and tamed.

Now behaviourism sees itself as being strongly opposed to psychoanalysis. In the eyes of the behaviourist, psychoanalysis is woolly and unscientific, hard to understand and impossible to check. How surprising it is to find, then, the same message coming out also from this source. We must distinguish between two different kinds of behaviourism, because they have different foundations.

The first kind of behaviourism is based on the classical conditioning theory of Pavlov. A good example of it is given by the British behaviourist Hans Eysenck (1965) where he says:

> [The young child] has to learn to be clean and not to defecate and urinate whenever and wherever he pleases; he has to suppress the overt expression of his sexual and aggressive urges; he must not beat other children when they do things he does not like; he must learn not to take things which do not belong to him. In every society there is a long list of prohibitions of acts which are declared to be bad, naughty and immoral, and which, although they are attractive to him and are self-rewarding, he must nevertheless desist from carrying out.

So activities like this have to be prohibited and suppressed from outside, by suitably designed punishment.

Often this is put in terms of biological drives. It is the drives which are basic, and push for immediate release. And it is only the strong conscience built up through conditioning, through good socialization or taming, which can cope with these strong forces, which have the whole power of evolution behind them. If we started looking deep inside ourselves, then, what we should find, if we went down far enough, would be these unregenerate drives with all their power and strength. So again, what we need if we want to do this at all for any reason is an expert behaviour therapist. This person knows about these things, and will know what to do if anything goes wrong.

The second form of behaviourism is based upon the operant conditioning theory of Skinner. It does not have any notion of drives, and is in many ways much less theoretically committed than the Pavlovian form. But in the classic book by Skinner (1974), he fortunately makes clear his view of how his own position differs from that of Freud. And it turns out that it does not differ at all – he merely wants to rename the Id to suit his own terminology:

> In Freud's great triumvirate, the ego, superego and id represent three sets of contingencies which are almost inevitable when a person lives in a group. The id is the Judeo-Christian 'Old Adam' – a man's 'unregenerate nature', derived from his innate suscepti- bilities to reinforcement, most of them almost necessarily in conflict with the interests of others.

So now it is the genetic endowment, a set of susceptibilities to reinforce- ment, which is what we find deep down underneath everything else. And it will not surprise us to find that this most fundamental layer of the personality is defined on another page as 'selfish behaviour', which needs to be limited and trained from outside so that it will become more acceptable to others.

And if we want to look inside ourselves to go into these matters, again what we need is – this time – a behaviour modifier. Only the behaviour modifier, unlike the other two experts we have met already – the psycho- analyst and the behaviour therapist – is even more cagey about the whole thing, and refuses to look inside at all, or to encourage anyone else to. All the work is done on the surface, without recourse to anything like depth. This seems in a way even more frightening than the other two – like it is something you had better not do even with an expert.

It can be seen that both the psychoanalyst and the behaviourist (in both varieties) have a pessimistic view of what is going on inside human beings. This seems to be helped, if anything, by the emphasis which both of them have on the biological and Darwinian basis of man's animal nature. As Maslow points out:

One expression of this world view has been to identify this animal within us with wolves, tigers, pigs, vultures or snakes, rather than with better, or at least milder, animals like the deer or elephant or dog or chimpanzee. This we may call the bad-animal interpretation of our inner nature, and point out that if we *must* reason from animals to men, it would be better if we chose those who were closest to us, i.e. the anthropoid apes. Since these are, on the whole, pleasant and likeable animals sharing with us many characteristics that we call virtuous, the bad-animal outlook is not supported by comparative psychology.

(Maslow 1987, p. 50)

So it is clear how humanistic psychology would reject psychoanalysis and behaviourism. But how would it reject the third form of psychology which has come up in the past 30 years and which now dominates academia – cognitive psychology? Cognitive psychology is perhaps one of the greatest con tricks ever perpetrated.

Back in the 1950s, cognitive psychology was one of the most promising and delightful parts of the whole psychological field. In the hands of people like Goldstein and Scheerer, it offered a very sophisticated critique of behaviourism, and said that to ignore emotions, imagination, consciousness and intentions for the future was absurd. I loved these people, and quoted them constantly. And of course, when I heard that cognitive psychology was getting popular in the universities, this was very cheering.

But it turned out that what was becoming popular was not the very cultivated European cognitive psychology which I had liked so much – it was a psychology which reduced people to the level of a computer. It was all about computer analogies of how the brain might work. One of its main branches was the study of artificial intelligence – how to make machines behave like human beings (Boden 1979). It was only willing to study those things about the person which could be set up in hardware and software.

Of course it is now terribly ingenious in doing this, and in its own way as sophisticated as any of the psychologies which had preceded it; but it is basically nonsense. I remember once doing a presentation about humanistic psychology at Warwick University, and in front of an audience I asked the professor there 'What is your model of the person?' He replied 'The computer'. I said 'Surely you can't really mean that?' but he assured me that he did. This is just obscene. A computer is a thing. To use a thing as a model of the person is to reduce the person to the level of a thing. It reduces something alive to something dead. And this is not OK.

This leads us into what is perhaps the main difference between humanistic psychology and these other forms which we have been looking at. For humanistic psychology, people are people all the way through – there is no point at which they turn into animals, or inanimate objects. Deep down underneath it all, where it really counts, there is the self. And the self is all right. There is nothing there to be afraid of. This is something which is held consistently by all those who are seen as central to humanistic psychology. Carl Rogers says: 'When we are able to free the individual from defensiveness, so that he is open to the wide range of environmental and social demands, his reactions may be trusted to be positive, forward-moving, constructive' (Rogers 1961, p. 194). His definition of adjustment is complete openness to experience, whether it comes from outside or from inside. And he says 'There is no beast in man. There is only man in man . . .' (Rogers 1961, p. 105).

Perls says that rather than try to change, stop, or avoid something that you don't like in yourself, it is much more effective to experience it fully and become more deeply aware of it. You can't improve on your own functioning, you can only interfere with it, distort and disguise it. When you really get in touch with your own experiencing, you will find that change takes place by itself, without your effort or planning. Beisser took up this idea and popularized it under the heading of 'the paradoxical theory of therapy'.

Maslow says that he sees people as living organisms with an inherent need to grow or change. This is their intrinsic motivation – it does not derive from other needs. And it leads to self-actualization – a never-ending process of going into the self and going beyond the self. It includes ecstasy, creativity and transpersonal experience, and not just everyday coping.

Mahrer (1989) says that if we delve beneath the surface of a person, what we come down to are the deeper potentials. These are often hated and feared when they first come into awareness, but when they are worked with and entered into fully, they turn out to be positive and full of energy and helpful meaning.

May (1980, 1983) says that the core, the centredness of a person is the bedrock on which we base all our attempts at therapy. We have to assume that it is all right, because neurosis is the attempt to deny it, to hide it, to get away from it. It is this that makes true love and real encounter possible. It is the 'I am!' experience.

All the detailed techniques and applications in this book are based on these assumptions. And they seem to form what is often called in social science a self-fulfilling prophecy: that is, if you act as if they were true, they seem to check out as true. But they are not just a self-fulfilling prophecy – they make a lot of logical sense too, as we shall see in the next section.

DEFICIENCY MOTIVATION AND ABUNDANCE MOTIVATION

Most psychology, most of the time, deals with deficiency motivation. Something happens, and we have to cope with it. We have to adjust to it in

some way, and we may do this well or badly, appropriately or inappro-
priately – often it will be possible to state quite objectively whether our
reaction met the situation or was inadequate to it in some way.

There is a word to describe this, taken from cybernetics, which is often
used in the literature and which is quite useful to remember: homeostasis.
Homeostasis simply means self-adjustment in accordance with a standard.
A thermostat, as found on the ordinary domestic iron, works on a homeostatic principle; so does the pupil of the eye. It is a principle of tension
reduction, and it works by relieving some kind of want or discomfort.

Now there is no doubt that dealing with this form of action is very
convenient for psychologists. It enables them to be very precise in their
measurements, and to set up experiments which enable strict control to be
kept and exact predictions to be made and checked.

Historically, the introduction of the notion of homeostasis in the 1950s
was a very progressive move. It enabled psychology to throw off all the
puzzles about 'the instinct of self-preservation', because homeostasis
replaces it completely. It enabled psychology to give mechanistic meanings
to such things as 'expectancy', 'purpose' and 'information', and in doing so
to revolutionize our whole notion of the word 'mechanistic'. It enabled us
to drop our puzzlement about free will and determinism, since it became
clear that we could construct machines which could rearrange their own
internal circuits in such a way that we could be sure that they would adapt
to their environment, but not sure at all of how they would do it. If
afterwards we wanted to know how they had done it, we would have to
take them apart to find out. If a machine could be as free as this, it was
obvious that animals and still more human beings could do this and more.
It is hard now to recall the excitement we felt on reading Ashby's fine book
(1952), which made all this so clear.

But now that all the hubbub has died down, it is easy enough to see that
homeostasis leaves out some very important things about human beings. In
particular, it leaves out virtually all the things which humanistic psychology
is interested in.

In terms of motivation, what it leaves out is abundance motivation. This
is the kind of motivation where we are not trying to relieve some
discomfort, but actively seeking fresh stimulation and new experiences. It is
sometimes called tension-seeking or tension-maintaining behaviour; Woodworth (1958) calls it outgoing motivation.

This has now been studied a great deal, and the classic by Fiske and
Maddi (1961) prints a number of papers which show that even by the very
strictest of scientific standards, deficiency motivation and homeostasis is
not enough to account for a great deal of animal behaviour, and still less of
human action.

Krech et al. (1969) explain very well the difference between deficiency and
abundance motivation, and make it clear that psychology needs both

concepts if it is to do justice to what we actually find. Coleman (1969) also deals with this in a helpful way.

Weiner (1985) in a very full and lengthy examination of the whole question of motivation from a modem psychological standpoint quotes Maslow as talking about Being-values as opposed to Deficiency-values (homeostatic drives); the B-values are more to do with needs which are not deficiency-driven, such as curiosity, appreciation, love, peak experiences and so on.

Supposing that we were to apply this thinking to Maslow's model, in a way which Maslow himself never apparently considered? Maslow says that we will expect to find abundance motivation (or growth motivation, or B-motivation, as he calls it) at the self-actualization level of development; as I read him, he tends to identify the two things, or run them together. (Weiner (1985) also takes this view.) Here and there he seems to suggest that we can find some abundance motivation at the self-esteem level and at the love and belongingness level, but he never says this, to the best of my knowledge, about the safety or the physiological levels.

Now it seems certainly and obviously true that we do find abundance motivation at the level of self-actualization. But I want to say two things about this. One, that we can also find deficiency motivation at this level; and two, that we can also find abundance motivation at the two lowest levels. In other words, I want to make a dividing line right down the middle of the Maslow chart.

Very young babies show exploratory tendencies, playful activity, curiosity and self-discovery, etc.; they do not have to wait to become self-actualizing adults before they can get away from deficiency motivation. And we all know we can eat or drink from purely aesthetic motives, or as a meditation, not only from hunger or thirst. So I think we can say that at every level of activity we can find deficiency motivation and abundance motivation side by side. Maslow himself says very clearly that there can be deficiency-motivated love, a kind of love-hunger; but there can also be abundance-motivated love, which is non-possessive and not need-oriented at all. But how about self-actualization sometimes being deficiency-motivated? To people who have studied Maslow this may seem something like heresy.

Funnily enough, it was Maslow himself who discovered this. One of the key things about the self-actualization level has always been, for Maslow, the fact that it was at this level that the peak experience most often appeared. But with the coming of LSD and the Esalen Institute, it appeared that perfectly authentic peak experiences were to be had simply and directly, almost for the asking. And Maslow turned back, appalled, from the new world he had helped to create:

> If the sole good in life becomes the peak experience, and if all
> means to this end become good, and if more peak experiences are

better than fewer, then one can force the issue, push actively, strive and hunt and fight for them. So they have often moved over into magic, into the secret and esoteric, into the exotic, the occult, the dramatic and effortful, the dangerous, the cultish.

(Maslow 1970, p. ix)

In other words, people could now start to say 'I'm a bit off and down at the moment, so I think I need a peak experience this weekend'. And this is precisely the language of deficiency motivation.

Instead of being 'surprised by joy', 'turning on' is scheduled, promised, advertised, sold, hustled into being, and can get to be regarded as a commodity . . . More and more exotic, artificial, striving 'techniques' may escalate further until they become *necessary*, and until jadedness and impotence ensue.

(Maslow 1970, p. x)

It seems, then, that this confirms our view that one can have deficiency motivation even at the level of self-actualization. The actual details shown in Table 15.1 are speculative, and have not been checked out by empirical research. They are there merely as possibly suggestive hypotheses, and not as authoritative pronouncements.

The advantage of putting it in this way, it seems to me, is that it shows more concretely how abundance motivation fits in to the whole picture. And it does seem to be an advantage to have a two-dimensional picture, rather than a one-dimensional one. But much more work needs to be done on this.

B-VALUES AND D-VALUES

Maslow's tendency to mix up self-actualization and abundance motivation extended also into his discussion of Being. He believed that Being was a kind of realm which one entered into by means of a peak experience, and that while in it (probably quite briefly) one found oneself living in terms of the Being-values (B-values) rather than the deficiency-values (D-values). Similarly one understood the world in terms of B-cognition rather than D-cognition, understood people in terms of B-love rather than D-love, and so on (Maslow 1973). This all makes perfectly good sense, but it does always sound as if we have to be at the self-actualizing level before any of this can happen.

How can we think about this in terms of the thought expressed in Table 15.1? It seems to me that there are two possibilities, which deserve to be mentioned. The first possibility is that we do indeed have to cross the gap (the 4–5 gap of Table 2.1) before we can enter the realm of Being. The

Table 15.1 Abundance motivation and the Maslow levels.

Deficiency motivated		Abundance motivated
Searching for peak experiences out of boredom; needing a 'turn-on' desperately; using the occult to control others; being driven by one's demons; comparing and evaluating peak experiences; using spiritual talk for sexual exploitation.	6	Letting peak experiences come; enjoying flashes of insight; finding non-punitive humour in many places; finding ecstasy in music; being genuinely creative; being inspired and inspiring; exploring spiritual realms.
Strong conscience with many guilt feelings; high personal standards which are rigid and must not be infringed; identity very important but precarious; need for consistency without ability to achieve it.	5	Strong connection between respect for one's own identity and respect for other's identity; sureness of identity leading to flexibility in action; awareness of some of the paradoxes of identity; authenticity.
Need for recognition from others; need for applause; need for commendation from important authorities; need for authorities to be important; need for system, law and order, hierarchy, stability.	4	Liking to be appreciated; warming to response from others; ability to receive respect as something appropriate to the situation; ability to set up 'virtuous circles' of interaction.
Need for approval; fear of the group; likely to conform; wants to be 'good'; need to please others; need to know what the others think; strong desire to belong to a definite group.	3	Love which overflows and reaches out to others; feeling of being part of a wider unity of people; love which gives space to the other person in which to grow; love which does not count the cost.
Need to do things the 'correct' way; need to be perfect; need to know the rules; desire for control 'over' things and people; manipulative and dominant; narrow concept of own advantage.	2	Control by integration of impulses and desires; control of situations by going with the flow; understanding of some of the paradoxes of control; mastery through enthusiasm; risk-taking.
Escaping danger; avoiding pain or harm; seeking protection in real threat situation; cutting down on stimulation; suppressing hurt; attempts to stop environment from changing; short-term thinking.	1	Seeking long-term protection; anticipating danger in imaginative ways; seeking vicarious danger so as to be ready for unfamiliar situations; playing games about dangerous situations.
Eating from real hunger; drinking from real thirst; excreting when necessary; having sex out of pressing bodily need; compensating for or escaping from heat or cold; sleeping when tired.	0	Eating for aesthetic pleasure; drinking for new sensations; excreting with full awareness; enjoying heat, cold or rain; luxuriating in a bath; laughing at the lightning.

suggestion would be that the lower levels are too heavily infused with fear and stereotyped thinking to be able to move. But after the leap has been made and the gap crossed, we can then come back down the levels and act at those levels, but now according to the principles of abundance motivation. So we would, on this supposition, go up the ladder on the left-hand side, and then come down it again on the right-hand side, 'redeeming' each level in terms of the values reached at the top. This seems to make a lot of sense, and be quite understandable.

The other possibility is that at any level we may, on a good day, move over to the left, and open ourselves up to abundance motivation, and that this may, in fact, be the way in which we do grow. Perhaps each leftward movement makes it easier for there to be an upward movement. Certainly we stand more chance of learning when we are open and receptive than when we are closed up and defensive. And it may be just this kind of self-owned learning which takes us up the levels. Perhaps each glimpse of what it would be like to cross the gap makes actually crossing the gap easier. This would make it easier to understand what happens in many encounter groups and other growth experiences, where we seem to have an intense experience at the time, which is however not reflected in our conduct outside the group. This would be a case of moving over to the left while in the group, and then moving back again once the special group atmosphere is removed. But with some more of this 'pump-priming' sort of experience, enough strength and insight may be achieved to cross the gap for ourselves, so that the group is no longer necessary. This would also fit in with Maslow's simple diagram:

GROWTH ◄──────── PERSONALITY ────────► SAFETY

Maslow says that the process of healthy growth can be considered as a never-ending series of free choice situations, confronting each individual 'at every point throughout his life, in which he must choose between the delights of safety and growth, dependence and independence, regression and progression, immaturity and maturity' (Maslow 1968, p. 45). This emphasis on choice is of course meat and drink to the more existentialist thinkers like May and Mahrer.

The two possibilities we have been considering both seem quite plausible, and only proper research can determine which of the two is true. Perhaps they both are. It would not take much change to see them as complementary rather than as competitive explanations of what we actually find in practice.

HUMANISTIC RESEARCH

And this takes us on to the general question of research method. We regard psychology as a social science rather than as a physical science. This seems so obvious as not to need arguing, though there are still many academic psychologists who have not got the message. There are many kinds of psychological research which are carried out in social science.

1 Pure basic research   Carried out in universities and institutions of higher learning. Concerned with high-level abstractions which may or may not have any practical relevance. Attempts to push forward the boundaries of some new or established theory. Tends to be very strictly controlled. Usually uses a reductionist view which says that science is built up from bricks of fact and truth – a false and misleading notion.

2 Basic objective research   Research which is designed to relate theory to real life situations. The results are intended to be relevant to the situation studied, and also to some theoretical framework. Again largely confined to universities, and usually irrelevant to the field it is supposed to be studying, because of its quality of distance and uninvolvement.

3 Evaluation research   Attempts to follow up some intentional course of action in an effort to determine whether what was intended to happen actually did happen (and possibly to what extent). The result almost always comes out as some kind of evaluative judgement on the course of action. Before-and-after measures are often used. In rare cases this measures something worth measuring.

4 Applied research   Covers a wide range of possibilities, but often takes the form of a survey of some kind. All the measures are within the four walls of the situation being researched, and ad hoc items may often be created. Can include exploratory studies, and may use factor analysis or other computer processing. Carried out by expert researchers. May include observation or unobtrusive measures. Here it is not only universities which use this – industry and commerce use it too, as well as large governmental and non-governmental bodies.

These first four methods are those dealt with in detail in most standard textbooks on research methods.

5 Qualitative research   There are two subspecies within this. The first is the kind of qualitative research which is just like the previous four types, only without numbers. There is just the same attempt at objectivity, just the same ownership of the data by the researcher. This is sometimes called 'small-q' qualitative research. It uses very open-ended types of questioning, which enable the research subjects to use their own categories of response. For a full description see Walker (1985).

The second is the kind of qualitative research which relies much more on the involvement and the personal interest of the researcher. Reflexivity is insisted on. This is 'Big-Q' qualitative research. It is described well in Denzin and Lincoln (1994); and there is an excellent journal which started at about the same time, called *Qualitative Inquiry*.

Often included under this heading is Grounded Theory, as described in Strauss and Corbin (1990), which seems to be more popular recently, though it is severely limited by an ambiguity or blurred quality which makes it unclear as to whether it is still trying to play the positivist game or to move all the way into the qualitative (Big-Q) sphere.

Also sometimes included here is Discourse Analysis, as described in Potter and Wetherell (1987). This is now beginning to produce some very interesting (Big-Q) work.

6 Participant observation   The researcher plays a role similar to the roles of the people being studied, either owning up to it or keeping it secret. Sometimes called symbolic interactionism. Well described in McCall and Simmons (1969).

7 Language and class research   Studies language by mixing with the people actually using that language, and entering into their world to some degree. See for example Labov (1972).

8 Personality and politics research   Studies the relationship between people's personality and the political positions they take up. Long interviews, sometimes over months, see Knutson (1973).

9 Ethogenic research   Studies carefully the accounts people give of their actions, and says that the explanation of such actions must be seen in terms of such accounts, but going quite deeply into them over extended periods of time, as Harré (1979) has discussed.

10 Phenomenological research   Examines very carefully the ground the researcher is standing on while conducting the research project; all the rules the researcher is taking for granted have to be rethought and re-examined, as Giorgi (1975) has outlined. This has become much more used recently, as described in the book edited by Valle (1998).

11 Ethnomethodology   Approach pioneered by Garfinkel, which again takes apart the taken-for-granted aspects of social life and re-examines them very fundamentally, experimenting sometimes with rule-breaking situations. Good summary in Turner (1974).

12 LSD research   Approach where a drug is administered and the thera-peutic results are carefully monitored, the researcher also having experience of the same drug. See Grof (1980).

13 Dialectical research   Good example in Esterson (1972) of someone who takes up an explicitly dialectical philosophical position when doing research within a family.

14 Action research   The researchers who do the work are people who will be affected by the results – often they live in the same place as those being studied. The process of doing the research is itself part of the action to be taken. Expert researchers may be used as advisers (Sanford 1981). This has developed very fast in recent years, as can be seen in the book edited by Peter Reason and Hilary Bradbury (2000).

15 Intervention research   A researcher acts in the situation as a complete person, aiming at the provision of valid and useful information, leading to free and informed choice, and internal commitment to a course of action. Research comes out in the form of shared experience, which may or may not be reducible to 'knowledge' which can be handed on to others (Argyris 1970).

16 Personal construct research   Research done according to the theory and precepts of George Kelly, as exemplified in Fransella (1972). Close cooperation between researcher and subject.

17 Existential research   The researcher acts as a measuring instrument, using thoughts, emotions, bodily reactions to register what is going on as fully and deeply as possible, as in Hampden-Turner (1977). An attempt is then made to play this back in such a form that it can be re-experienced by others. This may need a high degree of literary or other skill.

18 Experiential research   This is done by two people researching each other, and themselves. It involves a two-way, systematic but creative inter-action between persons who may take up the roles of agent and facilitator. Each session may be recorded and analysed afterwards, or this may only be done for certain agreed sessions. Hypotheses may be checked by an attempt to produce certain changes, in self or other, as Heron (1981) has described, and he has taken this much further now (Heron 1996). Further develop-ments have come from Barrell (1986) and his colleagues.

19 Endogenous research   Here the researcher turns the subjects, or some of them, into co-researchers who are equally concerned with the results of the project. See Maruyama (1981).

20 Participatory research   Pioneered by Hall (1981) in several different countries, this approach entails the cooperation of the research subjects in a very close and detailed way, such that they become co-owners of the research project. Sometimes called collaborative or cooperative research.

21 Transformational research   Here a more transpersonal attitude is taken up, which explicitly deals with the question of spirituality, and uses categories derived from that source (Rowan 1998a). This is now a fast-developing field, and people like Valerie Bentz and Jeremy Shapiro (1998) and William Braud and Rosemarie Anderson (1998) have made huge contributions to it.

The first four of these types tend to be alienated methods of research, which put people at some disadvantage, and treat them as objects to be described externally. They all belong to the field of Old Paradigm Research. Often the people studied are deceived in some way about the purpose of the study, and the extent of this massive deception has given rise to much worry in recent years, as Kelman (1968) has noted.

Types 5 to 16 are much more ambiguous. Depending on who is doing them, and for what purpose, they may be more or less alienated or deceptive. People involved in them may not be very clear themselves as to what paradigm of research they are following. However, these methods have in the past tended to be much more genuine, in that people are not deceived, and are allowed to express themselves in their own terms and in their own way.

The last five types are in the field of New Paradigm Research, which is relatively recent, and relates much better to humanistic psychology. It is described rather thoroughly in Reason and Rowan (1981). All the types of research from 17 to 21 seem particularly suitable for investigating theories of personal growth and human potential. Classic works here include Mitroff and Kilmann (1978), Part 2 of Darroch and Silvers (1982), Lincoln and Guba (1985) and Berg and Smith (1985). A challenging look at research in the field of counselling and psychotherapy is to be found in Mahrer (1985).

This whole field has undergone deep changes in the past ten years, and a recent fine text on research (Mertens 1998) presents a much more sophisticated picture than the books of even five years previously. Humanistic views now seem to be coming into their own in the research field.

CRITIQUES OF HUMANISTIC PSYCHOLOGY

Over the years, there have been a number of critiques of humanistic psychology. Most of them are quite weak, and hardly any of them show any real understanding of the fact that the whole thing is based on experience rather than abstract logic. Some of the criticisms are very well answered in Shaw (1974), who shows that the general theory of self-actualization holds up very well in answer to various criticisms made up to that time. Some more are to be found in the book edited by Donald Moss (1999), which has some sharp rejoinders to various critics.

Someone who has looked at humanistic theory from a sociological perspective is Roy Wallis, who examines the idea that the movement has gone in the direction of more spiritual concerns in recent years, and that this means a kind of failure, a substitution of false compensators for real rewards. He goes into this at some length, and in the end disagrees with it, saying that it seems rather that: 'Spirituality may be pursued as a way of providing an explanation for what has been achieved, and out of a desire to gain *additional*, rather than substitute, values and effects' (Wallis 1985, p. 39). But he says that the most consistent feature of the human potential movement is its epistemological individualism. I think what he means by this is quite acceptable, and reflects the emphasis on the real self which is so characteristic of humanistic theory.

Another critique comes from Leonard Geller, who takes a rather logical positivist position, and says that the whole theory is incoherent because it tries to mix biology and psychology in a way which does not logically hold water: 'Implicit in Rogers's view, I suspect, is the erroneous if not incoherent assumption that the true self is an immaterial, unchanging thing-like substance that can be an object of exploration and discovery but not a subject or agent' (Geller 1982, p. 59). This was answered very fully by Carl Ginsburg a couple of years later, who showed that this view was not sustainable, and was also based on a type of logic which could not even in principle work in the examination of humanistic psychology. He points out that 'Geller makes his argument against Rogers by converting phenomenological experiential statements into metaphysical propositions'. And he goes on to reply to Geller's point that authenticity is a logically incoherent notion by saying that:

> The test of whether one knows what it means when one says 'I am being authentic' or 'I am behaving according to the dictates of my inner self' is in the experience of doing so and the experience of difference in testing this strategy against previous possibilities. The difference is a difference in somatic experience of oneself, and is therefore empirically verifiable in the most direct sense.
> (Ginsburg 1984, p. 72)

So that even by Geller's own standards this has to be accepted as valid.

Geller (1984) tried to come back, but only made his own position more untenable, by making such a radical gulf between knowledge through language and knowledge without language that the two became quite impossible to relate together, never mind develop one out of the other, as must obviously be the case.

Again, we have had Lethbridge (1986) trying to attack humanistic psychology from a Marxist position. Unfortunately for him, there is no Marxist psychology – it keeps on turning into sociology, because of the extreme Marxist reliance on social determinism. He tries to show that Vygotsky, Leontyev and Lucien Sève have a valid alternative, but in my opinion fails completely. Leontyev is quoted as saying 'individual consciousness can exist only in the presence of social consciousness and language, which is its real substratum'. This again makes the error of Geller, of making too much of language. If language were so important, all the body therapies and all the regressive therapies would be impossible – they could not possibly work. It is only because experience is prior to language that we can have such therapies. Gendlin (1962) put forward long ago the basic story of how experience turns into language, and this account has never been bettered. We have seen some other examples of the difficulty of language imperialism all through the present text.

There has never been an attack on humanistic psychology which has really shown it to be either untenable or unscientific. Those who accuse humanistic psychology of being Cartesian are usually much more Cartesian themselves.

One of the more vague and general criticisms, which attracted a good deal of attention in its day, was the theme that humanistic psychology was narcissistic. Obviously the amount of time spent on discussing the self, and self-actualization, lends itself to this suspicion, but when we come to look at it closely, the plausibility of it departs. It is not about egotism or selfishness, and not much even about self-improvement in the sense of rational self-management. It is about the sort of movement towards a fuller sense of self which is very broad and unselfish and all-inclusive. As the very precise and hard-headed Mahrer (1989, p. 174) says: 'It involves the commitment to whatever there is within to be. This is the leap of faith, the tearing of one's self from what one is and the falling into whatever is there within'. This produces what he calls the 'integrating person' – the person who has taken up the challenge of self-actualization and has started moving in the direction of greater self-awareness and greater authenticity. He goes on to say:

> The ordinary person may be said to be engaged in a perpetual agonizing struggle to preserve the self, whereas, in stark and utter contrast, the integrating person is willingly engaged in suicidal self-destruction. These two persons are proceeding in opposite directions. The integrating person knows that the way to liberation, to integration, to metamorphosis, is through the eye of the nameless horror which the ordinary person desperately struggles to avoid.

With integration and actualization, a person is able to relate fully to another person. One of the crucial mistakes made by critics is to see the stress on autonomy as excluding relationship with another. But the whole point made by humanistic psychology is that it is only the autonomous person who can have real relationships. As Mahrer (1989, p. 579) says in his discussion of actualization:

> The highest levels of interpersonal relationships are those charac-
> terised by integration and actualization. This kind of relationship
> exceeds one of integrative love, mutual integrative oneness, and
> mutual integrative being-one-with. Because of the nature of actual-
> ization, these highest levels of interpersonal relationships are also
> characterized by mutual contexts enabling each participant toward
> increasing depth and breadth of experiencing. When relationships
> are of this order, they define the highest and most valued inter-
> personal relations available to human beings.

From this we can see that the various critiques of humanistic psychology are not such as to cause us any great misgivings about the basic direction of the enterprise. Of course we have a lot to learn still about the details. The forthcoming book edited by Kirk Schneider, James Bugental and Fraser Pierson and scheduled for early 2001 will help to fill out this story.

I wish you, the reader, well in your search.

JOURNALS AND MAGAZINES

Changes PCCS Books, Llangarron, Ross-on-Wye, HR9 6PT, UK

Consciousness & Experiential Psychology BPS, 48 Princess Road East, Leicester, LE1 7DR, UK

Energy & Character Benzenrüti 6, CH-9410 Heiden, Switzerland

Journal of Humanistic Psychology Sage Publications, 2455 Teller Road, Thousand Oaks, CA91320, USA

Journal of Transpersonal Psychology PO Box 4437, Stanford, CA94309, USA

Self & Society AHP(B), BM Box 3582, London WC1N 3XX, UK

The Humanistic Psychologist Psychology Dept, State University of West Georgia, Carrollton, GA30118, USA

Transpersonal Psychology Review Dept. of Psychology, The Open University, Walton Hall, Milton Keynes, MK7 6AA, UK

USEFUL ADDRESSES

Association for Humanistic Psychology, 1516 Oak Street, #320A, Alameda, CA94501-2947, USA

Association for Transpersonal Psychology, PO Box 3049, Stanford, CA94309, USA

Association for Humanistic Psychology Practitioners, BCM AHPP, London WC1N 3XX, UK

BIBLIOGRAPHY

Adams, John (ed.) (1986) *Transforming Leadership*. Alexandria: Miles River Press.

Adler, Margot (1986) *Drawing Down the Moon* (2nd edn). Boston: Beacon Press.

Adorno, Theodor W. (1973) *Negative Dialectics*. New York: Continuum.

Adzema, Mickel V. (1985) 'A primal perspective on spirituality', *Journal of Humanistic Psychology* 25(3): 83–116.

Albery, Nicholas (1983) *How to Save the Body*. London: Revelaction Press.

Alderfer, Clay (1972) *Existence, Relatedness, Growth*. New York: The Free Press.

Allen, R. F. (1980) *Beat the System! A Way to Create More Human Environments*. New York: McGraw-Hill.

Anderson, Rosemarie and Braud, William (1998) 'Additional suggestions, ethical considerations and future challenges' in W. Braud and R. Anderson (eds) *Transpersonal Research for the Social Sciences: Honouring Human Experience*. Thousand Oaks: Sage.

Anderson, Walter T. (1973) *Politics and the New Humanism*. Pacific Palisades: Goodyear.

Anderson, Walter T. (ed.) (1983) *Rethinking Liberalism*. New York: Avon.

Anthony, Dick, Ecker, Bruce and Wilber, Ken (eds) (1987) *Spiritual Choices: The Problem of Recognising Authentic Paths to Inner Transformation*. New York: Paragon House.

Arendt, Hannah (1958) *The Human Condition*. Chicago: University of Chicago Press.

Argyris, Chris (1970) *Intervention Theory and Method*. Reading: Addison-Wesley.

Ashby, W. Ross (1952) *Design for a Brain*. London: Chapman & Hall.

Aspy, David N. (1965) 'A study of three facilitative conditions and their relationship to the achievement of third grade students', unpublished doctoral dissertation, University of Kentucky.

Aspy, David N. (1969) 'The effect of teacher-offered conditions of empathy, positive regard and congruence upon student achievement', *Florida Journal of Educational Research* 11(1): 39–48.

Aspy, David N. (1972) *Toward a Technology for Humanizing Education*. Champaign: Research Press.

Aspy, David N. and Hadlock, W. (1967) 'The effect of empathy, warmth and genuineness on elementary students' reading achievement', reviewed in C. B.

Truax and R. R. Carkhuff, *Toward Effective Counselling and Psychotherapy*. Chicago: Aldine.

Aspy, David N. and Roebuck, Flora N. (1977) *Kids Don't Learn from People They Don't Like*. Amherst: Human Resource Development Press.

Assagioli, R. (1975) *Psychosynthesis: A Manual of Principles and Techniques*. London: Turnstone Press.

Atkinson, Rita L., Atkinson, Richard C., Smith, Edward E. and Bem, Daryl J. (1993) *Introduction to Psychology* (11th edn). Fort Worth: Harcourt Brace Jovanovich.

Bach, George R. and Wyden, P. (1969) *The Intimate Enemy*. New York: William Morrow.

Baerveldt, Cor and Voestermans, Paul (1996) 'The body as a selfing device', *Theory and Psychology* 6(4): 693–713.

Baldwin, Michele (2000) *The Use of Self in Therapy* (2nd edn). New York: Haworth Press.

Bales, R. F. (1958) 'Task roles and social roles in problem-solving groups' in E. E. Maccoby et al. (eds) *Readings in Social Psychology*. New York: Holt.

Balint, Michael (1968) *The Basic Fault*. London: Tavistock Publications.

Barnes, Hazel (1990) 'Sartre's concept of the self' in *Sartre and Psychology: Review of Existential Psychology and Psychiatry*. Seattle WA.

Barrell, James (1986) *A Science of Human Experience*. Acton, MA: Copley.

Barrett-Lennard, Godfrey (1998) *Carl Rogers' Helping System*. London: Sage.

Bateson, Gregory (1972) *Steps to an Ecology of Mind*. New York: Ballantine.

Bay, Christian (1965) 'Politics and pseudopolitics: a critical evaluation of some behavioural literature', *American Political Science Review* 59: 37–57.

Bay, Christian (1967) 'Needs, wants and political legitimacy', *Canadian Journal of Political Science* 1: 241–260.

Bay, Christian (1968) *The Structure of Freedom*. New York: Doubleday.

Bay, Christian (1971) '"Freedom" as a tool of oppression' in Bennello and Roussopoulos (eds) *The Case for Participatory Democracy*. New York: Viking.

Beck, Don E. and Cowan, Christopher C. (1996) *Spiral Dynamics: Mastering Values, Leadership, and Change*. Oxford: Blackwell.

Beckhard, R. (1969) *Organization Development: Strategies and Models*. Reading: Addison-Wesley.

Beisser, Arnold R. (1972) 'The paradoxical theory of change' in J. Fagan and I. L. Shepherd (eds) *Gestalt Therapy Now*. Harmondsworth: Penguin.

Belenky, Mary F., Clinchy, Blythe McV., Goldberger, Nancy R. and Tarule, Jill M. (1986) *Women's Ways of Knowing: The Development of Self, Voice and Mind*. New York: Basic Books.

Bennis, Warren G., Benne, K. D. and Chin, R. (eds) (1970) *The Planning of Change* (2nd edn). New York: Holt Rinehart and Winston.

Bentz, Valerie Malhotra and Shapiro, Jeremy J. (1998) *Mindful Inquiry in Social Research*. Thousand Oaks: Sage.

Berg, David N. and Smith, Kenwyn K. (eds) (1988) *The Self in Social Inquiry: Researching Methods*. Newbury Park: Sage.

Bergantino, Len (1981) *Psychotherapy, Insight and Style*. Boston: Allyn & Bacon.

Bergin, A. E. and Garfield, S. L. (eds) (1994) *Handbook of Psychotherapy and Behaviour Change*. Chichester: Wiley.

Berne, Eric (1964) *Games People Play*. Harmondsworth: Penguin.
Berne, Eric (1973) *What Do You Say After You Say Hello?* New York: Bantam.
Bischof, Leonard (1970) *Interpreting Personality Theories*. New York: Harper & Row.
Blake, Robert R. and Mouton, Jane S. (1964) *The Managerial Grid*. Houston: Gulf Publishing.
Blake, Robert R. and Mouton, Jane S. (1978) *The New Managerial Grid*. Houston: Gulf Publishing.
Blake, Robert R. and Mouton, Jane S. (1980) *The Grid for Sales Excellence* (2nd edn). New York: McGraw-Hill.
Blake, Robert R. and Mouton, Jane S. (1982) 'Theory and research for developing a science of leadership', *The Journal of Applied Behavioral Science* 18(3): 275–291.
Blake, Robert R. et al. (1970) 'The union-management intergroup laboratory: strategy for resolving intergroup conflict' in W. G. Bennis et al. (eds) *The Planning of Change* (2nd edn). New York: Holt Rinehart and Winston.
Blanco, Matte (1975) *The Unconscious as Infinite Sets*. London: Duckworth.
Blatner, Howard A. (1973) *Acting-in: Practical Applications of Psychodramatic Methods*. New York: Springer.
Blatner, Adam (1994) 'Tele' in P. Holmes, M. Karp and M. Watson (eds) *Psychodrama Since Moreno*. London: Routledge.
Blum, Thomas (ed.) (1993) *Prenatal Perception Learning and Bonding*. Berlin: Leonardo Publishers.
Boadella, David (1985) *Wilhelm Reich: The Evolution of his Work*. Arkana, London.
Boadella, David (1988) 'Biosynthesis' in J. Rowan and W. Dryden (eds) *Innovative Therapy in Britain*. Open University Press, Milton Keynes.
Boadella, David (1997a) 'Embodiment in the therapeutic relationship', *International Journal of Psychotherapy* 2(1): 31–44.
Boadella, David (1997b) 'Psychotherapy, science and levels of discourse', *Energy and Character* 28(1): 13–20.
Boden, Margaret (1979) *Artificial Intelligence and Natural Man*. Hassocks: The Harvester Press.
Bohart, Arthur C. and Tallman, Karen (1998) 'The person as active agent in experiential therapy' in L. S. Greenberg, J. C. Watson and G. Lietaer (eds) *Handbook of Experiential Psychotherapy*. New York: The Guilford Press.
Bolweg, L. F. (1976) *Job Design and Industrial Democracy*. Leiden: Martinus Nijhoff.
Bookchin, Murray (1986) *The Modern Crisis*. Philadelphia: New Society Publishers.
Boorstein, Seymour (ed.) (1996) *Transpersonal Psychotherapy* (2nd edn). Albany: SUNY Press.
Borton, Terry (1970) *Reach, Touch and Teach*. New York: McGraw-Hill.
Bourget, Linne (1988) *The Riches Within: Developing your Intuition for Success*. Alexandria: Positive Management Communication Systems.
Bower, Tom G. R. (1977) *A Primer of Infant Development*. San Francisco: W. H. Freeman.
Boydell, Tom and Pedler, Mike (1981) *Management Self-development*. Farnborough: Gower.
Bradford, Leland P., Gibb, J. R. and Benne, K. D. (eds) (1964) *T-group Theory and Laboratory Method*. New York: Wiley.

Brammer, Lawrence M., Abrego, Philip J. and Shostrom, Everett L. (1993) *Therapeutic Counselling and Psychotherapy* (6th edn). Upper Saddle River: Prentice-Hall.

Braud, William and Anderson, Rosemarie (eds) (1998) *Transpersonal Research for the Social Sciences: Honouring Human Experience*. Thousand Oaks: Sage.

Bridges, William (1973) 'Thoughts on humanistic education, or is teaching a dirty word', *Journal of Humanistic Psychology* 13(1): 5–13.

Broder, Michael (1976) 'An eclectic approach to primal integration', *Primal Integration Monographs*, 1(1).

Brooks, Charles V. W. (1974) *Sensory Awareness*. New York: Viking Press.

Brown, George I. (1971) *Human Teaching for Human Learning*. New York: Viking.

Brown, George I. (ed.) (1975) *The Live Classroom: Innovation Through Confluent Education and Gestalt*. New York: The Viking Press.

Brown, Phil (1973) *Radical Psychology*. London: Tavistock Publications.

Brown, Juliana and Mowbray, Richard (1994) 'Primal integration' in *Innovative Therapy: A Handbook*. Buckingham: Open University Press.

Brown, R. C. and Tedeschi, C. (1972) 'Graduate education in psychology: a comment on Rogers' passionate statement', *Journal of Humanistic Psychology* 12(1): 1–15.

Brown, S. D. and Lent, R. W. (eds) (1984) *Handbook of Counselling Psychology*. New York: John Wiley & Sons.

Bruyere, Rosalyn L. (1989) *Wheels of Light: A Study of the Chakras: Vol.1*. Sierra Madre CA: Bon Productions.

Buber, Martin (1975) *Tales of the Hasidim*. New York: Schocken Books.

Bugental, James F. T. (1981) *The Search for Authenticity* (enlarged edn). New York: Irvington.

Bugental, James T. (1987) *The Art of the Psychotherapist*. New York: W. W. Norton.

Cameron, Deborah (1985) *Feminism and Linguistic Theory*. Basingstoke: Macmillan.

Canfield, J. and Wells, F. C. (1976) *One Hundred Ways to Enhance Self Concept in the Classroom*. Englewood Cliffs: Prentice-Hall.

Capra, Fritjof (1983) *The Turning Point*. New York: Simon & Schuster.

Casriel, Daniel H. (1971) 'The Daytop story and the Casriel method' in L. Blank et al. (eds) *Confrontation*. New York: Collier-Macmillan.

Castillo, Gloria A. (1978) *Left-handed Teaching: Lessons in Affective Education*. New York: Holt Rinehart & Winston.

Chamberlain, David (1998) *The Mind of your Newborn Baby*. Berkeley: North Atlantic Books.

Cinnirella, Marco and Loewenthal, Kate Miriam (1999) 'Religious and ethnic group influences on beliefs about mental illness: a qualitative interview study', *British Journal of Medical Psychology* 72(4): 505–524.

Clark, Don (1972) 'Homosexual encounter in all-male groups' in L. N. Solomon and B. Berzon (eds) *New Perspectives on Encounter Groups*. San Francisco: Jossey-Bass.

Clarkson, Petruska (1989) *Gestalt Counselling in Action*. London: Sage.

Clarkson, Petruska (1995) *The Therapeutic Relationship*. London: Whurr.

Clatterbaugh, Kenneth (1990) *Contemporary Perspectives on Masculinity*. Boulder: Westview Press.

Cohen, David (1997) *Carl Rogers: A Critical Biography*. London: Constable.

Cohen, J. M. and Phipps, L.-F. (1979) *The Common Experience*. London: Rider.

Cohn, Hans (1997) *Existential Thought and Therapeutic Practice*. London: Sage.

Coleman, J. C. (1969) *Psychology and Effective Behaviour*. Glenview: Scott Foresman.

Connell, Robert W. (1987) *Gender and Power*. Cambridge: Polity Press.

Coover, V. et al. (1978) *Resource Manual for a Living Revolution*. Philadelphia: New Society Publishers.

Cortright, Brant (1997) *Psychotherapy and Spirit*. Albany: SUNY Press.

Crainer, S. (1998) *Guide to the Management Gurus*. London: Sheldon Press.

Culbert, Samuel A. and McDonough, John J. (1990) 'The concept of framing as a basis for understanding a blind spot in the way managers wield power' in F. Massarik (ed.) *Advances in Organization Development: Vol.1*. Norwood: Ablex.

Danziger, Kurt (1997) 'The varieties of social construction', *Theory and Psychology* 7(3): 399–416.

Darroch, V. and Silvers, R. J. (1982) *Interpretive Human Studies: An Introduction to Phenomenological Research*. Washington: University Press of America.

Davis, J., Lockwood, L. and Wright, C. (1991) 'Reasons for not reporting peak experiences', *Journal of Humanistic Psychology*, 31(1): 86–94.

DeCarvalho, Roy José (1991) *The Founders of Humanistic Psychology*. New York: Praeger.

Denzin, Norman and Lincoln, Yvonna (eds) (1994) *Handbook of Qualitative Research*. Thousand Oaks: Sage.

Doblin, Rick (1991) 'Pahnke's "Good Friday experiment": a long-term follow-up and methodological critique', *The Journal of Transpersonal Psychology* 23(1): 1–28.

Douglas, T. (1983) *Groups*. London: Tavistock Publications.

Dreyfuss, A. and Feinstein, A. D. (1977) 'My body is me: body-based approaches to personal enrichment' in McWaters, B. (ed.) *Humanistic Perspectives*. Monterey: Brooks/Cole.

Dryden, Windy (ed.) (1987) *Key Cases in Psychotherapy*. London: Croom Helm.

Dunayevskaya, Raisa (1982) *Rosa Luxemburg, Women's Liberation and Marx's Philosophy of Revolution*. Sussex: Harvester Press.

Duval, S. and Wicklund, R. W. (1972) *A Theory of Objective Self Awareness*. New York: Academic Press.

Eckert, Jochen and Biermann-Ratjen, Eva-Maria (1998) 'The treatment of borderline personality disorder' in L. S. Greenberg, J. C. Watson and G. Lietaer (eds) *Handbook of Experiential Psychotherapy*. New York: The Guilford Press.

Eisler, Riane (1987) *The Chalice and the Blade*. San Francisco: Harper & Row.

Eisler, Riane (1995) *Sacred Pleasure: Sex, Myth and the Politics of the Body*. Shaftesbury: Element.

Elliott, James (1976) *The Theory and Practice of Encounter Group Leadership*. Berkeley: Explorations Institute.

Elworthy, Scilla (1996) *Power and Sex: A Book about Women*. Shaftesbury: Element.

Emerson, William and Shorr-Kon, Stephan (1994) 'Somatotropic therapy' in D. Jones (ed.) *Innovative Therapy: A Handbook*. Buckingham: Open University Press.

Emery, Fred and Thorsrud, E. (1976) *Democracy at Work*. Leiden: Martinus Nijhoff.

Emmet, Dorothy (1966) *Rules, Roles and Relations*. London: Macmillan.

Enright, John (1970) 'Awareness training in the mental health professions' in J. Fagan and I. L. Shepherd (eds) *Gestalt Therapy Now*. Palo Alto: Science & Behaviour.

Ernst, Sheila and Goodison, Lucy (1981) *In Our Own Hands: A Book of Self-help Therapy*. London: The Women's Press.

Esterson, Aaron (1972) *The Leaves of Spring: A Study in the Dialectics of Madness*. Harmondsworth: Penguin.

Evans, Roger and Russell, Peter (1989) *The Creative Manager*. London: Unwin.

Evison, Rose and Horobin, Richard (1983) *How to Change Yourself and Your World*. Sheffield: Co-counselling Phoenix.

Eysenck, Hans J. (1965) *Fact and Fiction in Psychology*. Harmondsworth: Penguin.

Fagan, Joen and Shepherd, Irma L. (eds) (1970) *Gestalt Therapy Now*. Palo Alto: Science & Behaviour.

Faraday, Ann (1976) *The Dream Game*. New York: Harper & Row.

Farber, Barry A., Brink, Deborah C. and Raskin, Patricia M. (eds) (1996) *The Psychotherapy of Carl Rogers: Cases and Commentary*. New York: The Guilford Press.

Farrell, Warren (1974) *The Liberated Man: Freeing Men and their Relationships with Women*. New York: Random House.

Ferguson, Marilyn (1982) *The Aquarian Conspiracy*. London: Routledge.

Ferrucci, Piero (1982) *What We May Be*. Wellingborough: Turnstone Press.

Fiedler, Fred E. (1967) *A Theory of Leadership Effectiveness*. New York: McGraw-Hill.

Firman, John and Gila, Ann (1997) *The Primal Wound*. Albany: SUNY Press.

Fisher, Seymour (1973) *Body Consciousness: You Are What You Feel*. Englewood Cliffs: Prentice-Hall.

Fiske, D. W. and Maddi, S. R. (eds) (1961) *Functions of Varied Experience*. Homewood: The Dorsey Press.

Fletcher, B. (1990) *Organization Transformation Theorists and Practitioners: Profiles and Themes*. New York: Praeger.

Follett, Mary P. (1995) 'Constructive conflict' in P. Graham (ed.) *Mary Parker Follett: Prophet of Management*. Boston: Harvard Business School Press.

Fordyce, J. K. and Weil, R. (1971) *Managing with People. A Manager's Handbook of Organization Development Methods*. Reading: Addison-Wesley.

Fransella, Fay (1972) *Personal Change and Reconstruction*. New York: Academic Press.

Freud, Sigmund (1975/1900) *The Interpretation of Dreams*. Harmondsworth: Penguin.

Friedan, Betty (1965) *The Feminine Mystique*. Harmondsworth: Penguin.

Friedman, Maurice (1964) 'Problematic rebel: an image of modern man' in M. Friedman (ed.) *The Worlds of Existentialism: A Critical Reader*. Chicago: The University of Chicago Press.

From, Isador (1984) 'Reflections on Gestalt therapy after thirty-two years of practice: A requiem for Gestalt' *The Gestalt Journal* 7(1): 4–13.

Gaines, Jack (1979) *Fritz Perls Here and Now*. Millbrae: Celestial Arts.

Gallwey, W. (1974) *The Inner Game of Tennis*. London: Jonathan Cape.

Garfield, Patricia (1976) *Creative Dreaming*. London: Futura.

Garfield, Sol L. and Bergin, Alan E. (eds) (1978) *Handbook of Psychotherapy and Behaviour Change* (2nd edn). New York: John Wiley & Sons.

Gebser, Jean (1985) *The Ever-present Origin*. Athens: Ohio University Press.

Geller, Leonard (1982) 'The failure of self-actualization theory: a critique of Carl Rogers and Abraham Maslow', *Journal of Humanistic Psychology* 22(2): 56–73.

Geller, Leonard (1984) 'Another look at self-actualization', *Journal of Humanistic Psychology* 24(2): 93–106.

Gendlin, Eugene T. (1962) *Experiencing and the Creation of Meaning*. London: Collier-Macmillan.

Gendlin, Eugene T. (1981) *Focusing* (2nd edn). New York: Bantam.

Gendlin, Eugene T. (1996) *Focusing-Oriented Psychotherapy*. New York: The Guilford Press.

Georgaca, E. (2000) 'Reality and discourse: a critical analysis of the category of delusions', *British Journal of Medical Psychology* 73(2): 227–242.

Gergen, Kenneth J. (1972) 'Multiple identity: the healthy, happy human being wears many masks', *Psychology Today*, May.

Gergen, Kenneth J. (1985) 'The social constructivist movement in modern psychology', *American Psychologist* 40: 266–275.

Gergen, Kenneth J. (1997) 'The place of the psyche in a constructed world', *Theory and Psychology* 7(6): 723–746.

Gergen, Mary M. and Davis, Sara N. (1997) *Toward a New Psychology of Gender: A Reader*. London: Routledge.

Ginsburg, C. (1984) 'Toward a somatic understanding of self: a reply to Leonard Geller', *Journal of Humanistic Psychology* 24(2): 66–92.

Giorgi, Amedeo (ed.) (1975) *Duquesne Studies in Phenomenological Psychology*. Duquesne: Duquesne University Press.

Glenn, Michael (1971) 'Introduction' in the Radical Therapist Collective (eds) *The Radical Therapist*. New York: Ballantine.

Glouberman, Dina (1995) *Life Choices, Life Changes*. London: Thorsons.

Goffman, Erving (1974) *Frame Analysis: An Essay on the Organization of Experience*. New York: Harper Colophon.

Golembiewski, R. T. and Blumberg, A. (eds) (1970) *Sensitivity Training and the Laboratory Approach: Readings About Concepts and Applications*. New York: Peacock.

Golembiewski, R. T. et al. (1982) 'Estimating the success of OD applications', *Training and Development Journal*, April: 86–95.

Goodman, Paul (1962) 'Seating arrangements: an elementary lecture on functional planning' in P. Goodman, *Utopian Essays and Practical Proposals*. New York: Vintage.

Gopnik, Alison, Meltzoff, Andrew and Kuhl, Patricia (1999) *How Babies Think: The Science of Childhood*. London: Weidenfeld & Nicholson.

Graham, Pauline (ed.) (1995) *Mary Parker Follett: Prophet of Management*. Boston: Harvard Business School Press.

Gray, Elizabeth D. (1982) *Patriarchy as a Conceptual Trap*. Wellesley: Roundtable Press.

Gray, Harry (1985) *Organization Development in Education*. Stoke-on-Trent: Deanhouse.

Green, Elmer E. and Green, Alyce M. (1971) 'On the meaning of transpersonal: some metaphysical perspectives', *Journal of Transpersonal Psychology* 3(1): 27–46.

Greenberg, Ira A. (ed.) (1974) *Psychodrama: Theory and Therapy*. London: Condor.

Greenberg, Leslie S., Watson, Jeanne C. and Lietaer, Germain (1998) *Handbook of Experiential Psychotherapy*. New York: The Guilford Press.

Greer, Scott (1997) 'Nietzsche and social construction', *Theory and Psychology* 7(1): 83–100.

Grof, Stanislav (1979) *Realms of the Human Unconscious*. London: Souvenir Press.

Grof, Stanislav (1980) *LSD Psychotherapy*. Pomona: Hunter House.

Grof, Stanislav (1988) *The Adventure of Self-discovery*. Albany: SUNY Press.

Grove, David and Panzer, B. I. (1989) *Resolving Traumatic Memories: Metaphors and Symbols in Psychotherapy*. New York: Irvington.

Guignon, Charles (ed.) (1993) *The Cambridge Companion to Heidegger*. Cambridge: Cambridge University Press.

Gunther, Bernard (1969) *Sense Relaxation: Below Your Mind*. London: Macdonald.

Habermas, Jürgen (1979) *Communication and the Evolution of Society*. Boston: Beacon Press.

Hacker, H. (1951) 'Women as a minority group', *Social Forces* 30: 60–69.

Haigh, Gerald V. (1968) 'The residential basic encounter group' in H. A. Otto and J. Mann (eds) *Ways of Growth*. New York: Grossman.

Hall, Budd L. (1981) 'The democratization of research in adult and non-formal education' in P. Reason and J. Rowan (eds) *Human Inquiry*. Chichester: Wiley.

Halpin, A. W. and Winer, B. J. (1952) *The Leadership Behaviour of the Airplane Commander*. Columbus: Ohio State University Press.

Hamblin, Angela (1972) 'Ultimate goals', *Women's Liberation Review* 1: 23–46. (Reprinted in *Self & Society* 1975, 3(12): 1–6 and 1976, 4(2): 19–24.)

Hammond, John, Hay, David, Moxon, Jo, Netto, Brian, Raban, Nancy, Straugheir, Ginny and Williams, Chris (1990) *New Methods in RE Teaching: An Experiential Approach*. Harlow: Oliver & Boyd.

Hampden-Turner, Charles (1971) *Radical Man: The Process of Psychosocial Development*. London: Duckworth.

Hampden-Turner, Charles (1977) *Sane Asylum*. New York: William Morrow & Co.

Hampden-Turner, Charles (1981) *Maps of the Mind*. London: Mitchell Beazley.

Hampden-Turner, Charles (1983) *Gentlemen and Tradesmen: The Values of Economic Catastrophe*. London: Routledge.

Harman, Willis and Hormann, John (1990) *Creative Work: The Constructive Role of Business in a Transforming Society*. Knowledge Systems: Indianapolis.

Haronian, F. (1974) 'The repression of the sublime', *Synthesis* 1(1): 51–62.

Harré, Rom (1979) *Social Being*. Oxford: Blackwell.

Harrison, Roger (1984) 'Leadership and strategy for a new age' in J. D. Adams (ed.) *Transforming Work*. Alexandria: Miles River Press.

Hay, David (1982) *Exploring Inner Space*. Harmondsworth: Penguin.

Hay, David (1990) *Religious Experience Today: Studying the Facts*. London: Mowbray.

Hegel, George W. F. (1892) *The Lesser Logic* (ed. W. Wallace). Oxford: The Clarendon Press.

Hegel, George W. F. (1971) *Hegel's Philosophy of Mind* (trans. A. V. Miller). Oxford: The Clarendon Press.

Heidegger, Martin (1962) *Being and Time*. New York: Harper & Row.

Heider, Jon (1974) 'Catharsis in human potential encounter', *Journal of Humanistic Psychology* 14(4): 27–47.

Henderson, Hazel (1982) *Thinking Globally, Acting Locally: The Politics and Ethics of the Solar Age*. Berkeley: University of California Press.

Hendricks, Gay and Fadiman, James (1976) *Transpersonal Education*. Englewood Cliffs: Prentice-Hall.

Hendricks, Gay and Roberts, T. B. (1977) *The Second Centering Book*. Englewood Cliffs: Prentice-Hall.

Hendricks, Gay and Wills, R. (1975) *The Centering Book*. Englewood Cliffs: Prentice-Hall.

Henley, Nancy (1977) *Body Politics*. Englewood Cliffs: Prentice-Hall.

Herbst, P. G. (1976) *Alternatives to Hierarchies*. Leiden: Martinus Nijhoff.

Heron, John (1972) *Experience and Method*. Guildford: Human Potential Research Project.

Heron, John (1974) *Reciprocal Counselling*. Guildford: Human Potential Research Project.

Heron, John (1981) 'Experiential research methodology' in P. Reason and J. Rowan (eds) *Human Inquiry*. Chichester: Wiley.

Heron, John (1996) *Co-operative Inquiry*. London: Sage.

Hersey, Paul G. and Blanchard, Kenneth H. (1977) *Management of Organizational Behaviour: Utilising Human Resources* (3rd edn). Englewood Cliffs: Prentice-Hall.

Hersey, Paul, Blanchard, Kenneth and Natemeyer, Walter E. (1979) 'Situational leadership, perception and the impact of power', *Group and Organization Studies* 4(4): 418–428.

Hillman, James (1979) *The Dream and the Underworld*. San Francisco: Harper & Row.

Hoffer, Eric (1952) *The True Believer*. London: Secker & Warburg.

Hoffman, Bernard (1979) *No One is to Blame*. Palo Alto: Science & Behaviour.

Holmes, Paul and Karp, Marcia (eds) (1991) *Psychodrama: Inspiration and Technique*. London: Routledge.

Holmes, Paul, Karp, Marcia and Watson, Michael (eds) (1994) *Psychodrama Since Moreno*. London: Routledge.

Horne, J. R. (1978) *Beyond Mysticism*. Waterloo: Canadian Corporation for Studies in Religion.

Horney, Karen (1942) *Self-analysis*. London: Routledge.

Horney, Karen (1968) *The Neurotic Personality of Our Time*. New York: Norton.

Houston, Jean (1982) *The Possible Human*. Los Angeles: J. P. Tarcher.

Huang, Al Chung-Liang (1973) *Embrace Tiger, Return to Mountain*. Moab: Real People Press.

Huczynski, A. (1983) *Encyclopedia of Management Development Methods*. Aldershot: Gower.

Hunter, Elizabeth (1972) *Encounter in the Classroom: New Ways of Teaching*. New York: Holt Rinehart & Winston.

Huxley, Aldous (1963) *The Doors of Perception*. New York: Harper & Row.

Inglis, Brian (1964) *Fringe Medicine*. London: Faber.

Jackins, Harvey (1965) *The Human Side of Human Beings*. New York: Norton.

Jackins, Harvey (1970) *Fundamentals of Co-Counselling*. Seattle: Rational Island.

Jackins, Harvey (1973) *The Human Situation*. Seattle: Rational Island.

Janov, Arthur (1970) *The Primal Scream*. New York: Putnam.

Janov, Arthur (1990) *The New Primal Scream*. London: Abacus.

Johnson, David and Johnson, Roger (1975) *Learning Together and Alone*. Englewood Cliffs: Prentice-Hall.

Jones, F. and Harris, M. W. (1971) 'The development of interracial awareness in small groups' in L. Blank et al. (eds) *Confrontation: Encounters in Self and Interpersonal Awareness*. New York: Collier-Macmillan,

Jung, Carl G. (1933) *Modern Man in Search of a Soul*. London: Routledge.

Jung, Carl G. (1938) *Psychology and Religion* in Collected Works, Vol. 2. London: Routledge & Kegan Paul.

Jung, Carl G. (1959) *Basic Writings of C. G. Jung* (ed. V. S. de Laszlo). New York: Modern Library.

Jung, Carl G. (1966) *Two Essays on Analytical Psychology*. London: Routledge.

Jung, Carl G. (1971) *The Portable Jung* (ed. J. Campbell). New York: The Viking Press.

Kanter, Rosabeth M. (1985) *The Change Masters*. London: Unwin.

Kapleau, Philip (ed.) (1967) *The Three Pillars of Zen: Teaching, Practice and Enlightenment*. Boston: Beacon Press.

Karp, Marcia, Holmes, Paul and Tauvon, Kate B. (eds) (1998) *The Handbook of Psychodrama*. London: Routledge.

Kekes, John (1994) *The Morality of Pluralism*. Princeton: Princeton University Press.

Keleman, Stanley (1985) *Emotional Anatomy*. Berkeley: Center Press.

Kelman, H. C. (1968) *A Time to Speak: On Human Values and Social Research*. San Francisco: Jossey-Bass.

Kennedy, Carol (1991) *Guide to the Management Gurus*. London: Business Books.

Kirschenbaum, Howard (1978) *Advanced Value Clarification*. Mansfield: University Associates.

Knutson, J. K. (ed.) (1973) *Handbook of Political Psychology*. San Francisco: Jossey-Bass.

Kogan, G. (1980) *Your Body Works: A Guide to Health, Energy and Balance*. Berkeley: Transformation Press.

Kohlberg, Lawrence (1969) 'Stage and sequence: the cognitive-developmental approach to socialization' in D. Goslin (ed.) *Handbook of Socialization Theory and Research*. Chicago: Rand McNally.

Kohlberg, Lawrence (1981) *The Philosophy of Moral Development*. San Francisco: Harper & Row.

Kohut, Heinz (1984) *How Does Analysis Cure?* Chicago: University of Chicago Press.

Kornegger, Peggy (1975) 'Anarchism: the feminist connection' in Dark Star (ed.) *Quiet Rumours: An Anarcha-feminist Anthology*. London: Dark Star.

Kotler, P. (1973) 'The elements of social action' in G. Zaltman (ed.) *Processes and Phenomena of Social Change*. New York: Academic Press.

Krech, David, Crutchfield, Richard and Livson, Norman (1969) *Elements of Psychology*. New York: Knopf.

Krippner, Stanley (1972) 'Altered states of consciousness' in J. White (ed.) *The Highest State of Consciousness*. New York: Anchor.

Krippner, Stanley and Powers, Susan M. (1997) *Broken Images, Broken Selves: Dissociative Narratives in Clinical Practice*. Washington: Brunner/Mazel.

Kurtz, Ron and Prestera, Hector (1977) *The Body Reveals*. New York: Harper & Row.

Kutash, Irwin D. and Wolf, Alexander (eds) (1986) *Psychotherapist's Casebook*. San Francisco: Jossey-Bass.

Kutchins, Herb and Kirk, Stuart A. (1997) *Making Us Crazy: DSM: The Psychiatric Bible and the Creation of Mental Disorders*. New York: The Free Press.

Labov, W. (1972) 'The logic of nonstandard English' in P. P. Giglioli (ed.) *Language and Social Context*. Harmondsworth: Penguin.

Laing, Ronald D. (1967) *The Politics of Experience*. Harmondsworth: Penguin.

Laing, Ronald D. (1983) *The Voice of Experience*. Harmondsworth: Penguin.

Lawrence, P. R. and Lorsch, J. W. (1969) *Developing Organizations: Diagnosis and Action*. Reading: Addison-Wesley.

Leary, Timothy (1970) *The Politics of Ecstasy*. London: Paladin.

Leeds, Ruth (1970) 'The absorption of protest: a working paper' in W. G. Bennis et al. (eds) *The Planning of Change* (2nd edn). New York: Holt Rinehart & Winston.

Leonard, George B. (1968) *Education and Ecstasy*. New York: Dell.

Leonard, George B. (1977) *The Ultimate Athlete*. New York: Avon.

Lessing, Doris (1970) *The Four-gated City*. New York: Bantam Books.

Lester, David (1995) *Theories of Personality*. Washington: Taylor & Francis.

Lethbridge, D. (1986) 'A marxist theory of self-actualization', *Journal of Humanistic Psychology* 26(2): 84–403.

Leuner, Hanscarl (1984) *Guided Affective Imagery*. New York: Thieme-Stratton.

Levant, Ronald F. and Pollack, William S. (eds) (1995) *A New Psychology of Men*. New York: Basic Books.

Lewin, Kurt (1936) *Principles of Topological Psychology*. New York: McGraw-Hill.

Lewin, Kurt, Lippitt, R. and White, R. K. (1939) 'Patterns of aggressive behaviour in experimentally created social climates', *Journal of Social Psychology*, 10: 271–299.

Lilly, John C. (1973) *The Centre of the Cyclone*. London: Paladin.

Lincoln, Yvonna S. and Guba, Egon G. (1985) *Naturalistic Inquiry*. Beverley Hills: Sage.

Loevinger, J. (1976) *Ego Development*. San Francisco: Jossey-Bass.

Lowen, Alexander (1976) *Bioenergetics*. London: Coventure.

Lowen, A. and Lowen, L. (1997) *The Way to Vibrant Health*. New York: Harper Colophon.

McAllister, P. (ed.) (1982) *Reweaving the Web of Life: Feminism and Nonviolence*. Philadelphia: New Society Publishers.

McCall, G. J. and Simmons, J. L. (eds) (1969) *Issues in Participant Observation*. Reading: Addison-Wesley.

McGregor, Donald (1960) *The Human Side of Enterprise*. New York: McGraw-Hill.

McNamara, William (1975) 'Psychology and the Christian mystical tradition' in C. T. Tart (ed.) *Transpersonal Psychologies*. London: Routledge.

Macy, Joanna R. (1983) *Despair and Personal Power in the Nuclear Age*. Philadelphia: New Society Publishers.

Maddi, Salvatore (1996) *Personality Theories: A Comparative Analysis* (6th edn). Pacific Grove: Brooks/Cole.

Madison, P. (1969) *Personality Development in College*. Reading: Addison-Wesley.

Mahler, Margaret S., Pine, F. and Bergman, A. (1975) *The Psychological Birth of the Human Infant*. London: Hutchinson.

Mahoney, M. (1972) *The Meaning of Dreams and Dreaming*. New York: Citadel Press.

Mahrer, Alvin R. (1978) *Experiencing: A Humanistic Theory of Psychology and Psychiatry*. New York: Brunner/Mazel.

Mahrer, Alvin R. (1985) *Psychotherapeutic Change: An Alternative Approach to Meaning and Measurement*. New York: W. W. Norton.

Mahrer, Alvin R. (1986) *Therapeutic Experiencing: The Process of Change*. New York: W. W. Norton.

Mahrer, Alvin R. (1989) *Experiencing: A Humanistic Theory of Psychology and Psychiatry*. Ottawa: University of Ottawa Press. (Originally published in 1978 by Brunner/Mazel.)

Mahrer, Alvin R. (1994) *Dream Work: Psychotherapy and Self Change*. New York: W. W. Norton.

Mahrer, Alvin R. (1996) *The Complete Guide to Experiential Psychotherapy*. New York: John Wiley.

Mann, Richard D. (1975) 'Winners, losers and the search for equality in groups' in C. L. Cooper (ed.) *Theories of Group Processes*. London: Wiley.

Marmor, Judd (1974) *Psychiatry in Transition*. London: Butterworth.

Martin, Shan (1983) *Managing Without Managers*. Beverly Hills: Sage.

Maruyama, Magoroh (1981) 'Endogenous research: rationale' and 'Endogenous research: the prison project' in P. Reason and J. Rowan (eds) *Human Inquiry*. Chichester: Wiley.

Maslow, Abraham H. (1965) *Eupsychian Management*. New York: Irwin Dorsey.

Maslow, Abraham H. (1968) *Toward a Psychology of Being*. New York: Van Nostrand.

Maslow, Abraham H. (1969) *The Psychology of Science: A Reconnaissance*. New York: Henry Regnery (Gateway Edition).

Maslow, Abraham H. (1970) *Religions, Values and Peak Experiences*. New York: The Viking Press.

Maslow, Abraham H. (1973) *The Farther Reaches of Human Nature*. Harmondsworth: Penguin.

Maslow, Abraham H. (1987) *Motivation and Personality* (3rd edn). New York: Harper & Row.

Masters, Robert E. L. and Houston, Jean (1978) *Listening to the Body*. New York: Delacorte Press.

May, Rollo (1980) *Psychology and the Human Dilemma*. New York: W. W. Norton.

May, Rollo (1983) *The Discovery of Being*. New York: W. W. Norton.

May, Rollo (1989) *The Art of Counselling* (revised edn). New York: Gardner Press.

Meade, Michael (1993) *Men and the Water of Life: Initiation and the Tempering of Men*. San Francisco: Harper.

Mearns, Dave (1994) *Developing Person-centred Counselling*. London: Sage.

Mearns, Dave (1996) 'Working at relational depth with clients in person-centred therapy' *Counselling* 7(4): 306–311.

Mearns, Dave (1997) 'Achieving the personal development dimension in professional counsellor training', *Counselling* 8(2): 113–120.

Mearns, Dave (1999) 'Person-centred therapy with configurations of self', *Counselling* 10(2): 125–130.

Mearns, Dave and McLeod, John (1984) 'A person-centered approach to research' in R. F. Levant and J. M. Schlien (eds) *Client-centered Therapy and the Person-centered Approach*. New York: Praeger.

Melnick, Joseph and Nevis, Sonia M. (1998) 'Diagnosing in the here and now: a Gestalt therapy approach' in L. S. Greenberg, J. C. Watson and G. Lietaer (eds) *Handbook of Experiential Psychotherapy*. New York: The Guilford Press.

Merleau-Ponty, Maurice (1962) *The Phenomenology of Perception*. London: Routledge.

Mertens, Donna M. (1998) *Research Methods in Education and Psychology: Integrating Diversity with Quantitative and Qualitative Approaches*. Sage: Thousand Oaks.

Metcalf, Andy and Humphries, Martin (eds) (1985) *The Sexuality of Men*. London: Pluto Press.

Metcalf, H. C. and Urwick, L. (1941) *Dynamic Administration: The Collected Papers of Mary Parker Follett*. London: Pitman.

Miller, Alice (1985) *Thou Shalt Not be Aware*. London: Pluto Press.

Miller, Casey and Swift, Kate (1979) *Words and Women*. Harmondsworth: Penguin.

Miller, Leslie A. (2000) 'The poverty of truth-seeking: Postmodernism, discourse analysis and critical feminism', *Theory & Psychology* 10(3): 313–352.

Mindell, Amy (1995) *Metaskills*. Tempe: New Falcon Publications.

Mindell, Arnold (1985) *Working with the Dreaming Body*. London: Routledge.

Mintz, Elizabeth E. (1972) *Marathon Groups: Reality and Symbol*. New York: Avon.

Mintz, Elizabeth E. (1983) *The Psychic Thread: Paranormal and Transpersonal Aspects of Psychotherapy*. New York: Human Sciences Press.

Mitchell, Juliet (1974) *Psychoanalysis and Feminism*. New York: Pantheon Books.

Mitroff, Ian I. (1974) *The Subjective Side of Science*. Amsterdam: Elsevier.

Mitroff, Ian I. and Kilmann, Ralph H. (1978) *Methodological Approaches to Social Science*. San Francisco: Jossey-Bass.

Mittelman, Willard (1991) 'Maslow's study of self-actualization: a reinterpretation', *Journal of Humanistic Psychology* 31(1): 114–135.

Mittelman, Willard (1992) 'Openness and self-actualization: a reply to Tobacyk and Miller', *Journal of Humanistic Psychology* 32(2): 137–142.

Mittelman, Willard (1994) 'Openness, optimal functioning and final causes', *Journal of Humanistic Psychology* 34(2): 100–107.

Mittelman, Willard (1995) 'Openness: a final reply to Tobacyk', *Journal of Humanistic Psychology* 35(1): 102–107.

Montagu, Ashley (1986) *Touching* (3rd edn). New York: Harper & Row.

Moreno, Jacob L. (1964) *Psychodrama, Vol.1*. New York: Beacon House.

Moreno, Jacob L. (1966) *Psychodrama, Vol.2*. New York: Beacon House.

Moreno, Jacob L. (1969) *Psychodrama, Vol.3*. New York: Beacon House.

Moss, Donald (ed.) (1999) *Humanistic and Transpersonal Psychology: An Historical and Biographical Sourcebook*. Westport: Greenwood Press.

Moss, L. E. (1981) *A Woman's Way: A Feminist Approach to Body Psychotherapy*. Ann Arbor: University Microfilms International.

Mullender, Audrey and Ward, Dave (1991) *Self-directed Groupwork*. London: Whiting & Birch.

Müller, Bertram (1996) 'Isadore From's contribution to the theory and practice of Gestalt therapy', *The Gestalt Journal* 19(1): 57–81.

Murphy, Gardner (1950) 'Psychical research and personality', *Journal of the American Society for Psychical Research* 44(1): 3–20.

Murphy, Michael (1978) *The Psychic Side of Sports*. Reading: Addison-Wesley.

Negrin, Su (1972) *Begin at Start: Some Thoughts on Personal Liberation and World Change*. Washington: Times Change Press.

Newsome, Audrey et al. (1973) *Student Counselling in Practice*. London: University of London Press.

Nicholas, J. M. (1982) 'The comparative impact of OD interventions on hard criteria measures', *Academy of Management Review* 7(4): 531–542.

Nichols, Michael P. and Zax, Melvin (1977) *Catharsis in Psychotherapy*. New York: Gardner Press.

Nietzsche, Friedrich (1967/1901) *The Will to Power*. New York: Random House.

Noble, Vicki (1991) *Shakti Woman: The New Female Shamanism*. San Francisco: Harper.

O'Connor, Elizabeth (1971) *Our Many Selves*. San Francisco: Harper & Row.

Osho (1992) *Meditation: The First and Last Freedom*. Poona: Osho International Foundation.

Ouspensky, P. D. (1949) *In Search of the Miraculous*. New York: Harcourt Brace.

Pahnke, W. N. (1972) 'Drugs and mysticism' in J. White (ed.) *The Highest State of Consciousness*. Garden City: Doubleday/Anchor.

Painter, Jack (1986) *Deep Bodywork and Personal Development*. Mill Valley: Bodymind Books.

Palmer, Barry (1979) 'Learning and the group experience' in W. G. Lawrence (ed.) *Exploring Individual and Organizational Boundaries*. Chichester: John Wiley.

Palmer, Barry (1992) 'Ambiguity and paradox in group relations conferences' in M. Pines (ed.) *Bion and Group Psychotherapy*. London: Routledge.

Palmer, Stephen and Varma, Ved (eds) (1997) *The Future of Counselling and Psychotherapy*. London: Sage.

Perls, Frederick S. (1969) *Gestalt Therapy Verbatim*. Moab: Real People Press.

Perls, Frederick S. (1970) 'Four lectures' in J. Fagan and I. L. Shepherd (eds) *Gestalt Therapy Now*. Palo Alto: Science & Behaviour.

Perls, Fritz (1976) *The Gestalt Approach and Eyewitness to Therapy*. New York: Bantam Books.

Pierce, R. (1966) 'An investigation of grade-point average and therapeutic process variables', unpublished dissertation, University of Massachusetts. Reviewed in R. R. Carkhuff and G. B. Berenson, *Beyond Counselling and Therapy*. New York: Holt Rinehart & Winston.

Pierce, R. A. et al. (1983) *Emotional Expression in Psychotherapy*. New York: Gardner Press.

Pirani, Alix (1975) 'Creative relations in secondary education', *Self & Society*, 3.

Pleck, Joseph H. and Sawyer, Jack (eds) (1974) *Men and Masculinity*. Englewood Cliffs: Prentice-Hall.

Potter, J. and Wetherell, M. (1987) *Discourse and Social Psychology: Beyond Attitudes and Behaviour*. London: Sage.

Powell, A. (1986) 'Object relations in the psychodrama group', *Group Analysis* 19(2): 125–138.

Rajneesh, Bhagwan Shree (1979) *Roots and Wings*. London: Routledge.

Randall, Rosemary and Southgate, John (1980) *Cooperative and Community Group Dynamics: Or, Your Meetings Needn't be so Appalling*. London: Barefoot Books.

Rawson, Philip and Legeza, Laszlo (1973) *Tao: The Chinese Philosophy of Time and Change*. London: Thames & Hudson.

Reason, Peter and Bradbury, Hilary (eds) (2000) *The Handbook of Action Research*. Thousand Oaks: Sage.

Reason, Peter and Rowan, John (eds) (1981) *Human Inquiry: A Sourcebook of New Paradigm Research*. Chichester: John Wiley.

Reddin, William J. (1977) 'An integration of leader-behaviour typologies', *Group and Organization Studies* 2(3): 282–295.

Reich, Charles A. (1972) *The Greening of America*. Harmondsworth: Penguin.

Reps, Paul (1961) *Zen Flesh, Zen Bones*. Garden City: Doubleday.

Reynaud, Emmanuel (1983) *Holy Virility: The Social Construction of Masculinity*. London: Pluto Press.

Richards, Mary C. (1969) *Centering: In Pottery, Poetry and the Person*. Middletown: Wesleyan University Press.

Riegel, K. F. (1984) Chapter in M. L. Commons, F. A. Richards and C. Armon (eds) *Beyond Formal Operations: Late Adolescence and Adult Cognitive Development*. New York: Praeger.

Ring, Kenneth (1974) 'A transpersonal view of consciousness: a mapping of farther regions of inner space', *Journal of Transpersonal Psychology* 6.

Rogers, Carl R .(1942) *Counselling and Psychotherapy*. Boston: Houghton Mifflin.

Rogers, Carl R. (1951) *Client-centred Therapy*. Boston: Houghton Mifflin.

Rogers, Carl R. (1959) 'A theory of therapy, personality, and interpersonal relationships as developed in the client-centred framework' in S. Koch (ed.) *Psychology: A Study of a Science*, Vol. 3: *Formulations of the Person and the Social Context*, pp. 184–256. New York: McGraw-Hill.

Rogers, Carl R. (1961) *On Becoming a Person*. London: Constable.

Rogers, Carl R. (1972) 'Comments on Brown and Tedeschi's article', *Journal of Humanistic Psychology* 12(1): 16–21.

Rogers, Carl R. (1983) *Freedom to Learn for the 80s*. Columbus: Charles E. Merrill.

Rogers, Carl R. (1990/1968) 'Some thoughts regarding the current presuppositions of the behavioural sciences' in H. Kirschenbaum and V. L. Henderson (eds) *The Carl Rogers Reader*. London: Constable.

Rogers, Carl R. and Dymond, Rosalyn F. (eds) (1954) *Psychotherapy and Personality Change*. Chicago: University of Chicago Press.

Rogers, Carl R. and Freiberg, H. Jerome (1994) *Freedom to Learn* (3rd edn). New York: Macmillan.

Rogers, Carl R. and Ryback, David (1985) 'A psychological view of the Camp David meeting', *Counselling* No. 54.

Romey, William D. (1972) *Risk-Trust-Love: Learning in a Humane Environment*. New York: Charles E. Merrill.

Rothberg, Donald and Kelly, Sean (eds) (1998) *Ken Wilber in Dialogue: Conversations with Leading Transpersonal Thinkers*. Wheaton: Quest.

Rowan, John (1975) 'The four-way workshop', *Self and Society* 3(5): 16–19.

Rowan, John (1976a) *The Power of the Group*. London: Davis-Poynter.

Rowan, John (1976b) 'Ethical issues in organizational change' in P. B. Warr (ed.) *Personal Goals and Work Design*. Chichester: John Wiley.

Rowan, John (1983a) 'The real self and mystical experiences', *Journal of Humanistic Psychology* 23(2): 9–27.

Rowan, John (1983b) 'Person as group' in H. H. Blumberg et al. (eds) *Small Groups and Social Interaction* (vol. 2). Chichester: John Wiley & Sons.

Rowan, John (1985) 'Listening as a four-level activity', *British Journal of Psychotherapy* 1(4): 273–285.

Rowan, John (1987) *The Horned God*. London: Routledge.

Rowan, John (1990) *Subpersonalities: The People Inside Us*. London: Routledge.

Rowan, John (1992) 'Hegel and self-actualization', *The Humanistic Psychologist* 20(1): 58–74.

Rowan, John (1993) *The Transpersonal: Psychotherapy and Counselling*. London: Routledge.

Rowan, John (1997) *Healing the Male Psyche: Therapy as Initiation*. London: Routledge.

Rowan, John (1998a) 'Maslow amended', *Journal of Humanistic Psychology* 38(1): 81–92.

Rowan, John (1998b) *The Reality Game: A Guide to Humanistic Counselling and Psychotherapy* (2nd edn). London: Routledge.

Rowan, John (1998c) 'Transformational research' in P. Clarkson (ed.) *Counselling Psychology: Integrating Theory, Research and Supervised Practice*. London: Routledge.

Rowan, John (1999) 'Ascent and descent in Maslow's theory', *Journal of Humanistic Psychology* 39(3): 125–133.

Rowan, John (2000) 'Dialectics and humanistic psychotherapy', *Practical Philosophy* 3(2): 18–21.

Rowan, John (2000) 'The three bodies in psychotherapy', *European Journal of Psychotherapy, Counselling and Health* 3(2): 193–207.

Rowan, John and Cooper, Mick (eds) (1999) *The Plural Self: Multiplicity in Everyday Life*. London: Sage.

Rowan, John and Dryden, Windy (eds) (1988) *Innovative Therapy in Britain*. Milton Keynes: Open University Press.

Rowbotham, Sheila et al. (1979) *Beyond the Fragments*. London: The Merlin Press.

Rubin, Z. and McNeil, E. B. (1987) *Psychology: Being Human* (4th edn). New York: Harper & Row.

Rush, Anne K. (1973) *Getting Clear: Body Work for Women*. New York: Random House.

Russell, Peter (1982) *The Awakening Earth: Our Next Evolutionary Leap*. London: Routledge.

Samuels, Andrew (1989) *The Plural Psyche*. London: Routledge.

Sanford, Nevitt (1981) 'A model for action research', in P. Reason and J. Rowan (eds) *Human Inquiry*. Chichester: Wiley.

Sapriel, Lolita (1998) 'Can Gestalt therapy, self-psychology and intersubjectivity theory be integrated?', *British Gestalt Journal* 7(1): 33–44.

Sartre, Jean-Paul (1948) *Existentialism and Humanism*. London: Methuen.

Sartre, Jean-Paul (1963) *Search for a Method*. New York: Alfred A. Knopf.

Schmuck, R. (1966) 'Some aspects of classroom social climate', *Psychology in the Schools* 3: 59–65.

Schneider, Kirk J. (1998) 'Existential processes' in L. S. Greenberg, J. C. Watson and G. Lietaer (eds) *Handbook of Experiential Psychotherapy*. New York: The Guilford Press.

Schneider, Kirk J., Bugental, James F. T. and Pierson, J. Fraser (eds) (in press) *The Handbook of Humanistic Psychology*. Thousand Oaks: Sage.

Schrank, Jeffrey (1972) *Teaching Human Beings: 101 Subversive Activities for the Classroom*. Boston: Beacon Press.

Schutz, Will C. (1971) *Here Comes Everybody: Bodymind and Encounter Culture*. New York: Harper & Row.

Schutz, Will C. (1973) *Elements of Encounter*. Big Sur: Joy Press.

Schutz, Will C. (1977) 'Bodymind' in C. A. Garfield (ed.) *Rediscovery of the Body*. New York: Laurel/Dell.

Schutz, Will C. (1981) 'Holistic education' in R. J. Corsini (ed.) *Handbook of Innovative Psychotherapies*. New York: Wiley.

Schutz, Will C. (1989) *Joy: Twenty Years Later*. Berkeley: Ten Speed Press.

Segal, Julia (1985) *Phantasy in Everyday Life*. Harmondsworth: Penguin.

Seidenberg, Robert (1973) 'Is anatomy destiny?' in J. B. Miller (ed.) *Psychoanalysis and Women*. Harmondsworth: Penguin.

Shaffer, John B. P. and Galinsky, M. David (1989) *Models of Group Therapy* (2nd edn). Englewood Cliffs: Prentice-Hall.

Shane, Paul (1999) 'Gestalt therapy: The Once and Future King' in D. Moss (ed.) *Humanistic and transpersonal psychology*. Westport, CT: Greenwood Press.

Shapiro, Stuart B. (1976) *The Selves Inside You*. Berkeley: Explorations Institute.

Shapiro, Stewart B. (1998) *The Place of Confluent Education in the Human Potential Movement: An Historical Perspective*. Lanham: University Press of America.

Sharaf, Myron (1983) *Fury on Earth*. London: Andre Deutsch.

Shaw, John (1974) *The Self in Social Work*. London: Routledge.

Shiel, Barbara J. (1994) 'A teacher's diary' in C. Rogers and H. J. Freiberg (eds) *Freedom to Learn* (3rd edn). New York: Merrill.

Shohet, Robin (1985) *Dream Sharing*. London: Turnstone Books.

Shorr, Joseph E. (1983) *Psychotherapy Through Imagery* (2nd edn). New York: Thieme-Stratton.

Simon, Stewart B., Howe, L. W. and Kirschenbaum, Howard (1972) *Values Clarification*. New York: Hart Publishing Company.

Simpson, Elizabeth L. (1971) *Democracy's Stepchildren: A Study of Need and Belief*. San Francisco: Jossey-Bass.

Singer, Jerome L. (1974) *Imagery and Daydream Methods in Psychotherapy and Behaviour Modification*. New York: Academic Press.

Sjöö, Monica and Mor, Barbara (1987) *The Great Cosmic Mother: Rediscovering the Religion of the Earth*. San Francisco: Harper & Row.

Skinner, Burrhus F. (1974) *About Behaviorism*. London: Jonathan Cape.

Smith, M. Brewster (1974) *Humanizing Social Psychology*. San Francisco: Jossey-Bass.

Snodgrass, Jon (ed.) (1977) *A Book of Readings for Men against Sexism*. New York: Times Change Press.

Southgate, John (1989) 'Interactive self-analysis: the successor to psychotherapy', *Journal of the Institute for Self-Analysis* 3(1): 11–16.

Southgate, John and Randall, Rosemary (1989) *The Barefoot Psychoanalyst* (3rd edn). Ilford: Gale Centre.

Southwell, Clover (1988) 'The Gerda Boyesen Method: biodynamic therapy' in J. Rowan and W. Dryden (eds) *Innovative Therapy in Britain*. Milton Keynes: Open University Press.

Spender, Dale (1980) *Man Made Language*. London: Routledge.

Spinelli, Ernesto (1989) *The Interpreted World*. London: Sage.

Spinelli, Ernesto (1994) *Demystifying Therapy*. London: Constable.

Spinelli, Ernesto (1997) *Tales of Un-knowing*. London: Duckworth.

Spino, Mike (1976) *Beyond Jogging*. Berkeley: Celestial Arts.

Spretnak, Charlene (ed.) (1982) *The Politics of Women's Spirituality: Essays on the Rise of Spiritual Power Within the Feminist Movement*. Garden City: Anchor/ Doubleday.

Sprinker, Michael (1980) 'Fictions of the self: the end of *Autobiography*' in J. Olney (ed.) *Autobiography: Essays Theoretical and Critical*. Princeton: Princeton University Press.

Starhawk (1979) *The Spiral Dance: A Rebirth of the Ancient Religion of the Great Goddess*. San Fancisco: Harper & Row.

Starhawk (1982) *Dreaming the Dark: Magic, Sex and Politics*. Boston: Beacon Press.

Starhawk (1987) *Truth or Dare*. San Francisco: Harper & Row.

Starhawk (1989) *The Spiral Dance* (2nd edn). San Francisco: Harper & Row.

Stein, Murray I. (1974) *Stimulating Creativity* (2 vols). New York: Academic Press.

Steiner, Claude and Members of the Radical Psychiatry Collective (1975) *Readings in Radical Psychiatry*. New York: Grove Press.

Stenner, Paul and Eccleston, Christopher (1994) 'On the textuality of being', *Theory and Psychology* 4(1): 85–103.

Stern, Daniel N. (1985) *The Interpersonal World of the Infant*. New York: Basic Books.

Stevens, Barry (1970) *Don't Push the River*. Moab UT: Real People Press.

Stevens, Barry and Rogers, Carl R. (eds) (1967) *Person to Person*. Moab: Real People Press.

Stevens, John O. (1971) *Awareness: Exploring, Experimenting, Experiencing*. Moab: Real People Press.

Stone, Hal and Winkelman, Sidra (1989) *Embracing our Selves*. San Rafael: New World Library.

Strauss, Anselm L. and Corbin, J. A. (1990) *Basics of Qualitative Research: Grounded Theory Procedures and Techniques*. Newbury Park: Sage.

Sturgess, D. (1972) 'Happenings in a primary school' in D. Rubinstein and C. Stoneman (eds) *Education for Democracy* (2nd edn). Harmondsworth: Penguin.

Tart, Charles T. (1969) *Altered States of Consciousness*. New York: John Wiley.

Tart, Charles T. (ed.) (1975) *Transpersonal Psychologies*. London: Routledge.

Tart, Charles T. (1986) *Waking Up: Overcoming the Obstacles to Human Potential*. Boston: Shambhala.

Tart, Charles T. (ed.) (1990) *Altered States of Consciousness* (3rd edn). San Francisco: Harper.

Taylor, Eugene I. (ed.) (1998) *Benchmarks in the History of Humanistic and*

Transpersonal Psychology: Reconstruction of the First Old Saybrook Conference, November 28–30, 1964. A Commemorative Edition. Manuscript in preparation.

Taylor, Susie (1998) 'The warm-up' in M. Karp, P. Holmes and K. B. Tauvon (eds) *The Handbook of Psychodrama.* London: Routledge.

Thomas, H. F. (1970) 'Encounter – the game of no game' in A. Burton (ed.) *Encounter.* San Francisco: Jossey-Bass.

Thorne, Brian (1992) *Carl Rogers.* London: Sage.

Tichy, Noel M. (1977) 'Demise, absorption or renewal for the future of organization development' in W. W. Burke (ed.) *The Cutting Edge: Current Theory and Practice in Organization Development.* La Jolla: University Associates.

Tichy, Noel M. and Devanna, Mary Anne (1986) *The Transformational Leader.* New York: John Wiley.

Tompkins, Penny and Lawley, James (1997) *Principles of Grovian Metaphor Therapy.* London: The Developing Company.

Torbert, William (1972) *Learning from Experience. Toward Consciousness.* New York: Columbia University Press.

Totton, Nick and Edmondson, Em (1988) *Reichian Growth Work.* Bridport: Prism Press.

Turner, R. (ed.) (1974) *Ethnomethodology: Selected Readings.* Harmondsworth: Penguin.

Valle, Ron (ed.) (1998) *Phenomenological Inquiry in Psychology: Existential and Transpersonal Dimensions.* New York: Plenum Press.

Van Deurzen, Emmy (1999) 'Heidegger's challenge of authenticity', *Journal of the Society for Existential Analysis* 10(1): 115–125.

Van Deurzen-Smith, Emmy (1997) *Everyday Mysteries: Existential Dimensions of Psychotherapy.* London: Routledge.

Varela, J. A. (1971) *Psychological Solutions to Social Problems.* New York: Academic Press.

Vargiu, James (1974) 'Psychosynthesis workbook: subpersonalities', *Synthesis* 1(1): 74-page section.

Vaughan, Frances (1986) *The Inward Arc.* Boston: New Science Library.

Verny, Tom (1982) *The Secret Life of the Unborn Child.* London: Sphere.

von Eckartsberg, Rolf (1981) 'Maps of the mind: the cartography of consciousness' in R. S. Valle and R. von Eckartsberg (eds) (1981) *The Metaphors of Consciousness.* Plenum Press, New York.

von Franz, Marie-Louise (1964) 'The process of individuation' in C. G. Jung (ed.) *Man and His Symbols.* London: Aldus Books.

Wade, Jenny (1996) *Changes of Mind.* Albany: SUNY Press.

Walker, Barbara G. (1983) *The Woman's Encyclopaedia of Myths and Secrets.* San Francisco: Harper & Row.

Walker, Barbara G. (1986) *The I Ching of the Goddess.* San Francisco: Harper & Row.

Walker, R. (ed.) (1985) *Applied Qualitative Research.* Aldershot: Gower.

Wallis, R. (1985) 'Betwixt therapy and salvation: the changing form of the Human Potential Movement' in R. K. Jones (ed.) *Sickness and Sectarianism.* Aldershot: Gower.

Warmoth, Art (1997) Personal communication.

Warnock, Diana (1982) 'Patriarchy is a killer: what people concerned about peace and justice should know' in P. McAllister (ed.) *Reweaving the Web of Life*. Philadelphia: New Society Publishers.

Watts, Alan W. (1951) *Psychotherapy East and West*. New York: Pantheon Books.

Watts, Alan W. (1957) *The Way of Zen*. London: Thames & Hudson.

Weiner, B. (1985) *Human Motivation*. New York: SpringerVerlag.

Wells, B. (1973) *Psychedelic Drugs: Psychological, Medical and Social Issues*. Harmondsworth: Penguin.

West, William (1994) 'Post-Reichian therapy' in D. Jones (ed.) *Innovative Therapy: A Handbook*. Buckingham: Open University Press.

West, William (2000) *Psychotherapy and Spirituality*. London: Sage.

Wheeler, Gordon (1998) 'Towards a Gestalt developmental model', *British Gestalt Journal* 7(2): 115–125.

Wheelis, Alan (1972) 'How people change' in L. F. Glass and J. R. Staude (eds) *Humanistic Society Pacific*. Palisades: Goodyear.

Wheway, John (1997) 'Dialogue and intersubjectivity in the therapeutic relationship', *British Gestalt Journal* 6(1): 16–28.

Whitfield, Geoffrey (1988) 'Bioenergetics' in J. Rowan and W. Dryden (eds) *Innovative Therapy in Britain*. Milton Keynes: Open University Press.

Whitmore, Diana (1991) *Psychosynthesis Counselling in Action*. London: Sage.

Whitmore, Diana (1999) *Psychosynthesis Counselling in Action* (2nd edn). London: Sage.

Wibberley, Mike (1988) 'Encounter' in J. Rowan and W. Dryden (eds) *Innovative Therapy in Britain*. Milton Keynes: Open University Press.

Wilber, Ken (1975) 'Psychologia Perennis: the spectrum of consciousness', *Journal of Transpersonal Psychology* 7(2): 105–132.

Wilber, Ken (1977) *The Spectrum of Consciousness*. Wheaton: Quest.

Wilber, Ken (1979) *No Boundary*. Boulder: Shambhala.

Wilber, Ken (1980) *The Atman Project*. Wheaton: Quest.

Wilber, Ken (1982) 'Reflections on the New Age paradigm' in K. Wilber (ed.) *The Holographic Paradigm and Other Paradoxes*. Boulder: Shambhala.

Wilber, Ken (1983) *Eye to Eye: The Quest for the New Paradigm*. Garden City: Anchor.

Wilber, Ken (1986a) 'Treatment modalities' in K. Wilber, J. Engler and D. P. Brown (eds) *Transformations of Consciousness*. Boston: Shambhala.

Wilber, K., Engler, J. and Brown, D. P. (eds) (1986b) *Transformations of Consciousness*. Boston: Shambhala.

Wilber, Ken (1995) *Sex, Ecology, Spirituality*. Boston: Shambhala.

Wilber, Ken (1996a) *The Atman Project* (2nd edn). Wheaton: Quest.

Wilber, Ken (1996b) *Up from Eden* (2nd edn). Wheaton: Quest.

Wilber, Ken (1997) *The Eye of Spirit*. Boston: Shambhala.

Wilber, Ken (1998) *The Marriage of Sense and Soul: Integrating Science and Religion*. New York: Random House.

Wilber, Ken (1999a) 'An approach to integral psychology', *The Journal of Transpersonal Psychology* 31(2): 109–136.

Wilber, Ken (1999b) 'Where It was, there I shall become: human potential and the boundaries of the soul' in *Collected Works, Vol.1*. Boston: Shambhala.

Wilber, Ken (2000) *A Theory of Everything* (unpublished draft).

Willis, Ellen (1981) *Beginning to See the Light*. New York: Alfred A. Knopf.

Winnicott, Donald W. (1975) *Through Paediatrics to Psychoanalysis*. London: Hogarth Press.

Woodcock, Mike (1979) *Team Development Manual*. Aldershot: Gower.

Woodworth, Robert S. (1958) *Dynamics of Behaviour*. New York: Henry Holt.

Wright, Betty (1982) 'Sunpower/Moonpower/Transformation' in P. McAllister (ed.) *Reweaving the Web of Life*. Philadelphia: New Society Publishers.

Wright, David L. (1973) 'Images of human nature underlying sociological theory: a review and synthesis', Annual Meeting of the American Sociological Association.

Wright, David L. (1974) 'On the bases of social order: indoctrinated control versus voluntary cooperation', Annual Meeting of the American Sociological Association.

Wyckoff, Hogie (1975) 'Problem-solving groups for women' in C. Steiner et al. (eds) *Readings in Radical Psychiatry*. New York: Grove Press.

Yontef, Gary (1993) *Awareness, Dialogue and Process: Essays on Gestalt Therapy*. Highland: The Gestalt Journal Press.

Zaltman, G. (1973) *Processes and Phenomena of Social Change*. New York: Academic Press.

Author index

Subject index

acceptance 39, 44, 60
alienation 45, 46
anomie 45, 46
archetypes 107, 166
authenticity 20, 33, 36, 37, 40, 42–45, 46, 50, 51, 103, 124, 134, 166, 176, 218–223, 250, 256, 257
autonomy 9, 38, 39, 42, 46, 80, 118, 174, 218, 221, 227, 258

birth 102, 104, 223
body therapies 42, 85, 89–98, 115, 257

catharsis 92, 95, 102, 105, 118
Centaur consciousness 33, 35, 36, 41, 45, 48, 49, 50, 51, 56, 166, 167, 168, 217, 221, 222, 223, 227, 228, 238–241
client-centred, see person-centred
COEX system 104, 113
conflict 143, 144, 147, 152–154, 217, 227, 238, 240, 244
confrontation 117, 124, 125–126
constructivism 3, 83, 179–186, 189, 205, 218–223
counselling 37, 55–76, 129, 131, 173, 255
countertransference 114, 119
creativity 9, 13, 21, 27, 32, 40, 45, 99, 100, 118, 144, 147, 158, 159, 162, 216, 230, 233, 246, 250

diagnosis 81, 82, 84, 85, 143, 147
dialectics 1, 2, 3, 4, 5, 15, 16, 31, 33, 46, 48, 49, 59, 73, 109, 121, 138, 145, 159, 161, 184, 189, 206, 209, 213, 214, 223, 238–241, 254

dialogue 80, 81, 83, 172, 218, 219
dream work 42, 75–76

ecstasy 4, 95, 109, 162, 163, 165, 222, 246, 250
empathy 59–60, 64, 83, 85, 125, 129, 158
encounter 38, 98, 138, 142, 147, 163, 237, 246, 251
encounter group 110–124, 131, 138, 147
existentialism 3, 33, 37, 42, 43, 44, 45, 49, 51, 65, 75, 81, 83, 85, 93, 94, 114–117, 122, 124, 166, 182, 202, 205, 251, 254
experiential approach 42, 82–86, 94, 135–137
experiential knowledge 19, 20

feminist approach 42, 85, 122, 175, 182, 183, 184, 185, 186, 187, 219
focusing 82, 83, 85, 94, 128
freedom 43–44, 51, 56, 118, 134, 141, 227, 240, 241
fully-functioning person, see self-actualization

genuineness 44, 58–59, 62, 129
Gestalt approach 42, 73, 77–82, 83, 85, 94, 99, 105, 106, 110, 111, 115, 204
growth 9, 24–26, 38
guided fantasy 72, 73, 104, 105, 106, 107

imagery 103, 112, 118, 166
individualism 37, 56
intentionality 41, 213, 214

transformation 4, 142, 157–159, 172,
200, 227, 255
transpersonal 1, 23, 34–36, 38, 64,
72–73, 75, 82, 93, 102, 104, 107, 108,
118–119, 136, 158, 159, 162–173,
246
trauma 102, 103, 104, 202, 223
trust 114, 124–125, 130, 148

unconscious, collective 106, 119
unconscious, higher 104, 105, 106,
118
unconscious, lower 104, 105, 106, 112,
181, 230, 231, 235, 237, 243

vision-logic 1, 33, 41, 161, 166, 214,
223, 238–241